Advance Praise for
China into the Future:
Making Sense of the World's Most Dynamic Economy

With so much contemporary writing on China taking a cultural, biographical or "how-to-do-business" approach, it is significant that the contributors to *China into the Future* have carefully examined the myriad of business, economic, social and political issues shaping China's future.

John Kuzmik
Partner, Baker Botts LLP, Hong Kong & Beijing

This book is critical reading for all senior business executives and government policymakers seeking a simple but incisive look into the dynamics shaping China.

Serge Dumont
Senior Vice President
President Asia Pacific
Omnicom Group Inc.

No other China book frames the interplay of dynamic forces underlying the threats and opportunities debate of engaging China more clearly for senior business and public policy decision-makers.

Firth Griffith
Senior Advisor – Strategic Development
Mitsui & Co. (Asia Pacific) Pte Ltd., Singapore

Many books on China take an over-arching view of China's future. The thoughtful approach of this book is to identify the different forces and issues that will shape China's future and to analyze from a number of expertly informed perspectives how they may converge. For those of us who make almost daily choices that affect the future of our business in China, this book provides a valuable understanding of the forces at play and their possible outcomes.

Kenneth Macpherson
Managing Director
Diageo Greater China

China Into the Future

Making Sense of the World's Most
Dynamic Economy

China Into the Future
Making Sense of the World's Most Dynamic Economy

Edited by
W. John Hoffmann
Principal, XRG- Exceptional Resources Group
Co-founder, China Dialogues Network

and

Michael J. Enright
Director, Competitiveness Programs, Hong Kong
Institute of Economics and Business Strategy
Sun Hung Kai Professor, University of Hong Kong
Director, Enright, Scott & Associates

WILEY

John Wiley & Sons (Asia) Pte. Ltd.

Other Wiley Editorial Offices

John Wiley & Sons, Inc., 111 River Street, Hoboken, NJ 07030, USA
John Wiley & Sons Ltd., The Atrium, Southern Gate,
    Chichester PO19 BSQ, England
John Wiley & Sons (Canada) Ltd., 5353 Dundas Street West, Suite 400, Toronto, Ontario
    M9B 6H8, Canada
John Wiley & Sons Australia Ltd., 42 McDougall Street, Milton, Queensland 4064, Australia
Wiley-VCH, Boschstrasse 12, D-69469 Weinheim, Germany

Library of Congress Cataloging-in-Publication Data:

ISBN 13: 978-0-470-82244-9

Typeset in 12-13 point, Perpetua Regular by Superskill Graphics Pte. Ltd.
Printed by Saik Wah Press Pte. Ltd.
10 9 8 7 6 5 4 3 2 1

Contents

Preface

This book grew out of our experience in operating as consultants, researchers, and analysts of China over many years. In that time, we have seen interest in China grow dramatically and the production of books on China become an industry in itself. However, the more we worked on China-related strategies with major multinational companies, government agencies, investors, and others, the greater the disconnect we found between what was generally available and what was useful to these organizations as they wrestled with the enigma that is China. We concluded that while China is much studied and much discussed, it is not well-understood, particularly by an outside world that seems to predict China's emergence as a superpower one day and its imminent collapse the next.

The wide variations in perceptions reflect the fact that China is full of contradictions and apparent contradictions that can be difficult to reconcile. It takes years of experience to even begin to understand how China works and how its system has held together through periods of rapid change. Complexity and contradictions make it difficult to understand the individual pieces to the puzzle, no less the puzzle itself. In China, it is important to avoid preconceived notions of what it should be. Instead, it is crucial to focus on what China is today, the driving forces that have shaped its past, and the driving forces that will shape its future.

A focus on these driving forces leads us to several conclusions:

- China's future will be profoundly different from its past
- China has been far more resilient than many expected
- China's leaders have a very different world view than leaders in the West
- China will not simply follow the path suggested by others
- China is not a monolith, but is comprised of numerous actors and groups with their own agendas
- Despite greater market-orientation, government will continue to play an immensely important role in China's economy
- For businesses in China, rapid economic development need not necessarily correspond with profits
- Success in China requires a deep and broad understanding of a multifaceted economy and society

China has embarked on a transformation of unprecedented scale and scope. It has shown itself to be distinctive, independent, complex, and adaptable. Yet China remains fraught with internal contradictions that make it immensely challenging. China's future will be the result of a confluence of forces rather than a single master plan. In our experience, success in China and in dealing with China requires an understanding of the intricacies and subtleties of these forces and the ability to cope with their ebb and flow. It is an examination of these forces that provides the focal point for this volume.

Writing about China and its future development is a substantial challenge. The complexity, inconsistencies, and pace of change in China make it difficult to compose a nuanced picture that will withstand the test of the time. In order to achieve this, it was necessary to assemble a group of leading China experts who could draw upon their vast experience of working at the highest levels within China and of writing about China for outside audiences.

Fortunately, we were able to convince a group of top-flight experts with whom we have worked for many years to contribute to the volume. The contributors have impressed us over the years with the depth of their insights, their constant quest to augment their own knowledge, and their ability to communicate China's complexity in ways understandable to officials, analysts, and business people around the world.

This volume has been the result of the efforts of two organizations, the China Dialogues Network (CDN) and the Hong Kong Institute of Economics and Business Strategy (HKIEBS). CDN is a network of leading China scholars, analysts, consultants, and businesspeople that provides information and bespoke advice on China and its development. Based in Hong Kong, CDN is actually a global network, with associates and knowledge resources who live and work in China and all over the world. HIEBS is an Area of Excellence affiliated with the University of Hong Kong, and founded with initial grants by the Hong Kong University Grants Committee. While Asia-wide in its scope, HIEBS has developed a particular specialty in sponsoring and organizing international research projects and conferences focused on China.

Most of the chapters in this volume were written by CDN members and were sponsored by CDN as part of its efforts to extend our knowledge of forces influencing business in China. In addition, several of the authors attended a conference titled "China in the 21st Century" organized by HIEBS, where earlier versions of some of the chapters were presented and discussed, and the idea of a volume on China that dealt with its multiple facets was first raised. The editorial work on the present volume was also supported by HIEBS. The collaboration that has resulted in the present volume, which brings together academics, analysts, consultants, and other professionals on issues of importance to business people and policy makers, is exactly the sort of collaboration both organizations seek to foster.

We would like to thank Mr. Jay Chen, Mr. Willy Lam, Mr. Tim Collard, Ms. Bonnie Yeung, Professor Richard Wong, Professor Alan Siu, and Ms. Edith Scott for their help and support throughout this project. We also wish to thank Mr. Nick Wallwork and Ms. C. J. Hwu of John Wiley & Sons for their encouragement throughout the project. We would also like to thank the many clients, officials, colleagues, analysts, and experts that have shared their insights on China with us over the years. Finally, we owe a special thanks to the contributors to this volume. We have benefited greatly from ongoing collaboration and sharing of ideas with the contributors and look forward to more in the future. We are proud to have the present group as contributors to this volume. We are even prouder to have them as colleagues and friends.

W. John Hoffmann
Principal, XRG — Exceptional Resources Group
Co-Founder, China Dialogues Network

Michael J. Enright
Director, Asia-Pacific Competitiveness Programs, Hong Kong Institute of
Economics and Business Strategy
Sun Hung Kai Professor, University of Hong Kong
Director, Enright, Scott & Associates

Hong Kong, China

List of Contributors

Jonathan Anderson

Jonathan Anderson is Managing Director and Chief Economist, Asia, at UBS. He is also Head of Asia-Pacific Economics. Before joining UBS in 2003, he worked at Goldman Sachs; he also spent eight years at the International Monetary Fund, including three years as Resident Representative in China and three years as Resident Representative in Russia. Since joining UBS, Anderson and his Asian team have been top-ranked in a wide range of broker polls, including *Asiamoney, Institutional Investor, The Asset*, and *FinanceAsia*. He is the author of *The Five Great Myths About China and the World*, and speaks fluent Mandarin Chinese and Russian. Anderson received his MA and Ph.D. Candidacy in Economics from Harvard University.

Robert C. Broadfoot

Robert C. Broadfoot is the founder and Managing Director of Political & Economic Risk Consultancy, Ltd. (PERC), located in Hong Kong, Asia's premier country risk consulting firm. He has been working on Asian country risk-based analyses and scenario-planning for more than 28 years. Broadfoot has developed a system for combining scenario planning with surveys of businessmen working in Asia to quantify country risks and develop a fuller understanding of how perceptions of risks are affected by specific developments. In addition to consulting work, he also publishes regular risks reports on nine different East and Southeast Asian countries. Beside co-coordinating PERC's overall operations, Broadfoot is directly responsible for managing PERC's research and consulting on mainland China and the Greater China region. PERC's clients include over 1,000 multinational companies active in Asia and China. Broadfoot graduated with honors in economics from Oberlin College in the United States in 1972. Broadfoot became a CDN Founder Core Associate in 2003.

Kenneth J. DeWoskin

Kenneth J. DeWoskin is an independent senior consultant in Strategy and Business Development for PricewaterhouseCoopers in China, working in transaction services. A former Partner in PwC, former professor of International Business and Asian Languages and Cultures at the University of Michigan, Ann Arbor, former Chair of his department and Associate Director of the Center for Chinese Studies, DeWoskin has been involved with China for nearly 40 years. He has lived and worked extensively in both China and in Japan. He received his B.A. from Columbia College and his Ph.D. from Columbia University. He has also studied at National Taiwan University and Kyoto University. He is a fluent speaker of Mandarin Chinese and Japanese. He is a Founder Core Associate of the China Dialogues Network (CDN).

Michael J. Enright

Michael Enright is the Sun Hung Kai Professor at the School of Business of the University of Hong Kong, Director of Competitiveness Programs at the Hong Kong Institute of Economics and Business Strategy, and Director of Enright, Scott & Associates Limited, a Hong Kong-based economic and strategic consulting firm. Enright has directed or co-directed major competitiveness studies in 20 countries on five continents, has co-authored 10 books or monographs, has written numerous papers for academic and practitioner publications, and frequently has his work featured in the international press. Enright has been a consultant to numerous companies, governments, and multilateral organizations and economic development and has appeared in 33 countries as an invited speaker. Enright received his A.B., his M.B.A., and his Ph.D. from Harvard University. Before moving to Hong Kong in 1996, he spent six years on the faculty of the Harvard Business School. He is a CDN Founder Core Associate.

W. John Hoffmann

John Hoffmann is a Founder and Principal of XRG- Exceptional Resources Group Limited, a China-based strategy and transactional consultancy, and Co-founder of the China Dialogues Network. Hoffmann has over 27 years working experience in China, primarily in first-mover, breakthrough strategy formulation and venture execution. His main areas of expertise are breakthrough strategy development and venture negotiation, government relations and relationship building, project finance, mergers and acquisitions, and restructuring/workouts. Since 1990, as a co-founder and Principal of XRG, he has worked on multiple China projects for government and multinational clients.

Cheng Li

Cheng Li is the William R. Kenan Professor of Government at Hamilton College and Visiting Fellow at the Brookings Institution in Washington, D.C. Li grew up in Shanghai during the Cultural Revolution. In 1985, he went to the United States where he received an M.A. at the University of California, Berkeley, and a Ph.D. at Princeton University. Li has authored or edited several books and scholarly articles on China's leadership and reforms and is a columnist for Stanford University's journal *China Leadership Monitor*. He has been featured by numerous media outlets and leading publications. Dr. Li is a director of the National Committee on U.S.-China Relations, a trustee of the Institute of Current World Affairs, a member of the Academic Advisory Group of the Congressional U.S.-China Working Group, a member of the Committee of 100, a member of the Council on Foreign Relations Task Force on U.S. policy toward China, a council member of the Institute for International Research at the Hopkins-Nanjing Center, and a member of the U.S. National Committee of the Council for Security Cooperation in the Asia Pacific. Li became a CDN Core Associate in 2006.

Tony Saich

Anthony J. Saich is the Daewoo Professor of International Affairs and Faculty Chair of the Asia Programs and the China Public Policy Program at the Kennedy School of Government, Harvard University. He is also Director of the University Asia Center. This work includes significant training programs for national and local officials from China, Vietnam, and elsewhere in Asia. From 1994 until July 1999, he was the Representative for the China Office of the Ford Foundation. Prior to this he was the director of the Sinological Institute, Leiden University, the Netherlands. Saich first visited China as a student in 1976-77 and has been there for longer or shorter trips almost each year since. He has advised a wide range of government, private and not-for-profit organizations on work in China. His current research focuses on the interplay between state and society in China and the respective roles they play in the provision of public goods and services at the local level. He has written several books on developments in China. Professor Saich is a CDN Core Associate.

Robert A. Scalapino

Robert A. Scalapino received his BA degree from Santa Barbara College and his MA and Ph.D. degrees from Harvard University. From 1949 to 1990, he taught in the Political Science Department at the University of California at Berkeley, where he founded the

Institute of East Asian Studies. He is currently Robson Research Professor of Government Emeritus at Berkeley. Scalapino has been awarded the Medal of Highest Honour from the Graduate Institute of Peace Studies, Kyung Hee University; the Order of Diplomatic Service Merit, Heung-In Medal from the Government of Korea; and the Order of the Sacred Treasure by the Government of Japan. Scalapino is a Fellow of the American Academy of Arts and Sciences, a Berkeley Fellow, a Director of the Pacific Forum-CSIS, Founder and first Chairman of the National Committee on U.S.-China Relations, a Trustee of The Asia Foundation, Director Emeritus of the Council on Foreign Relations and the Japan Society of Northern California, Co-Chairman of the Asia Society's Asian Agenda Advisory Group; and a member of numerous other editorial boards and committees for educational and government agencies. He has published over 500 articles and 40 books or monographs on Asian politics and U.S. Asian policy. Scalapino became a CDN Core Associate in 2003.

List of Abbreviations

ARF	ASEAN Regional Forum
ASEAN	Association of Southeast Asian Nations
ASEAN Plus Three	ASEAN plus China, South Korea and Japan
ASEM	The Asia-Europe Meeting
BoC	Bank of China
CBRC	China Bank Regulatory Commission
CCP	Chinese Communist Party (The Party)
CCYL	Chinese Communist Youth League
CNOOC	China National Offshore Oil Corporation
DPP	Democratic Progressive Party of Taiwan
DPRK	Democratic People's Republic of Korea
EU	European Union
FDI	Foreign Direct Investment
FIE	Foreign Invested Enterprise
Forex	Foreign Exchange
FYP	Five Year Program, formerly Five Year Plan
G8	Group of Eight
GDP	Gross Domestic Product
GM	Genetically Modified

IP	Intellectual Property
IPO	Initial Public Offering
IPR	Intellectual Property Rights
IT	Information Technology
KMT	Kuomintang (or Nationalist) Party of Taiwan
LDP	Liberal Democratic Party of Japan
LME	London Metal Exchange
MNCs	Multinational Companies
NATO	North Atlantic Treaty Organization
NDRC	National Development and Reform Commission of China
NGO	Non-Governmental Organization
NSB	National Statistics Bureau of China
OECD	Organization for Economic Cooperation and Development
PBoC	People's Bank of China
PLA	People's Liberation Army
Politburo	Political Bureau of CCP Central Committee
PPP	Purchasing Power Parity
PRC	People's Republic of China
R&D	Research & Development
RMB	Renminbi or yuan, China's national currency
ROK	Republic of Korea
SAIC/NAG	Shanghai Automotive Industry Corporation/Nanjing Automotive Group
SAR	Special Administrative Region, e.g. Hong Kong or Macau SAR

SARS	Severe Acute Respiratory Syndrome
SASAC	State-owned Asset Supervisory and Administration Commission of China
SCO	Shanghai Cooperation Organization
SFXIC	State Foreign Exchange Investment Corporation
SIPO	State Intellectual Property Office of China
SOEs	State-Owned Enterprises
UBS	Union Bank of Switzerland
UN	United Nations
US	United States of America
USD	United States Dollar
WTO	World Trade Organization

1

China Into the Future

W. John Hoffmann
Principal, XRG – Exceptional Resources Group
Co-Founder, China Dialogues Network

Introduction

China's rise as an economic and political power has generated enormous attention in halls of government, in boardrooms, and on Main Streets all around the world. Hardly a day goes by without the publication of another report on the most recent "China miracle" or the latest "China threat." Readers are left to conclude that either China is on the verge of imminent collapse, or that it is on the brink of economic or political dominance. How can a single nation be the source of so much contradictory information and confusing conclusions? The reality is that China is a large, complex nation, with internal differences across regions, cities, and industries that are often wider than differences across nations. China is not a single actor moving in a single, well-specified direction. Instead it contains a multitude of actors all finding their way in the midst of unprecedented change. China is a place where good information is hard to come by and even more difficult to interpret. As a result, China has become a mirror, reflecting the hopes and fears of those that experience it. It is a place much observed, but little understood, with the search for headlines often obscuring the search for the bottom line.

China's Growing Importance

China's importance on the world stage has grown dramatically in the last twenty five years. In industry after industry, China is increasingly assuming a critical—if not dominant—position as a producer, competitor, investment location, market, and/or investor. From garments, to shoes, to housewares, to consumer electronics, China is becoming an essential producer. In steel, copper, aluminum, cement, mobile phones, and household appliances, China has become a world-leading market. An economy that once exported only simple goods is now exporting automobiles. A consumer market that once focused only on low-quality, price-sensitive goods is rapidly becoming one of the world's leading markets for luxury brands. China seems to be moving ahead on all fronts, expanding its position in low-end price-sensitive sectors, while increasing its position in technology-based sectors and research and development. Nations that find themselves complementary to China on the production side find themselves competing with China for energy, raw materials, and other commodities in the marketplace. Numerous companies from around the world have raced to enter China because they know that they cannot be or will not be number one or number two globally in their industry without an important production base, market position, or both in China.

Of growing importance as well is the fact that for the first time, China's leadership is encouraging Chinese companies to "Go Global." In parallel with its domestic economic imperatives, China's leadership believes it is critically important that Chinese companies take a more active role competing in developed as well as developing markets around the world. In some cases, such as energy and minerals, the imperative is to source abroad what China does not have at home. In other cases, it is to purchase brands and access to markets that comes with foreign acquisitions, or to obtain or develop the skills and capabilities that will allow large Chinese companies to remain important players domestically as they become major players internationally. Just as with other Chinese imperatives, the "Go Global" campaign must be seen as a political as well as business initiative. Favored Chinese companies are already receiving strong state support as they carry out their overseas forays. For the first time, Chinese companies are engaged in substantial competition and collaboration with foreign companies overseas, as well as in Mainland China markets.

China's growing importance has also created a number of geopolitical challenges. On international economic issues, China's very prominence has made it difficult to deal with in traditional ways. When producers elsewhere in the world attempt to obtain protection against Chinese imports, they find themselves battling local retailers who claim they need Chinese-made goods to serve their customers, as well as other local companies that have successfully moved their production to China. China's active investment and diplomatic efforts have resulted in many developing nations viewing China—not the United States or the European Union—as their market of choice and as their preferred friend. The fact that Chinese investment, aid, and accompanying diplomatic and military support has come without the strings often attached by traditional international donors has made China a virtual ally of nations considered "rogue states," and has made it difficult or impossible for the West to impose meaningful sanctions on such nations. Through the Shanghai Cooperation Organization in Central Asia, new initiatives in South Asia, diplomatic and commercial overtures in Africa and the Middle East, and new investments and relationships in Latin America, China is outflanking any efforts at containment of its diplomatic and investment strategy. China has used its position as a Permanent Member of the United Nations Security Council in ways that often frustrate the West. At the same time, China has become increasingly adept at leveraging bilateral relations, using access to its vast markets to drive wedges between members of traditional alliances.

China Under Hu Jintao and Wen Jiabao

Under "Fourth Generation Leaders" Hu Jintao (President of the People's Republic of China and Secretary General of the Chinese Communist Party) and Wen Jiabao (Premier of the People's Republic of China), China has continued the basic path of development set out by their predecessors from the "Third Generation," Jiang Zemin and Zhu Rongji—but with some new wrinkles of their own. China has continued to make progress in opening its economy, consistent with its commitments under its World Trade Organization accession agreement. Inward foreign direct investment has remained high, the financial sector has been opened to a significant extent, and progress has been made on a number of fronts. On the other hand, foreign critics claim that China has not moved ahead rapidly enough in clarifying legal arrangements for the economy, protecting intellectual property, ending subsidies to favored companies and sectors, and ensuring that local jurisdictions follow national commitments.

The Hu-Wen leadership has been much more careful than their predecessors in attempting to minimize the negative fallout of fast-paced growth on "disadvantaged groups," such as farmers and the urban unemployed. Abolition of rural taxes, greater support for agriculture, additional funding for the urban poor, new initiatives in the Northeast, and attempts to reign in housing prices have been only some of the features of the leadership's approach. In essence, the Hu-Wen leadership has offered a new social contract compared to its predecessors, one which promises a more equal distribution of wealth and national resources than in the past. A major social challenge facing the leadership will be the movement of some 300-plus million people from rural areas into urban and peri-urban areas in the coming 15 to 20 years. The success of what will be one of the world's largest ever social engineering projects depends on whether industrial and service sector jobs can be created for the migrants. Under the Hu-Wen leadership, the focus remains on "putting people first," "building a harmonious society," and "forestalling danger in the midst of stability."

Despite progress on many fronts, the Hu-Wen team has yet to come up with new initiatives in domestic political reform, especially where such initiatives might concern power-sharing among the country's disparate sectors and participation by all Chinese in governmental affairs. Such changes are seen as inimical to the Chinese Communist Party's (CCP's) goal of monopolizing authority. After the "velvet revolutions" in Central Asia, the CCP leadership masterminded a clampdown on non-governmental organizations and political dissidents. NGOs and institutes with close ties to Western counterparts are kept under tight surveillance. Journalists and lawyers who have represented people in human rights cases have also found themselves targets. Instead of liberalizing the political system, Hu, a career Party affairs specialist, has used political campaigns to ensure the viability of the CCP. This stems from the belief that if the Party remains competent and uncorrupt, it can solve the nation's problems more effectively. High profile ideological campaigns and corruption investigations within the Party have been aimed at the "purification" of the Party and to enhance public support. Nationalism, especially anti-Japanese nationalism, has also been used as a tool to promote internal cohesion and to strengthen the position of the Party.

Given the growing interdependence of China's economic development with the international community, its geopolitical relations are of utmost importance. China's relations with the United States, which have been strained over China's burgeoning trade surplus with the U.S., have found areas for cooperation in negotiations involving nuclear developments in North Korea and Iran. Ultimately, however, the United States may be frustrated by China's milder approach to these rogue states. China has also been favoring the European Union over the United States, by discussing a "multipolar" world (one without U.S. domination), with European powers. It appeared that China had nearly won E.U. agreement to end its post-Tiananmen arms embargo in 2005, but China's enactment of a tough anti-secessionist law, targeted at Taiwan in March 2005, put such discussions off the table for the time being. Relations with Japan seemed to improve with the departure of Japan's Prime Minister Koizumi, though his successor Abe is noted as being even more conservative when it comes to discussions over past difficulties between the two nations. Elsewhere in the world, the Hu-Wen team has put in an impressive performance. This has not only resulted in a much-enhanced position for China in the Asia-Pacific and other regions, but it has also opened up markets for Chinese products and secured new supplies of energy and minerals. To ensure a favorable climate for economic growth, which includes finding new markets and energy suppliers, Beijing needs to follow up on its initial success in befriending nations and regional blocs such as ASEAN, India, Russia, the E.U., Brazil, and other developing nations.

What is clear is that the Hu-Wen team has taken China in some directions that might have been expected, and some that were not. Continuation of the economic reform program has been combined with a greater sense of economic nationalism, leading to the view that the quality of China's development has not matched its quantity, that foreign companies are taking too much advantage of Chinese consumers, and that China's own companies need to be nurtured to achieve world standards. China's diplomatic overtures in the Third World have sometimes caught Western officials off-guard, as China's investment and market opening initiatives are not conditioned on behavioral modifications in the same way that Western aid is often tied. In China's case, pragmatism is combined with a greater sense of ideology, and the recognition that the Party must strengthen and broaden its contacts with all its constituencies. The result is a China that is different in many ways to that which might have been predicted a few years ago.

Part of the contrast is due to a difference in the backgrounds and formative experiences of the present leadership compared with its predecessors. Hu Jintao's career was built in China's poorer Western areas (Gansu, Guizhou, and Tibet) and through positions in the Chinese Communist Youth League (CCYL) and within the Party. This background has made him more sensitive to the plight of China's interior provinces and more ideological in mindset than Jiang Zemin and Zhu Rongji, whose most notable formative experiences were in Shanghai. Like Hu Jintao, Wen Jiabao also started his career in Gansu Province, and although he has been a Beijing insider (Wen has served as de facto Chief of Staff to two General Secretaries of the Chinese Communist Party, Hu Yaobang and Zhao Ziyang, and was Vice Premier under Zhu Rongji), he has been able to work with all major Party factions and has developed a reputation as a "man of the people." The fact that he survived the purges of both Hu Yaobang and Zhao Ziyang is testament to his political acumen and survival skills.

Hu and Wen preside over a government and Party whose top positions are split virtually down the middle between a group of elitist cadres (many of whom have close ties to Shanghai), and a more conservative group (many of whom have close ties to the CCYL). Despite their different backgrounds, the two groups generally share views on the need to maintain Party supremacy, ensure domestic stability, and enhance national security. The CCYL group, led by Hu and Wen, tends to call for a more "balanced" development, defined as trading off some economic growth in return for a more even distribution of wealth, along with greater concern for the environment, and greater efforts to invest in economically disadvantaged areas. This group is also somewhat more "economically nationalist," and places less emphasis on foreign investment as an engine of China's development. In international relations, members of this group tend to lean away from the United States and more towards Central Asia, Russia, and Third World nations. They are also inclined to look inward, rather than to foreign examples, in efforts to find solutions.

A full exposition of the traits of the "Fourth Generation" is beyond the scope of this essay (see Chapter 7 for a detailed discussion). The point rather is that even though Hu and Wen are China's principal leaders, they are not China's only leaders. This is of crucial importance as China's "Fifth Generation" leaders start to emerge. In China, sometimes contradictions (or seeming contradictions) arise as different groups jockey for position. Accepting that there are contradictions in a country of China's size and diversity is the first step to coming to grips with China's essential truth: there is no single leader; there is no single overarching master plan; there is no simple explanation for what China will become in the future. The Chinese Communist Party is still in the process of transitioning from a revolutionary party to a ruling party and there is wariness of the potential for a "cult of personality" to surround a leader. As a result, China's future will be shaped by a variety of actors, all with their own interests and their own views of what is best for the country.

China Into the Future

While an understanding of China is critical to policy makers, business people, investors, workers, consumers, and others around the world today, it will be even more critical in the future. This is true for business people, whose success globally will be linked ever closer with their success in competing in China, and competing with China in the international marketplace. It is true for policy makers concerned about how China will use its growing economic and geopolitical strength to shape world affairs. It is true for investors interested in taking advantage of one of the world's leading growth stories. It is true for workers whose jobs might be relocated to China, and consumers whose own household costs are influenced by China's emergence.

For each of these groups, it is important to base their view of China's future on detailed information, careful analysis, realistic assessments, and appropriate frames of reference. In this regard, there are a number of key points that need to be kept in mind by anyone dealing with China in the future.

China's future will be profoundly different from its past. The China of today is vastly different from the country ten or even five years ago. Business managers operating in China have told us that one of their biggest managerial challenges is managing across different generations of Chinese workers, since Chinese people of different generations have grown up in completely different worlds, and have profoundly different outlooks. From the Chinese leadership's perspective, the past two and a half decades have been devoted to opening up the economy and moving away from central planning, while still retaining one-party control. The next 25 years will be directed towards sustainable economic and social development. This will involve trying to manage growth in the context of regional disparities, rising expectations, and challenging political conditions. Meanwhile, key Party and state leaders at the national and local levels move on, circumstances change, and coalitions need to be constantly maintained and rebuilt. Thus, simply extrapolating from the past to reach conclusions about China's future could result in false assumptions and false conclusions.

China has been far more resilient than many expected. China's imminent collapse has been forecast many times since the country began its reform process in the early 1980s. Indeed there have been many versions of the imminent collapse scenario: China's political system would implode under the pressure of change; China would not be able to deal with the dislocation caused by the reform process; there would be a backlash against market-oriented reforms that would bring the economy down; China's state-owned enterprises would make meaningful reform impossible; regional disparities and jealousies would result in provinces and cities trying to pull away from the center; the backlash against corruption among government and Party officials would create public disorder and chaos; progress would not be possible without a more democratic society; an insolvent financial sector would cause rapid collapse; environmental degradation would derail China's development; and so on. While all of these issues remain important, no single issue or combination of issues has caused the much-touted collapse so far, despite arguably the most far-reaching economic reform program in recent history. While critics may claim it is simply a matter of time before the collapse comes or before growth limits set in, one cannot help but be impressed by the way that China and its leaders have been able to manage the reform process so far. While mistakes have been made, China's leaders have shown themselves to be astute, pragmatic, patient, open to new ideas, and able to strike out in new directions. China's resilience and ability to effect change when change is necessary should not be underestimated.

China's leaders have a very different worldview than leaders in the West. The formative experiences, intellectual environment, and realities faced by China's leaders have resulted in a worldview different from those found in other nations. One example of differing worldviews is over the "China threat." In many overseas circles, it is believed that China is creating disruption in economies around the world, is responsible for resource scarcities and pollution problems, is engaged in a massive military buildup, is causing regional neighbors concern, and is becoming more assertive and less easy to contain. Having such economic and military power in the hands of an undemocratic government with a poor domestic human rights record is viewed in the West as at best problematic, and at worst dangerous. Elsewhere, particularly in the developing world, China's strength is viewed with awe and envy.

From a Chinese standpoint the picture looks rather different. For 18 of the last 20 centuries, China had the world's largest economy. Although dramatic, its recent rise has not yet restored China to its earlier position among nations and its per capita income is only a small fraction of that of the Organization for Economic Cooperation and Development (OECD) countries. China is consuming vast amounts of resources, but far less in aggregate than the U.S. or Western Europe, and far, far less on a per capita basis. Its environmental record is poor, but so were those of today's advanced economies in their early days of industrialization. In other spheres, China sees itself as simply asserting its interests as any "normal country" would do.

In geopolitical terms, many in China view the "U.S. threat" as much more ominous. The U.S. has the preponderance of military firepower. American leaders speak openly of efforts to foster a change in China's government. The U.S. has troops stationed in countries neighboring China and a navy that can cut off China's seaborne energy imports and trade if it chooses. The U.S. also has a history of arming and supporting what China considers to be a renegade province (Taiwan), and is engaged in extensive discussions of how to constrain China's rise. Given China's recent history of a century of foreign domination and invasion, followed by decades of isolation from much of the rest of the world, it is easy to see how China's leaders could view China as more threatened than threatening. The point here is not so much to justify one view or another, but rather to point out that different worldviews mean that the same facts can be interpreted in very different ways in China than in other nations.

China will not simply follow the path suggested by others. While Chinese leaders, individuals, and organizations seek to learn from the rest of the world, there is a profound sense of the need for a Chinese strategy of development in economic and political circles. China has shown itself willing and able to chart its own path, sometimes in the face of foreign opposition and at the expense of internal division. There is no compelling reason for it to adopt a foreign model for either its economy or its political system, and thus projections of China's future based on the experience or hopes of others may have limited utility. We have already seen, for example, the Western optimism that each generation of Chinese leadership would be somehow more "Western" or "open" in outlook has not been realized. On a whole range of issues, such as the role of government in the economy, the role of foreign investors, economic openness, outlooks toward intellectual property, the role of markets in allocation of natural resources, and on basic issues of governance, we should expect that China will seek to develop its own models and resist those outsiders might wish to impose.

China is not a monolith. Although there is a tendency in the outside world to view China as a monolithic state, with a unified leadership issuing edicts and directives that are followed to the letter across the country, nothing could be further from the truth. In economic terms, China is more a set of loosely coupled regional economies rather than a single unified national economy. Historically, policies promoting local self-sufficiency created local economies that were, for the most part, isolated from each other. Even as improved infrastructure links China's cities and provinces closer together, local protectionism and favoritism creates substantial barriers to trade, transportation, and investment. Political edicts from Beijing are often interpreted to mean different things in different places, and the level of enforcement of directives is at best uneven. Many directives concerning economic activities—such as land conversions, new industrial investments, or orders to shut down plants—are simply ignored. Local branches of national banks often ignore directives from headquarters. On the governmental side, in many instances, funds allocated from the center are diverted to completely different purposes. "The mountains are high and the emperor is far away" is still a fitting description of significant portions of local administration. China's leadership is also made up of a number of factions. Although a unified face is shown to the outside world, intense internal discussion and debate over major policy measures often takes place within the CCP and between central and local officials.

Government will continue to play an immensely important role in China's economy. Although China is becoming more market-oriented, government and regulatory policy remains critically important to doing business in China. Many important sectors are still dominated by state enterprises and many others remain under strict regulatory control. Companies owned by the central government, provincial governments, and municipal governments can be competitors, buyers, and/or suppliers. Approvals for many projects are only forthcoming if they meet policy criteria. Finally, China continues to emphasize subservience of the legal system to the Chinese Communist Party. This means that important legal disputes will be resolved in ways that are considered in China's best interest, i.e. on policy grounds, rather than on equity or a precise reading of the law. None of these features is likely to change anytime soon.

China's rapid economic development does not necessarily correspond with business profits. For most companies, the biggest challenge in China has not been gauging the macroeconomy or overall policy directions, but making profits. China's rapid growth and development has fostered a gold rush mentality, in which an enterprise's initial success frequently breeds imitation, excess investment, and margin collapses. In many industries, competition is fiercer in China than anywhere else in the world because the shakeouts have yet to take place, and no one knows who the eventual winner will be. In addition, the central government frequently issues directives concerning individual industries that it wishes to encourage or discourage. The speed and extent to which they are enforced often varies by locality and can change suddenly. The result can be rapid changes in fortune for an enterprise or a sector, even in the context of rapid growth. Thus organizations that fail to keep abreast of the specific local and sectoral programs or wishes of government are often blindsided.

China is multidimensional. Many interpretations of what is going on in China are focused too much on a single perspective or dimension of the multidimensional reality that is "now" in China. Analyses of modern China often focus on partial answers to superficial questions about what is going on in China today rather than seeking to derive knowledge in depth and formulate careful analyses. The challenge for all external analysts is how to adopt a balanced approach to determine what is truly critical to China's continued development and what is actually just "smoke and mirrors." China has both an ancient culture as well as a modern post-Imperial history of less than 100 years. Some of what the current Chinese leadership is trying to achieve will take decades or generations to complete. China is undertaking experimentation on a massive scale: some of it will work, some of it will fail. This trial and error process that has so far produced the spectacular success of modern China will continue.

China's future is best understood as the result of a confluence of forces rather than a single master plan. Although to the outside world, China's development appears to be determined by a single, unified plan, the reality is somewhat different. In economic terms, the former quasi-dictatorial "Five Year Plans" have been replaced by indicative "Five Year Programs" that provide direction and aspiration as much as mandatory hard targets. The design process now involves large numbers of officials at the municipal, provincial, and central levels and reflects input from all those levels. As has been discussed, China is not monolithic and China's leaders have shown themselves adept at taking up new issues and adjusting course as circumstances change—at least in areas other than the non-negotiable "absolutes" of Communist Party authority and the Taiwan sovereignty issue. China's economic reform has progressed by "feeling the stones," resulting in remarkable flexibility as to how goals are achieved. As new forces emerge, or as old forces change in importance, adjustments are made. It will be the confluence of a variety of forces, from both inside and outside the Chinese Mainland, and the leadership's subsequent response, that will shape China's future.

Moving Beyond the Sound Bites

Given the complexities inherent in China's economic and political systems, the only way to hope to understand China and its future evolution is to go beyond the headlines and sound bites and into the details. It is only then that the apparent contradictions concerning China's development begin to fall away, and facts seemingly at odds with each other begin to reflect the same reality. Only with such a basis can one begin to assess China's likely future development.

One of the purposes of this volume is to provide such a basis. The chapters in this volume, written by leading international China analysts, provide a comprehensive overview of China's geopolitical, domestic political, social, and economic developments. While the major current trends and issues are identified, the main thrust of the volume is very much forward looking. We do not have a crystal ball to see what the future holds, but the chapters provide a good idea of the key driving forces and the most important issues and challenges facing China over the next ten years. They highlight the biggest uncertainties that exist in China's ongoing development and identify the key variables that need to be understood and monitored in order to be able to evaluate how successfully the Chinese authorities and the outside world are dealing with those uncertainties. We believe that this approach provides far better insights into China's present and future developmental possibilities than trying to map out a single, linear future for China's development—although this might make for good sound bites, it would not be particularly useful in reality.

Rather than argue for one future scenario or another, our approach has been to seek a deeper understanding of selected critical aspects of what is happening in China today, what is fundamental to China's longer term development, and what will remain of importance to China in the future. While different chapters focus on different aspects of China's development, and do so from different perspectives, many of the issues, forces, and uncertainties they identify are similar. It is these issues, forces, and uncertainties that are then combined into a number of possible scenarios for China. In our view, this is the best way to embrace the contradictions that constitute China today and will continue to exist in the China of tomorrow.

The next two chapters set the scene with discussions of China's economy and the key business issues facing companies active in China, or dealing with Chinese competition in overseas markets.

China's most obvious influence on the global stage is its impact on the world economy and global business. Professor Michael J. Enright, Director of Competitiveness Programs at the Hong Kong Institute of Economics and Business Strategy of the University of Hong Kong, Sun Hung Kai Professor at the University of Hong Kong, and Director of Enright, Scott & Associates, sets the scene with a view of China's future economic development. Domestic consumption, expanding exports, and strong foreign investment will continue to be hallmarks of China's economy. Improved transportation, greater urbanization, and the rise of second and third-tier cities will create an additional growth potential. In policy, emphasis will shift from the "quantity" to the "quality" of growth, with a focus on innovation, brand building, and the internationalization of Chinese companies. Greater attention will be paid to the coastal-interior and urban-rural disparities in development and living standards. The Chinese leadership is likely to retain control over strategic sectors and its influence will remain pervasive. The main threat to overall economic development could be the Chinese government's efforts to reign in some regions to reduce disparities. According to Enright, the main challenges for international companies in China will not involve China's macroeconomic conditions, but sector-specific issues, such as overcapacity, cutthroat competition, and sector-specific policies.

Dr. Kenneth J. DeWoskin, Professor Emeritus of International Business and Asian Languages and Cultures at the University of Michigan and a former Partner of PricewaterhouseCoopers China, identifies several of the key issues that will influence China's attractiveness for the global business community. He argues that the key forces that will drive China in the future include population dynamics, marketization dynamics, value chain dynamics, institutional dynamics, and environmental dynamics. He also notes that China is likely to continue to develop its economy in the future, leading to the internationalization of Chinese firms, the reduction of protectionism within China, the construction of a harmonious society, nurturing of national champion companies, and efforts to reduce the value and cost of intellectual property. Dr. DeWoskin analyzes these issues and strategies and provides a view of how they might play out in the future. While not identifying a single issue that is likely to derail China's development, DeWoskin cautions that one cannot rule out the possibility that confluences of forces could deal China significant setbacks.

The next three chapters focus on areas that could potentially serve as constraints on China's development. The global geopolitical environment, China's internal socio-political environment, and potential internal economic weaknesses are cited by many analysts as such constraints.

Professor Robert A. Scalapino, the Robson Research Professor Emeritus of the University of California, Berkeley, is uniquely positioned to examine the forces shaping China's key international relations and its reaction to globalization. In his chapter, Professor Scalapino focuses on six critical aspects of international relations confronting China in its quest for an effective global status: China's interaction with the U.S., its expanding relations with the E.U. and the G8, Sino-Russia relations, China's expanding outreach in South Asia, and its growing relations in the Middle East, Africa, and Latin America. The chapter also examines the role that Chinese nationalism plays as a force for unity within the country and asks if the Chinese government can control this force so that its negative dimension does not damage relations with important partner nations. Professor Scalapino traces China's expanded ties with numerous nations around the world and how China's diplomacy reflects and is reflected in China's domestic political environment. He posits a growing complexity in China's international relations as China becomes a great power.

China's socio-political environment will also have an important influence on the nation's development. Professor Tony Saich, the Daewoo Professor of International Affairs, the Chair of Asia Programs, and Chair of the China Public Policy Program at Harvard University, examines the key socio-political issues China will face over the next 10 years. The demographics of an aging population, worrying employment trends, and income inequality are creating enormous challenges for the Chinese government. There is a huge disjunction in China between the professed belief system of the Chinese Communist Party and the way many people in China are experiencing their everyday lives. There is an overwhelming desire to preserve social stability, yet people lack channels to express legitimate grievances, which has contributed to a rise in social unrest. This raises the critical question of whether sufficient governing capacity can be developed to deal with legitimate grievances of the population. Professor Saich describes three potential paths for China's socio-political development and offers a number of milestones that might serve as early indicators of which path this development may take.

Many analysts view China's banking system, by far the most important portion of China's financial sector, as a weak spot that may eventually jeopardize China's development. Jonathan Anderson, Managing Director of Asia Research for UBS, exposes several myths concerning China's banking sector, including predictions of its imminent collapse, its supposed inability to stand up to competition from foreign banks, and the purported futility of Chinese bank bailouts. He concludes that China's bank cleanup is real and is being accomplished with minimal macroeconomic fallout. He also maintains that bank performance in China has improved significantly, that foreign entry is a "red herring" unlikely to place much pressure on China's domestic banks, and that privatization of China's major banks is coming at the right time. He also concludes that China's banks face new challenges, particularly those linked to the liberalization of China's financial sector. How the banks meet these challenges will have a tremendous influence on China's future development.

The final two chapters take us further into the future, first by assessing the potential make up of China's future leadership, and then by developing a series of scenarios for China's future. These scenarios can in turn be used by analysts, business people, investors, and policy makers to enhance their own analysis and assessments.

Each generation of China's leaders has made its own imprint on China's policies. Professor Cheng Li, the William Kenan Professor of Government at Hamilton College and a non-resident senior fellow of the Brookings Institution, analyzes the internal political changes taking place in China and identifies the leading contenders for future leadership positions from the Chinese Communist Party, Chinese government, and corporate sectors. In his chapter, Professor Li analyzes how Hu Jintao is putting his own mark on China's future leadership. One of the key questions will be whether Hu is able to promote sufficient numbers of people with ties to the Chinese Communist Youth League and who share Hu's populist vision for China's development to overcome the more elitist, technocratic faction led by the so-called "Shanghai Gang." The outcome of the interfactional rivalries will shape China's "Fifth Generation" of leaders, including Hu Jintao's ultimate successor, and will influence Chinese policy for decades. Professor Li also profiles several leading candidates for leadership of the Fifth Generation.

Predicting the exact path of China's development is an impossible task, yet government officials, business people, investors, analysts, and others around the world must have some way to look at and track the potential outcomes of the uncertainties and contradictions associated with China's internal and external dynamics if they are to plan for the future. In the final chapter, Robert C. Broadfoot, Director of Political and Economic Risk Consultancy (PERC), and Michael Enright define several scenarios for China's future development. The goal is not to predict a single future for China, but rather to work through the logical outcomes of the critical uncertainties facing China, and how these could influence China's future political, social, and economic development. The chapter provides a mechanism to assess specific commercial strategies against China's potential future scenarios, as well as a framework which allows the reader to monitor key developments over time, to provide a sharper picture of which scenario is actually evolving. In this way, Broadfoot and Enright bring together and analyze the forces and uncertainties identified in the preceding chapters and place them in a framework that can be used to track China's development into the future.

The intention behind *China Into the Future* is not to hype the "China opportunity" or the "China threat," nor is it to provide a single view of China's future. In fact, the chapters represent a range of different perspectives, often viewing similar facts or events through different lenses. The goal of the volume, rather, is to identify the key forces and issues that need to be understood and monitored in China in the coming decade, and to analyze how those forces and issues interact with each other. The chapters not only show the current trajectory of the main forces that are shaping China, but also discuss how and why that trajectory could change, and the types of critical uncertainties that will have to be managed both inside and outside China. If everyone knew what China is going to be like 10 years from now, it would be easy to formulate and implement a strategy that would maximize benefits while minimizing risks. But the China story is not preordained. The plot will have twists and turns, many of which may not be currently part of the consensus view. Success in dealing with China will be determined by an ability to anticipate those twists and turns, and to understand their potential implications. That is precisely what we hope the present volume enables the reader to do.

2

China's Economy Into the Future[1]

Michael J. Enright
Director, Competitiveness Programs,
Hong Kong Institute of Economics and Business Strategy
Sun Hung Kai Professor,
School of Business of the University of Hong Kong
Director, Enright, Scott & Associates, Ltd.

Introduction

China's economic development since the onset of its reform program in 1979 has been nothing short of remarkable. Its development over the next several years is likely to be no less remarkable. While the Eleventh Five Year Program (FYP) provides an overall outline for developments from 2006 to 2010, the Program should be viewed as indicative rather than binding, or even as a reasonable forecast. The re-estimation of Chinese economic statistics resulting from the National Economic Census released in 2005 shows a stronger Chinese economy than had been known before, both in terms of economic size and the sustainability of the composition of the economy. While pressures for *renminbi* (RMB) appreciation remain, they are likely to be met with gradual movement against the U.S.

dollar for the foreseeable future. China's export economy will continue to grow and deepen as new assembly industries develop, as greater value is added in existing industries, as more activities are performed in China, and as capacity investments turn China into a net exporter in some heavy and materials industries in which it had previously been a net importer. China will remain one of the world's leading destinations for foreign direct investment and will become a more significant international investor itself, particularly in resource sectors.

China's importance as a market will continue to grow. China increasingly will be influencing world commodity markets and prices, and will become an important consumer market for a much wider range of goods than has been the case to date. China's regional economic differences will remain, as the more dynamic regions within the country power ahead, even in the face of the rise of a number of second and third-tier cities as significant economic entities. Urbanization will have a substantial impact on the production side as more and more people leave the farm and become employed in more productive manufacturing and service occupations, and on the market side as the new urban residents become far more accessible as consumers to local and foreign companies. Generating employment for the large number of migrants, however, will remain a significant challenge. Reform in the financial sector will improve the allocation of financial resources and reduce to a degree the constraint that a poorly performing financial sector has placed on China's development. The downsides associated with China's development, including environmental pollution and an increasing number of disaffected people, will continue to be major issues, but are not likely to derail China's economy to any significant extent over the next several years. Ironically, it is a potential overreaction to these pressures that is more likely to put a brake on economic development over the next five years or so.

As in the last five years, the most difficult challenges faced by companies operating in China in the next several years are unlikely to be challenges associated with China's macroeconomic development. Instead, problems are likely to stem from the challenges associated with combining political and administrative strategies with business and economic strategies, with the boom and bust cycles (and resulting policy responses) found in individual industries, and with the fierce industry-level competition found in a nation in which many industries are relatively new and competitive positions are not well-established. In essence, the biggest challenges will be microeconomic and micropolitical, rather than macroeconomic or macropolitical. It is these challenges that companies will have to overcome if they are to obtain maximum benefit from China's macroeconomic development over the next several years. It is these challenges that most analysts and companies ignore at their peril.

The Five Year Program

The reference point for China's development from 2006 to 2010 is the Eleventh Five Year Program. The shift from the word "Plan" to the word "Program" reflects a change of emphasis away from setting mandatory quantitative targets. Instead, the targets in the Program are important as indicators of the wishes of China's leadership as well as forecasts of what the leadership believes can be achieved. The Program adopted at the National People's Congress meetings in March 2006 calls for a doubling of per capita income from the 2000 level by 2010. The Program departed from earlier versions by not calling for specific targets for growth of the gross domestic product (GDP), but rather an expectation of real growth of around 7.5% per year, a change that is supposed to focus attention more on the "quality" than "quantity" of growth. The projections are that China's GDP would reach USD 3.23 trillion by 2010 (up from

USD 2.25 trillion in 2005) in current U.S. dollars and that per capita income would reach nearly USD 2,500 per year. Given that GDP growth in 2006 was actually on the order of 10.6%, and that growth in 2007 is also expected to exceed 10%, China will overshoot the 2010 projection handily.

The Program calls for more "balanced development," an emphasis on the "quality" of economic growth rather than the "quantity" of growth, greater investment in innovation, and greater energy efficiency. "Balanced development" is a catchphrase used to mean development that limits the economic disparities across regions and between the urban and rural economies. The Northeast joins the West as focal points of national attention, with increased transfer payments and infrastructure expenditures designed to help jump start those economies. The elimination of agricultural taxes and increases in farm incomes will be extended to help provide better balance between the urban and rural areas. Attempts will be made to raise the efficiency of agriculture and improve public services to rural areas, many of which are hardly touched by public services at present.

The focus on the "quality" of development derives from the view that much of China's manufacturing development, particularly export-oriented manufacturing, is low value-added and that foreign companies capture the bulk of the economic benefits from China's manufacturing. Indeed, the Chinese value-added component in most export industries is on the order of 20% to 25%, and few Chinese companies have their own technology or brands that allow them to obtain above-average profits. As a result, most Chinese enterprises are left to compete on price, resulting in cutthroat competition and low margins. This, in turn, leaves them with limited resources to invest in developing their own technology and brands. Such a commitment to "quality" of development is supposed to come with increased protection for intellectual property, though it seems Chinese policy, overall, is to minimize the payment for foreign intellectual property while improving overall intellectual property protection.

In order to ensure higher value-added production at home, the Chinese leadership wishes to foster investment in innovation. While "innovation" in China was once taken to be synonymous with "technological innovation," increasingly (if grudgingly) China's leaders appear to accept investments in new processes, new brands, and new management systems as forms of "innovation" as well. The typical focal point for investments in "innovation" in China has been research and development investments by state-owned enterprises, universities, and institutes. While these have led to success in terms of technological development (consider China's ability to put men into space for example), they have a spotty record of generating commercially successful innovations. Part of the reason is that the lack of intellectual property protection in China makes it very difficult for local companies to benefit from their own research and development. In the absence of sufficient incentives for the private sector to engage in research and development due to a lack of intellectual property protection, the R&D function tends to fall back to the state. While China is perfectly willing to ramp up state "innovation" investments, it appears less willing to set up an intellectual property regime that safeguards local or foreign companies in a meaningful way.

"Energy efficiency" is another phrase that is heard much more frequently in China. China has one of the world's least efficient economies in terms of energy utilization per dollar of GDP. This is due in part to relatively low levels of productivity across the economy, and to the fact that higher value manufacturing and services are not well-developed, so that while China is a leading producer in energy intensive products like steel and cement, in these industries China's level of technological sophistication is mixed and there are large numbers of highly inefficient facilities still in operation. In addition, domestic heating in many parts of China still relies on individual coal-fired stoves, and many factories use inefficient diesel generators to fill gaps in local power grid supply.

There are three main reasons why China's leaders are looking to improve the economy's energy efficiency. The first is simply to reduce the energy bill. China already is the world's second leading importer of oil after the United States. Oil price increases in 2005 showed the potential vulnerability of a Chinese economy increasingly reliant on foreign oil. The second reason is to ensure that China has energy resources sufficient to continue its economic expansion. Increasing energy efficiency would reduce the quantity of energy required for China's development, regardless of price. The third reason is to reduce the pollution inherent in the inefficient use of energy resources. Cleaner and more completely burning fuels, the elimination of obsolete plant and equipment, and shifts to more efficient plants and processes could also dramatically reduce the pollution that is starting to choke several of China's major cities. In any case, the stated intent of improving China's energy efficiency by 20% over the Eleventh Five Year Program is at best optimistic and at worst unrealistic. Of course, some areas might "meet" the target by underreporting energy utilization.[2]

The Eleventh Five Year Program also calls for further improvements in the economic system, reforms to the role of government in the economy, faster fiscal and financial reform, development of a modern market economy, improvements in human capital and education, improvements in income distribution and the social safety net, as well as enhanced investment in health and culture, among others. Most of these reforms can be viewed as continuations of existing policies rather than completely new departures—and the changes are largely in terms of emphasis rather than completely new ideas.

Over the 2006 to 2010 period, we would expect movement in the direction of "balanced development," "higher quality growth," "greater innovation," and higher "energy efficiency." This movement will be in part so that officials can show that they have been acting in a way consistent with the Program and in part it will be significant. However, these slogans should be regarded as aspirational and no one, not even China's leadership, believes that the issues will be resolved within a five-year period. Instead, these objectives should be viewed as important long-term goals of the State—along with rapid economic development, preserving national security, and assertion of national prestige.

Re-Estimation of Economic Figures

Going forward, China starts from a stronger economic base than had been previously imagined. The results of the National Economic Census conducted by the National Statistical Bureau (NSB) were announced in late 2005. The main result of the census was to increase the estimate of China's GDP by nearly 17%. The principal reason for the revision was the underestimation of the service sector and private sector activity by the previous estimation methods. While in the mid-1990s, there was some concern raised by foreign economists that the Chinese GDP numbers might have been overstated, in recent years, most reputable analysis considered the figures understated by more or less the 17% figure estimated by the National Statistical Bureau. The NSB also re-estimated GDP figures for the previous decade, adding about a percentage point to the growth rate in most years, placing China's real GDP growth rate over the 1990 to 2004 period at 10.5% per year.

One result of the revision is that when combined with robust real growth of just under 10% in 2005 and 10.6% in 2006, China's GDP (at around USD 2.512 trillion in 2006), is now the fourth highest in the world, behind that of the United States, Japan, and Germany. At present growth rates, China's GDP will surpass Germany's in 2008 and that of the United States by around 2035.[3] It should be noted that the revised estimates were not necessarily welcomed in all quarters within China, since many believed the revised figures would provide more ammunition to foreign "China Threat" proponents who believe that China's economic rise may be harmful to other economies.

The revised estimates also showed a healthier and more sustainable economic profile for China's economy than did the older estimates. In addition to new aggregate GDP figures, there were also new estimates of the various components of GDP. In particular, the new estimates revised down the portion of GDP accounted for by investment and revised up the portion of GDP accounted for by consumption. Under the new estimates, investment was estimated to have accounted for roughly 38% of GDP in the early 2000s, as opposed to around 45% of GDP. The former figure is considered much more sustainable than the latter. The revised estimates showed consumption roughly equal to 60% of GDP, up from prior estimates of around 50%, providing some evidence that consumer spending power is becoming a major engine of economic growth in China. Again, this is viewed as healthier than a situation in which net exports and investment were the main engines of economic growth.

Over the next several years, we would expect the trends seen in the re-estimation of the GDP figures to continue. That is, the service sector and private consumption will become more important contributors to China's economic growth. These are consistent with a modernization of the Chinese economy. In addition, any signs that China's enormously high savings rate will be somewhat reduced and turned into consumer demand raises the chances that a national market of more than 1 billion consumers will soon be a reality.

The RMB

China revalued the RMB against the U.S. dollar by 2.1% in July 2005 and indicated that it would manage the RMB exchange rate against an unspecified "basket of currencies." This move, plus the promise of eventual further liberalization, reduced the political pressure on China to do more on currency reform for much of 2005. Since that time, however, the RMB has appreciated slightly against the U.S. dollar (to RMB 7.5 per USD by mid-2007) and has followed the dollar's performance against essentially all other currencies. Thus, there is every indication that the RMB is being managed solely against the U.S. dollar, or against a currency basket that is so weighted toward the U.S. dollar that it is essentially the same thing. Given the relative strength of the U.S. dollar against other currencies in the latter portion of 2005, this reduced some of the pressure on the RMB, except of course against the U.S. dollar and from the U.S. Treasury. With the Chinese trade surplus reaching USD 178 billion for 2006 and its bilateral trade surplus with the United States reaching USD 235 billion in the same year, pressure for China to allow a sharper appreciation of the RMB versus the dollar and the currencies of other trading partners has been mounting.

China is likely to continue to resist this pressure for three basic reasons. The first is that it can. In the absence of a freely convertible currency, China can more or less do what it wants to in terms of exchange rate, as long as it is willing to pay the price for sterilizing its U.S. dollar inflows and is willing to put up with the geopolitical backlash. The second is that there is a sense that if China's exchange rate mechanism is not broken (at least for China), there is no reason to fix it. This is combined with fear of managing something more complicated than a fixed exchange rate, which is something that China has no real experience doing. The third is that the RMB is not kept at present levels against the U.S. dollar so much to support exports as it is to protect inefficient heavier industry from imports. Thus the exchange rate mechanism is far more defensive in actual use than offensive. After all, it is China's relatively poor regions with their disproportionate representation of heavy industry that are vulnerable to competition in the domestic market from imports from Korea, Taiwan, and Japan that pose the potential dilemma for China—not the affluent regions with booming exports, which China's leaders would just as soon reign in.

Over the next several years, we would expect China to manage a gradually appreciating RMB. While it is difficult to forecast, we would not be surprised to see a total appreciation on the order of a few percent per year or slightly more against the U.S. dollar, and to see the RMB track the U.S. dollar to a greater extent against other currencies. While China might diversify its basket of currencies somewhat, any wholesale movement away from the dollar, which would logically be accompanied by a change in its reserve portfolio, could see the value of China's large stash of U.S. Treasuries fall. However, we do not expect to see sudden shifts in the exchange rate, given the Chinese tendency to go slow on currency matters and China's lack of experience in managing anything but a fixed exchange rate. Nor do we expect a freely convertible RMB any time soon. We also expect that China's flexibility on the exchange rate will have more to do with the modernization of heavy industry in China and with the development of the economies of the West and the Northeast regions rather than with a cave-in to pressure from the rest of the world. Should China's less affluent regions start to prosper, there will be far less reason for China to maintain an exchange rate that most analysts consider undervalued. At the same time, the recognition of enormous "off balance sheet" liabilities, in terms of unfunded pensions and continued challenges in turning tax revenues into a sufficient social safety net, will start to temper economic pressures for appreciation, and could place limits on the amount of appreciation.

The RMB value is tied to China's growing reserves and investment capital that is expecting future appreciation. China's leadership has tried to stem the flow of some of the investment capital by making it more difficult for foreigners to buy and profit from the real estate market. It also is in the process of developing a strategy to hire international fund managers to manage a sizeable portion (on the order of USD 200 billion by some estimates), in a global investment portfolio. These funds would have the advantage of putting the money to work outside China and to yield potentially higher returns than U.S. Treasuries. Such a fund could become a substantial player if it were to concentrate its investments in certain areas.

China's Export Economy

China's position in the international economy is likely to continue to grow in importance. China is both the world's third leading exporter and importer. China's trade surplus ballooned from approximately USD 30 billion in 2004 to around USD 100 billion in 2005 and USD 178 billion in 2006. According to U.S. figures, China ran a trade surplus of just over USD 200 billion in 2005 and USD 235 billion in 2006. At the same time, however, China ran a sizeable trade deficit with the rest of Asia. This represents a situation in which goods stamped "Made in China" often have only approximately 25% or less Chinese value added. Instead of being the sole production location for a wide range of goods, China has become the last stop in a Pan-Asian production system in which advanced inputs and capital goods come from Japan, Korea, and Taiwan; other components and sub-assemblies come from Southeast Asia; and final goods are assembled in China for export to other markets around the world. This system can be seen not only in China's export rise, but also in the fact that many East Asian economies have seen their exports to China, mostly in industrial intermediates, grow by 20% or 25% or more per year in recent years.

Another important feature of China's export economy is that the bulk of China's exports, nearly 60% by value in recent years, have been produced by foreign-invested enterprises. When the exports mediated by international sourcing offices of multinational retailers and Hong Kong trading companies are also factored in, it becomes clear that many of the activities associated with China's export industries, such as research, development, design, marketing, logistics management, and so on, are not performed by Chinese companies, and in fact are not performed in China at all. This again serves to limit the value added in China itself. China's export success is more a matter of assembly in particular industries, rather than the presence of complete production chains. For example, the export of consumer electronics from China, where most of the companies exporting are foreign-owned, most of the advanced components are imported, and most of the distribution and marketing is done by non-Chinese companies, is a very different phenomenon than exports of consumer electronics products from Japan, which is often the source of the original technology, as well as the home of the most advanced component makers, the brand builders, and the companies doing distribution and marketing.

There is no significant indication that China's export growth will slow anytime soon. The burst of garment exports in early 2005, when quotas were reduced or eliminated, shows that China is still enormously competitive in light manufactured goods. While China's export growth in garments and textiles was slowed by the imposition of safeguard measures, these measures are only temporary. Most will be gone by 2008 or 2010. At that point, China will be able to leverage its competitiveness, limited only by the desire to reduce potential trade frictions, cost increases, and by the natural tendency of buyers to use more than one source to mitigate risk. In other light manufactured goods, China's growth will be increasingly limited only by global demand, as China becomes the de facto production location for a wide range of products.

China is also improving its position in other manufactured goods. China is already the assembly point for more than 50% of the world's consumer electronics production, a figure that is only likely to increase. An example is the notebook computer sector, in which a huge portion of the world's production capacity was shifted to a single city in China, Suzhou, in less than 18 months. In addition, as more and more electrical and electronic components are produced in China, China's component import bill is likely to be reduced sharply. This, in turn, may result in significant portions of the Pan-Asian production system being absorbed into China with concomitant fallout for other economies in the region.

At the same time, China is likely to emerge as a net exporter in other industries in which it historically has been a sizeable net importer. The growth in automotive exports indicates that China will eventually become a major supply base for automotive components as well as completed automobiles. Massive capacity investments in the steel sector have already transformed China from a sizeable net importer to a net exporter. While one might imagine that China's advantage in labor-intensive goods would lead to a comparative disadvantage in capital-intensive industries, it is not quite as straight forward as that. China is a capital-surplus nation which has been a net exporter of capital. In addition, labor intensity and capital intensity are not necessarily mutually exclusive. China's labor cost advantages in the construction of capital-intensive facilities means that the cost of constructing large-scale facilities in capital-intensive sectors like chemicals, steel, and cement can be a third or more lower than those found in other nations. Going forward, China's comparative advantages and disadvantages are more likely to be framed in terms of the sophistication of the business activities performed inside and outside of China, rather than a simple labor-intensive versus capital-intensive split.

Over the next several years, we would expect to see movement in China's export economy in several directions. China's position in industries formerly restricted by quotas will improve. China will become an assembly location for more and more industries, an example would be the auto sector. China will produce more and more of the components for its traditional export sectors, an example would be the electronics sector. An increasing number of activities will be performed in China in its traditional export industries, as skills and capabilities within China improve. This is already happening as production engineering, quality control, logistics, and some research and design are done in China. China will become a net exporter in a number of heavy and materials-related industries in which it is already a leading producer and consumer. The geographic profile of China's export sector will diversify to encompass more than just a few coastal regions. Finally, we expect to see Chinese firms themselves taking on greater prominence in the export sector with their own brands, international marketing, and global distribution. This is happening to a certain extent as companies like Haier and Huawei start to penetrate international markets, as TCL and Lenovo acquire foreign competitors, and as China's leaders encourage Chinese companies to go international, learn from the experience, and capture more value from the business system.

Each of these directions should result in higher value being added in China than is the case with today's export profile. Expansion to new assembly industries is the easiest step, and we would expect to see considerable movement in this direction in the next few years (for example, it took China less than five years to ramp up exports of furniture to world beating levels). Within the next decade, vertical integration is likely to displace foreign suppliers of all but the most advanced components for China's existing export industries. Japan and Korea (and perhaps Taiwan) will stay ahead, but the rest of the pan-Asian production system may be absorbed into China. The third direction, additional activities, will see some expansion, particularly in the upstream development, design, and applications research, but there are limits on the research side in China due to gaps in capabilities and intellectual property protection, and some downstream activities have to be done close to the customer.

The fourth direction, shifting from net importer to exporter in heavy industries is already happening in some sectors. The fifth direction will take time, but is starting to take place. As costs increase along China's coasts, some production is moving inland, following new infrastructure development, and seeking lower costs. Chinese firms becoming world leaders will be the most difficult and time consuming step, and probably well over a decade will be required to achieve widespread success. Chinese companies still lack the systems, capabilities, and resources to compete effectively in global markets, and it is not clear that purchasing complementary assets from competitors will shorten the process appreciably. In any case, the expansion of China's export economy is expected to move it from the world's third leading exporter in 2006 to the world's leading exporter by 2010.

Foreign Direct Investment

Inward foreign direct investment into China has been on the order of USD 60 billion per year for the last few years. Such levels should be sustainable for the foreseeable future. China is still an opening market with vast opportunities for foreign-invested companies that get their political/administrative and business/economic strategies right. In many sectors, China is the perhaps the best opportunity in the world today to enter and obtain a sizeable share of a large and growing market. China's World Trade Organisation (WTO) accession is making more and more sectors of China's economy open to foreign investment and its overall economic growth is fostering the development of new product markets and regional markets for both local and foreign companies. While China is actually a capital surplus nation, and therefore does not "need the money" associated with foreign direct investment, it continues to need the technology, market knowledge, business systems, and managerial expertise that accompanies the investment.

Even though the phase-in of China's WTO accession agreement has made foreign investment easier, there are still numerous sectors that are off-limits for foreign investors, or in which foreign companies are limited to minority shares. There is no reason to expect that China will go beyond its WTO commitments in these sectors. Other sectors, even if technically open to foreign companies, are still subject to approvals for everything from factory sites to employment and business practices. It is not surprising that the draft competition law that has been circulating seems largely to be a tool to limit the positions of foreign companies. Labor legislation is also seen to target foreign firms. In addition, under legislation passed by the National People's Congress in March 2007, the preferential tax treatment that many foreign firms have received in China will be replaced by a unified corporate tax rate of 25% for both domestic and foreign firms. Overall, there is an increasing sense among some Chinese elites that foreign investors have made substantial profits from their investments in China, that China needs foreign investors less than it used to, and that Chinese consumer, worker, and corporate interests need greater protection against foreign companies. The team of Hu Jintao and Wen Jiabao is viewed as more economically nationalist than their predecessors, and while there are no signs of significant rollbacks of policies toward foreign investment (other than the ones mentioned), many believe that China's environment for inbound foreign investment may get less friendly for many companies. On the other hand, companies that are able to find ways in which their investments can contribute to China's national goals will still be welcomed.

Perhaps the biggest change in terms of China's international investment position in the next several years will be in its position as an outward investor. Historically, China's outbound investment has been dwarfed by its inbound investment. This trend is likely to continue in the foreseeable future. However, there are already signs that China and Chinese companies will become far more aggressive as foreign investors over the next several years. The leading external investors from China to date have been in the energy and minerals sectors. Despite the high profile rejection of the CNOOC offer to purchase Unocal, China's oil companies have been doing deals in several countries around the world, including Ecuador, Sudan, Venezuela, Kazakhstan, and Russia. China National Petroleum Corporation already has oil and gas assets in 22 countries. Chinese minerals and metals companies have bought into mineral resources in Australia, Brazil, Chile, the Philippines, and Papua New Guinea, to name a just a few.

While the oil and mineral investments can be understood as China Inc. attempting to safeguard raw materials supplies, other Chinese companies invest abroad for other reasons. We would expect that sectors dominated by Chinese production would soon see internationalizing Chinese companies. The most logical industries for such initial forays are garments, footwear, appliances, and even electronics and automobiles. Haier's foreign investments are best understood as attempts to leverage competitive cost structures into world markets. The purchase of the IBM PC division by Lenovo and the TCL purchase of Thomson's European TV set business are best understood as attempts by Chinese companies to obtain the complementary resources and capabilities necessary to move from China-based companies focused on assembly manufacturing to internationally competitive companies with the full set of development, design, branding, marketing, and distribution activities. Teething pains indicate that such acquisitions are going to be a challenge for Chinese enterprises to manage effectively. It is yet to be seen whether a strategy of buying struggling foreign companies in profit-poor industries is the best way for Chinese enterprises to proceed.

Over the next several years, we are likely to see significant increases in outward investment from China. This is in part a natural economic phenomenon and in part the result of a "Go Out" or "Go Abroad" policy in which the central government is encouraging Chinese companies to become international competitors. In some cases, the clear impetus is to obtain resources and materials that the Party and state leadership believe are crucial to China's continued development. In other cases, there is a desire on the part of the firms and the central government to build up the capacity of Chinese enterprises to understand international markets, develop international brands, master international distribution, and develop internationally capable management systems.

China as a Market

China is becoming a market of increasing importance in a wide range of sectors. In several resource sectors, such as copper, iron ore, cement, oil, coal, aluminum, and others, China is either the world's leading or second leading consumer. The emergence of Chinese demand has influenced commodity prices around the world. In some cases, China is viewed as the main factor behind historically high prices. China's rise also has raised the specter of resource competition and resource shortages. China is expected to be importing about as much oil as Saudi Arabia exports by around 2012. If China starts to consume on a per capita basis the same quantity of resources as most middle-income economies, there is a fear that the world's supplies will simply run out. What is clear is that China will be a major influence on resource prices, policies, and strategies around the world and the approach that China takes, cooperative or not, toward other major resource consumers will have a major influence on how these markets develop. China seems to believe that the only way to ensure resource security is to own the resources themselves, i.e., it does not appear to believe that global markets by themselves will provide adequate supplies. This explains in part the outward investment by Chinese entities attempting to purchase resources or resource rights. Competition for resources can already be seen in the discussions over the terminus of a Russian oil pipeline, and over oil and gas exploration in the sea between China and Japan.

China also is becoming a market for a wide variety of other goods. The number of people living in households with a household income in excess of USD 5,000 per year has been growing at an estimated rate of over 18% per year, while the number of people living in households with household incomes greater than USD 15,000 per year has been growing at an estimated rate of 34% per year. China had less than 14 million mobile telephone subscribers in 1997, but had more than 390 million by 2005, and over 430 million by 2006. More people own a mobile phone in China than live in the United States (plus Mexico and Canada). The number of passenger cars sold in China grew from around 500,000 in 1997 to nearly 4 million in 2005. The value of outstanding home mortgages went from roughly USD 1.6 billion in 1997 to over USD 200 billion by 2004. According to Goldman Sachs, by the year 2015 China will account for approximately 29% of the world's sales of luxury branded goods, a figure that would put it on par with Japan, which was by far the world leader in 2006. China's outbound international tourism, which was on the order of 31 million person times in 2005, is expected to exceed 100 million person times by 2015. Economies all over Asia are gearing up to meet the demand.

China will become increasingly important as a market. There is no sign that its appetite for resources will diminish. In fact the demand appears to be accelerating in some sectors. China's position as a leading producer of light manufactured goods, electronics, and other goods will make it an industrial market of enormous size. In terms of consumer markets, by the year 2010, China's per capita income (likely to be USD 3,000 or higher in much of the country) will be at the level at which there is typically very rapid growth of the middle class and consumption of all sorts of goods. In purchasing power parity terms (PPP), China's per capita income is already well above the USD 3,000 level. As more of

China's population moves to the cities and becomes employed in the manufacturing and service sectors, and thus accessible to retailers, China's consumer markets should exhibit rapid growth.

China's Regional Economies

China's economy is more a series of loosely coupled regional economies, rather than a single national economy. There are several reasons for this phenomenon. In the past, efforts were made to ensure that cross-city and cross-provincial flows of information were restricted to the Chinese Communist Party, the central government, and the People's Liberation Army. Another reason was the desire to make each local economy self-sufficient in order to make China less vulnerable to outside attack. Another was a command and control economic system administered by local officials. In the absence of markets, inter-provincial and inter-city trade was often limited to raw materials, staples, and a few specialized goods. Still another reason was a lack of sufficient infrastructure to link the various city and provincial economies together into a coherent whole.

Even after more than 25 years of reform and greater market-orientation, the regional nature of China's economy remains pronounced. The national highway and rail networks are only now beginning to knit the country together. For example, a truck trip from Wuhan to Shenzhen, which would have taken several days a few years ago, can now be done in under 12 hours. However, barriers to trade and investment between cities and provinces in China still prevent the formation of a single market. The 12 hours can turn back into days if city and provincial governments require changes of trucks or impose regulations or costs on inter-provincial travel. Calls in the Eleventh Five Year Program for greater economic integration in the Yangtze River Delta and Bohai regions show how little has actually happened in terms of linking together cities, even within China's main economic regions. Only in the Greater Pearl River Delta (Hong Kong plus Macao plus the Pearl River Delta Economic Zone of Guangdong Province) has economic integration proceeded across municipal jurisdictions to any great extent, and that is largely due to the strong role played by Hong Kong. Even there, however, the relationship between different jurisdictions is best characterized as fiercely competitive and self-interested rather than enlighteningly cooperative. The "Pan-Pearl River Delta" or "Nine plus two" initiative to link together economically the nine provinces of Southern China and the two Special Administrative Regions of Hong Kong and Macao pushed by Zhang Dejiang, Communist Party Secretary of Guangdong Province and a member of the Politburo of the Central Committee of Chinese Communist Party, is the first attempt to create a true multi-provincial regional economy in China. Even the proponents of this plan indicate that it may be a decade or more before it bears fruit.

The regional nature of China's economy provides some of its starkest contrasts, and biggest challenges. The Greater Pearl River Delta, the Yangtze River Delta, and (to a certain extent) the Bohai Rim have been powering ahead, while the Northeast and the West have been falling further behind. Some coastal cities like Shenzhen and Shanghai have per capita incomes on the order of USD 6,000 or USD 7,000 per year, while some interior provinces, such as Guizhou, barely crack USD 500 per year. Nearly 70% of China's exports come from (and nearly 70% of China's inward FDI is invested in) approximately 3% of its land mass. In the early days of China's reform period, such regional disparities were viewed as necessary or even favorable. China did not have the resources to build the infrastructure to link the whole nation to the global economy at once. Moreover, national leaders wished to confine economic experiments to relatively small areas, and it was felt that the learning and resources developed along the coast would then be used to develop the interior.

The obvious issues arising from regional disparities are uneven development, regional jealousies, and potential social disruption. In recent years, fearing such results, the central government has turned more of its attention to the West and Northeast, engaging in transfer payments to help develop these regions and to supplement incomes of those displaced by the reform process. The "Go West" program has resulted in massive transfers from the central government as well as vast investments in infrastructure, education, and training in order to help stimulate development. More recently, similar programs are being instituted in the Northeast, China's rust belt and home to thousands of relatively inefficient state-owned enterprises. In pursuing this objective, the government has an eye toward preventing the spread of social discontent in one of the few areas in China in which there are arguably large numbers of people that have been made worse off by the reform process, rather than better off.

There are other, less obvious, impacts of regional disparities as well. China's leadership has not been able to employ macroeconomic policies as if the country had a single economy growing at 10.5% per year. Instead, it has had to manage a situation in which some coastal areas have been growing much faster than that and some interior areas much slower than that. Faced with the choice between "playing it down the middle," and having nonsensical macro policies for everyone all of the time, and flip-flopping in order to have optimal policies for everyone at least some of the time, the tendency has been to choose the latter. As central control over the economy is reduced, it is becoming more and more difficult to stimulate the less developed areas without having inflation along the coast. Recent efforts to limit investments in aluminum and cement and to reduce consumer expenditures on autos and housing show attempts to use micro tools to address macro problems. These attempts are unlikely to lead to satisfactory results and could well exacerbate the problems they were designed to solve.

While most of the efforts to reduce regional disparities have focused on improving the performance of the economically backward regions, there are some signs that the more dynamic regions might actually be constrained in order to generate a more equal spread of the economy. While analysts believe that the sacking of Shanghai Communist Party Secretary Chen Liangyu in September 2006 was due in part to corruption investigations and in part to factional infighting, some observers noted Chen's opposition to reining in Shanghai's booming property market, despite orders from the central leadership to do so, as a contributing factor. Similarly, Du Shicheng, who was widely associated with Qingdao's construction boom, was stripped of his posts as Party Secretary of Qingdao and Deputy Party Secretary of Shandong Province in December 2006 under corruption charges. By early 2007, officials in most coastal cities and towns appeared far more conservative in their development plans and far more focused than before on enforcing a series of measures enacted in 2005 and 2006 to stem property price increases. In some places, efforts to limit economic growth rather than to maximize economic growth appeared to be coming into play. If the attempts to rein in coastal development were to go too far, China would be in danger of stifling its main economic growth engine, something it can ill afford to do.

Over the next several years, we would expect to see some movement towards the development of a national economy. The national highway and rail infrastructure will start knitting the economy together. Municipal and provincial boundaries to trade and investment, however, are likely to come down only slowly. Efforts to integrate the economies of the Greater Pearl River Delta, the Yangtze River Delta, and the Bohai Rim will continue. The Pan-Pearl River Delta initiative is likely to evolve into a national test case for the creation of the linkages between provinces and the reduction of barriers between provinces necessary to create national markets in China. The Bohai Rim should firmly join the Greater Pearl and Yangtze River Deltas as a third growth engine for China. Elsewhere, a range of second-tier cities will start to develop and become interesting business cities and markets in their own right to a much greater extent than has been the case to date. While these cities will pull some areas along, we do not expect to see any appreciable diminution of regional disparities over the next several years. Instead, the dynamic regions are likely to race ahead further with other areas of China forced to content themselves with an "all boats rising" situation. The alternative of actually throttling the coastal economies in order to achieve greater balance would be more likely to happen inadvertently than by design.

Urbanization

China's urban development is having an increasing impact on its economy. In the days of the command economy, each city and even each district within each city was designed to be economically self-sufficient or nearly so. The result was absolutely horrendous land planning whereby each major district of each major city would often have commercial, residential, industrial, and agricultural land. In order to create modern commercial centers, virtually every city in China has to be ripped apart and redeveloped from scratch. This is one reason for the massive redevelopment that can be seen in many of China's major cities. The economic value generated by the creation of modern cities that can serve as commercial centers in their own right, as commercial centers for their hinterlands, and as part of a network of urban nodes, is enormous and in most cases easily sufficient to fund redevelopment.

Another major issue associated with urbanization is population distribution. Roughly two-thirds of China's population is still in the rural setting. These people are generally stuck in non-productive agricultural employment, whereas China will eventually require only approximately one-fifth the number of farmers that it has today. The rural economy has been a drag on overall development in China for two main reasons. The first is that the rural economy is relatively less productive than the urban economy. The second is that people living in the rural settings have been generally inaccessible to major domestic and foreign companies as consumers or producers due to their low income and the logistical difficulty in reaching them.

The Chinese Academy of Social Sciences expects that 350 million or more people will leave the rural setting in the next 15 years. Many of these people will move from less affluent interior cities and provinces toward the coast, continuing a phenomenon that has been going on for more than two decades. While the magnitude of the influx has been greater in the Greater Pearl River Delta, where cities such as Shenzhen and Dongguan, which hardly existed 20 years ago, today have populations on the order of 11 million to 12 million each, while China's other economically dynamic regions, such as the Yangtze River Delta and the Bohai Rim, have also seen significant influxes of people. In all three regions, urban development is proceeding rapidly and is likely to continue to do so.

It is expected that in addition to migration to the coast, there will be substantial migration to cities all over China. As of 2004, China already had more than 100 cities with a population of more than one million people. Virtually all of these cities are likely to see significant increases in population over the next 15 years and many more cities will join the ranks of cities with more than one million population. There are likely to be four major impacts on China's economy. The first is that in China when workers leave the farm for urban or suburban settings, they generally enter occupations more productive than subsistence farming and thus add to total productivity in the country. The second is that the vast numbers of unskilled and semi-skilled workers that move to the cities and suburban areas will add to the manufacturing workforce and serve to keep wages in many manufacturing activities low for the foreseeable future. This in turn will enhance China's competitiveness in labor-intensive manufactured goods. The third is that once the people are in the cities they are increasingly reachable as consumers. This will be particularly true with the completion of the national trunk highway and rail network. The fourth is that there will be substantial pressure on the economy to provide employment for these people, reducing the chances that government will impose policies that will stifle economic growth.

Over the next several years, we expect the various aspects of urbanization, urban development, redevelopment, and migration to the cities to accelerate. The impact on the economy will be largely positive, as more people are brought into higher productivity occupations and as more people become consumers. We expect that the development will spread from the first-tier cities of Shanghai, Beijing, Guangzhou, and Shenzhen to several cities in the more dynamic regions (the Greater Pearl River Delta, the Yangtze River Delta, and the Bohai Rim) as well as to second and third-tier cities elsewhere in China. In fact, the rise of the second and third-tier cities will be a major theme of the next 20 to 30 years. The ability to predict which cities will be the next to develop will be enormously valuable going forward.

Urbanization will not be without its challenges. There will be problems associated with urban redevelopment and the displacement of people that redevelopment entails. There will be issues associated with providing the urban services and amenities required for growing urban populations. There will also be environmental strains created by more and larger urban centers. While the challenges will be major, we expect that they will remain manageable over the next several years.

Reform in the Financial Sector

While China's financial sector has a long way to go, there has been substantial progress. By far the most important part of the financial sector is the banking sector, which typically supplies on the order of 87% of the capital deployed in China, according to the People's Bank of China (PBoC). While non-performing loans (NPLs) have been the bane of the sector, approximately 60% of the non-performing loans run up by the banking sector have been hived off to asset management companies, which by 2006 had managed to sell off 69% of the loans under their purview. Despite what must be considered an optimistic set of NPL numbers issued by China's big banks, analysts estimate that China's NPLs at the end of 2005 were equal to around 25% of GDP.[4]

Tens of thousands of state-owned companies have been shut down or shifted out of the state sector and millions of employees have been laid off from state-owned enterprises, thereby reducing the drain on the banking sector. Major international banks have been taking strategic stakes in China's big state-owned banks and have promised to help instill proper credit and risk analysis. The process of preparing three of the big four banks for overseas listings instilled greater discipline than had been the case in the past. The Hong Kong listings of the China Construction Bank, Industrial and Commercial Bank, and Bank of China were themselves landmarks in China's financial history. So too were the licenses granted in December 2006 to the first foreign banks incorporated in China under its WTO market opening pledge. The banks, all registered in Shanghai, were Bank of East Asia (Hong Kong), Standard Chartered Bank (UK with a strong Hong Kong hub), HSBC (UK with a strong Hong Kong hub), Mizuho Corporate Bank (Japan), Hang Seng Bank (Hong Kong, a subsidiary of HSBC), Bank of Tokyo-Mitsubishi UFJ (Japan), DBS Group (Singapore), ABN-Amro Bank (Netherlands), and Citibank (U.S.). While we should not expect a Western-style banking sector to develop any time soon, all indications are that we are seeing real reform in the financial sector. Since allocation of financial resources has been a significant hindrance on China's economy to date, we might expect the easing of what has been a major constraint to China's growth. A more detailed analysis of the banking sector can be found in Chapter 6 in this volume.

Another positive factor has been the recent economic performance of the large state-owned enterprises whose shares are held by SASAC, the State-owned Assets Supervision and Administration Commission. Taken as a whole, SASAC companies registered record profits in 2005 and 2006, on the back of monopoly positions in infrastructure industries and increases in values of raw materials stocks among others. The importance of the profitability of the SASAC companies is that the sooner these companies are consistently profitable, the sooner they will be able to fund themselves through the capital markets, and the less reliant they will be on capital from the state banking sector. In addition, the more profitable they are, the more likely they will be able to pay back whatever loans they have outstanding to the banking sector.

The rest of China's financial sector remains relatively underdeveloped. The stock markets in the Chinese Mainland are still not a game for the timid. China's stock markets were among the world's worst performers from 2000 to 2005, before seeing a spectacular rise in 2006 (the Shanghai Index went up 130%) and early 2007, before some market adjustments mid-year. Attempts to float some of the "untradable" state shares, which accounted for approximately two-thirds of the shares of the companies listed on China's exchanges, failed in 1999 and 2001, but succeeded starting in 2005 with a plan to gradually bring those shares onto the market while compensating investors for losses incurred as a result. In 2006, in addition to new initial public offerings, which had been banned during a period of reflection and planning, the Chinese government also started to push the development of a bond market as an alternative to bank finance. At the same time, however, the Chinese government has bailed out several of the country's largest securities companies in an effort to quell concern over the poorly managed and regulated securities sector.

The outlook over the next several years is for a gradually improving financial sector with more and more state-owned companies allowed to rise and fall on their own merits and with fewer and fewer bailed out by state-owned banks. This will allow China to open the financial sector to a greater extent without the fear that foreign banks will somehow eclipse the local banks. Instead, we expect to see the big Chinese banks become allied with foreign banks where the Chinese bank has the branch network, the access to RMB deposits, and the retail presence, while foreign partner banks are involved in corporate and investment banking, credit cards, and value added services in conjunction with the Chinese banks. In the process, the private sector is likely to obtain much easier access to bank credit, although it may still be blocked from a significant presence in the equity markets. The securities sector is likely to be a tougher nut to crack in terms of creating long term confidence in the market. A gradual unwinding of the non-tradable share overhang, a gradual increase in access of foreign shareholders to China's A-share market (first through the QFII or Qualified Foreign Institutional Investor plan), and eventual access to the A-share market by foreign issuers is the most likely evolution.

While there has been a great deal of progress, China's financial sector is likely to continue to be an inefficient allocator of resources and therefore a major constraint on China's overall development. While the banking sector is far less likely to be a source of economic collapse than many outside China tend to believe, nascent capital markets remain a risk for the unwary investor.

Downsides to China's Economic Emergence

There are of course downsides to China's economic development that will continue into the foreseeable future. The environmental impact of China's rapid development has been substantial. According to the World Bank, China has 16 of the world's 20 most polluted cities and the health impact of environmental pollution already costs China tens of billions of dollars per year. A number of protests have occurred in China over polluting factories and industrial complexes. However, the truth of the matter is that relatively few places in China have the levels of income at this point at which environmental considerations are viewed as comparable in importance to economic growth. Thus, while environmental rules and regulations exist, it is often easier for companies either to pay the minimal fines involved or to ignore environmental regulations altogether. Local governments, many of which have investments in polluting facilities, do not necessarily see enforcement of environmental regulations as a first priority. While improving the environment is a clear goal of the Eleventh Five Year Program, in reality, we do not expect that there will be substantial overall improvement soon. The best we can probably hope for is that environmental degradation will be slowed and eventually reversed. The question is whether China will adopt an approach that will yield environmental benefits, or lessen the environmental impact of its development over the longer term. It is worthy of note that some of the more affluent cities in China are starting to take up an environmental mantle in order to provide a better place for higher technology, higher value-added industries, and mobile professionals and workers.

For the first 25 years of the reform process, the Chinese Communist Party and the Chinese government could point to the fact that the vast majority of Chinese people benefited from the reform process. However, middle-aged and elderly workers displaced from traditional state-owned enterprises have had a very difficult time becoming gainfully employed in the modern market-oriented economy. Many rural households have not seen their incomes increase in years. Sprawling cities have displaced many people, many of whom have not received the compensation to which they are entitled. Local corruption is a major issue in the privatization process and in the land clearance process. In addition, while for the first few decades of the reform period most people in China appeared to compare their present state (favorably) with their own past, the growth of conspicuous consumption and a wealthy class has shifted the comparison for many from their own past to the new-found present wealth of others. The fact that many of the individuals involved have amassed their wealth in questionable ways only adds to the discontent. The potential for social backlash has become a major focal point for China's most senior leaders. Preventing and dealing with so-called "public order disturbances" has become a major concern. While few expect that these protests will spiral out of control, they are receiving attention at the very highest levels of the Chinese leadership.

China's economic rise, and its policies that limit foreign access to China's own markets, have resulted in a backlash in some quarters. Many in the international community believe that China is benefiting asymmetrically from its contact with the international economy. Some of the concern can be seen in the re-imposition of restrictions on Chinese garment exports after the rapid rise in Chinese exports in early 2005, in the political furor that emerged in the United States when CNOOC attempted to purchase Unocal, when Spanish shoemakers torched a warehouse storing "Made in China" shoes in late 2004, and in the fact that China has been subject to more anti-dumping actions than any other country by a wide margin over the last few years. In 2006 and early 2007, the United States and the European Union both ratcheted up their attempts to get China to change its policies. The U.S. filed unfair subsidy actions against a range of Chinese industries at the WTO, and the E.U. issued a trade paper that was noteworthy for its non-diplomatic tone. Ironically, while the loudest voices concerning the "China threat" come from the United States and Western Europe, the greatest concerns are in developing economies whose producers have been displaced from global markets, and even from their home markets. Developing nations that do not have significant natural resource deposits and have not found a way of benefiting from China's own growth are in danger of being left behind. However, it is in the U.S. and the E.U. that China's burgeoning trade surplus makes it potentially vulnerable to a protectionist backlash.

Despite these downsides, there is no apparent force that will derail China's economy anytime soon. The underlying dynamic appears to be powerful enough to ensure strong growth for at least the next five to ten years. This does not mean that China will see no bumps along the road, or that it is immune to business cycles. It just means that it still is operating from a low base and many of the issues that could become problematic are either improving or at least receiving attention from the central leadership. Perhaps the greatest threat to China's continued economic growth over the next several years actually comes from the leadership itself. If China becomes too redistributionist, if it throttles the coastal economies in efforts to bring them under control, if it makes China an unattractive place for foreign firms, if it slows down the reform process, if it emphasizes "quality" of growth beyond which China can reasonably produce and sacrifices "quantity" in the process, if it fosters inefficient land use by trying to reign in property prices, and if, as a result, it fails to deliver sufficient employment to absorb migrants from the rural sector, then it could have significant problems in both the economic and social spheres.

Challenges for Companies in China

Despite the attention focused on China's macroeconomic development, the biggest challenges for companies operating in China are often not macroeconomic at all. While China exhibited substantial macroeconomic fluctuations in the 1980s and 1990s, these have subsided somewhat in the 2000s. Overall macroeconomic growth has been healthy in recent years and is expected to remain healthy over the next several years, in excess of 8% real GDP growth per year. For most companies, aggregate macroeconomic growth in China has not been the most difficult issue they have faced over the last several years. Instead, the challenges of convincing consumers to spend, the challenges of getting things done in China, the challenges of dealing with government and the Party at all levels, the challenge of attracting and retaining key personnel in China, the challenges of microeconomic development in individual sectors, and the challenge of ferocious competition have been far more difficult.

Despite China's movement towards a market economy and its accession into the World Trade Organization, China remains an extremely challenging place from a regulatory and political standpoint. While the rules and regulations are becoming clearer over time, how they are interpreted and enforced is still subject to great uncertainty and potential inconsistency over time and place. In addition, numerous industries still require a range of permissions or special arrangements for both domestic and foreign firms. When combined with a WTO accession process that is considered to be moving in the right direction (but slowly), the business landscape remains potentially treacherous for foreign companies. This means that it is still essential for foreign companies to try to find win-win solutions in which the company's investments bring some knowledge or expertise that China needs if they are to receive favorable treatment.

Among the leading challenges faced by all types of companies in China is the ability to attract and retain key employees. While people with basic skill levels are relatively easy to find and there are a vast number of university graduates available to take up positions requiring a basic college education, the stock of key managerial, financial, professional, technical, and multilingual staff is still quite limited. It is estimated that China needs hundreds of thousands more trained managers than it produces, and China has distinct shortages of people with world-class financial or professional experience. Even in technical fields where China graduates tens or hundreds of thousands per year, only a small fraction of these graduates are viewed as suitable hires by leading companies. The result is that major foreign and domestic companies are chasing the same pools of people and are bidding up salaries in some categories. Many foreign companies talk of the costs associated with investing heavily in developing high-fliers only to have them poached by rivals.

While China's overall macroeconomic growth rates have been relatively predictable in recent years, microeconomic developments in individual industries have been far less so. Industries in China have shown a tendency to take off, grow rapidly, attract massive investment, start overheating, and perhaps attract a policy response that reduces demand just as new capacity comes on line. This was the pattern in the automobile sector, in which rapid growth attracted massive capacity investments, where the central government stepped in to reduce auto loans, and where much new capacity has remained idle. As a result, sales value grew by 40%, 5%, and 30% in consecutive years. Even though the macroeconomic picture was stable with 10% growth, the volatility and competition in the auto sector has made it very difficult for any company to hit its profitability targets. The same phenomenon has been seen in industry after industry, in which a five-year growth rate of 20% or 25% per year often masks massive volatility. The inability to predict and deal with such volatility often means companies miss their profit targets even if their medium-term industry forecasts are accurate. Dealing with volatility involves not just an understanding of the marketplace and of competition, but also of potential policy moves and political imperatives.

Finally, perhaps the single most important reason that many companies find it difficult to turn China's rapid development into profit is competition. Given the size and importance of China's markets, local and foreign companies are willing to make investments and take risks in order to become established. While sometimes the magnitude of investment seems irrational, we must remember that most modern industries in China are still very early in their histories. The shakeouts in most industries in China have not yet taken place and we simply do not know who the winners and losers will eventually be. It will take time for the cycle of investment, competition, and shakeout to occur. Until the shakeouts occur in a given sector, we are likely to see boom and bust cycles, or simply bust cycles. While the presence of companies backed by the central government or by local governments in China (many of which may have goals beyond profit maximization) complicates matters, the potential and unsettled nature of Chinese markets would attract large investment anyway. In many industries, competitive positions achieved in the next five to ten years could become entrenched for decades. Of course, the willingness to fight for such positions makes it difficult for companies in several industries to show profits today. The home appliance industry as a whole lost money in China for six consecutive years before a true shakeout began. Three years later, after significant consolidation and exit, a reasonable level of profitability was being restored.

Over the next several years, we expect that most of these major challenges will remain. China will become more market-oriented, but political and administrative analysis and strategies will remain as important as business and economic analysis and strategies. Attracting and retaining key personnel will continue to be major challenges as the shortages of highly skilled individuals are only gradually reduced. Microeconomic and sectoral developments will remain far more difficult to predict and deal with than macroeconomic developments. Competition in many industries in China is likely to continue to be fiercer than found elsewhere.

Despite its rapid economic growth, China will remain a very challenging environment for most companies for the foreseeable future. Major challenges involve sectoral level policies, overinvestment in particular industries, and resulting ferocious competition. In addition, the continued importance of governments of different levels and the Party in China's economy make it essential for companies to understand the nature of China's leadership, and the forces that will influence policies going forward. This in turn, requires an understanding of China's international relations, its socio-political issues, its potential economic weak spots, the outlook of China's present and future leaders, and how related issues and forces can shape China's future. It is the ability of companies and organizations to understand these forces, in addition to the nation's underlying economic conditions, that will determine the overall performance of enterprises in China-related activities in the years to come.

Notes

1. The author wishes to acknowledge the support of the Hong Kong Institute for Economics and Business Strategy of the University of Hong Kong for this work.
2. In the late 1990s, a number of Western economists began to claim that China's GDP growth had to be less than that reported because the energy utilization figures would not support such growth. It turned out that China was moving to a somewhat less energy-dependent economic structure, and many local governments responded to central government edicts to close inefficient, polluting, dangerous coal mines by reporting the

closure of mines that were never actually closed. The result was not an overstatement of growth, as the later Economic Census showed that growth was actually understated, but an understatement of energy utilization. This shows the challenges of trying to reach conclusions based on Chinese numbers without knowing the underlying facts.

3. Few analysts believe that China can continue at 10+% growth rates for that long. Instead, forecasters generally come up with dates in the 2040s for China's GDP to pass that of the United States.

4. See, for example, Syetarn Hansakul, "China's Banking Sector: Ripe for the Next Stage?," *Deutsche Bank Research Report*, December 7, 2006 and Jonathan Anderson's chapter in this volume.

Bibliography

Anderson, Jonathan 2005, "How to Think About China," UBS Investment Research, Asian Economic Perspectives, Hong Kong: UBS.

China Daily 2006, "The Eleventh Five Year Program," www.chinadaily.com.cn.

China Statistical Press various years, *China Statistical Yearbook*, Beijing: China Statistical Press.

The Economist Intelligence Unit various editions, *China Country Report*, London: The Economist Group.

The Economist Intelligence Unit 2004, *Coming of Age: Multinational Companies in China*, London: The Economist Group.

Enright, Michael J. 2004, "China and International Competitiveness," Deutsche Bank China Expert Series, Hong Kong: Deutsche Bank.

Enright, Michael J. 2005, "Competitiveness Examined: China's Regional Disparities," Deutsche Bank China Expert Series, Hong Kong: Deutsche Bank.

Enright, Michael J. 2005, "Rethinking China's Competitiveness," *Far Eastern Economic Review, 168,* 9, October, pp. 16-20.

Enright, Michael J., Edith E. Scott, and Ka-mun Chang 2005, *Regional Powerhouse:The Greater Pearl River Delta and the Rise of China,* Singapore: John Wiley & Sons.

Hansakul, Syetarn 2006, "China's Banking Sector: Ripe for the Next Stage?," *Deutsche Bank Research Report*, Frankfurt: Deutsche Bank.

Wilson, Dominic and Roopa Purushothaman 2003, "Dreaming with BRICs: The Path to 2050," *Goldman Sachs Global Economics Paper No. 99*, New York: Goldman Sachs.

Websites of the Chinese Government, the Chinese Communist Party, the Chinese Ministry of Commerce, the National Statistical Bureau of China, *China Daily, People's Daily,* and the U.S. Department of Commerce.

Articles in the *China Daily, People's Daily, Xinhua, Financial Times, New York Times,* and *South China Morning Post.*

3

China: Key Issues for Business

Kenneth J. DeWoskin
*Professor Emeritus of International Business and
Asian Languages and Cultures, University of Michigan
Former Partner,
PricewaterhouseCoopers, China Ltd.*

Introduction

In recent years, China's stunning momentum in economic growth, trading power, wealth accumulation, regional power, and prestige has continued to charge ahead. Double digit GDP growth has been fueled by even more rapid growth in fixed asset investment and money supply. By 2006, China's GDP was the fourth largest in the world, behind only the U.S., Germany, and Japan. China's trade surplus grew six-fold from 2004 to 2006. China's foreign exchange reserves passed Japan's in the first half of 2006 and broke through USD 1 trillion in October 2006. In addition to double-digit expansion of exports and imports, China's outbound investment has increased rapidly, reaching USD 16.1 billion in 2006. Savings rates have remained very high, by some estimates in excess of 50% of income, and liquidity throughout the economy has reached new heights. Acceleration of this momentum in 2006 and 2007 has shown that the efforts of the central government to cool the economy are not achieving the desired results and unless China is charting new territory in economic development, the rate of growth and resulting imbalances could be reaching a precarious point.

Although the strategic impact of China's rise on all aspects of global life (carbon, iron ore, pandemics, information technology, merger and acquisition activity) is widely discussed in the international media, the meaning of China's rise for China and the rest of the world is often unclear. Depending on the commentator, China has become a wakened dragon, the world's factory, an economic miracle, an opportunity, a threat, a strategic partner, a strategic enemy, an exporter of deflation, and an exporter of inflation. Some writers predict an unstoppable rise of Asia, powered by China, to dominate the world. Others predict imminent collapse.

As China's economic growth has continued to outpace the other three-fourths of the world, China's formidable challenges, domestically and internationally, have yet to be persuasively or fundamentally addressed by its leadership. President Hu Jintao and Premier Wen Jiabao have consolidated their power and made their mark on all aspects of domestic policy. Nonetheless, the implementation of economic, social, and political initiatives across the country has remained fragmented, uncertain, and incomplete. Some of the most cherished concepts of the previous administrations have died a quiet death (such as Jiang Zemin's "Three Represents") and some of the most noteworthy programs have been abandoned or replaced (such as the "Go West" campaign). At the National People's Congress in early 2007, three strong themes representing the vision of the current leadership were promoted consistently: "Building the Harmonious Society," "Building the New Socialist Countryside," and "Achieving Green Growth."

Social turbulence, and the government's aggressive responses to it, has appeared to escalate in recent years, with a number of high profile encounters, many with reported deaths at the hands of the military police, public security, or unidentified thugs. These incidents are almost all eruptions by aggrieved rural citizens who have no other avenue to expose and constrain local corruption. Severe cases have combined land expropriation with deadly environmental degradation, such as farmers being driven off their land for the construction of a polluting insecticide factory. Such disturbances feature local Communist Party officials, in collusion with developers, converting agricultural land to industrial use, without adequate consultation, compensation, or safeguards for pubic health or the environment.

It has also become evident that a new battle line has emerged between the Party and a growing army of Internet bloggers seeking to blow open China's information flows, which are still throttled in the traditional print and broadcast channels and are under the monopoly control of the Party's propaganda apparatus. Considerable pressure continues to be exerted on the Internet, SMS message system, and other non-traditional means of communication and virtual assembly; and China has pressed forward with technologies and manpower to enable surveillance, as well as documentation of the wide range of crimes related to current broad concepts of state secrets, and other content seen as undermining the stability of the state.

With the completion of China's WTO phase-in period, trading partners are showing impatience with commitments they argue remain unmet. The coming years will be punctuated with trade disputes, as the rest of the world takes measure of China's development success and wealth and, as a result, seems less inclined to be tolerant of what they perceive as unfair practices. The upshot will be a period marked by protracted tension, negotiation, and dispute resolution processes. While the particulars of the complaints vary—subsidies, preferential treatment, intellectual property rights—all are rooted in the profound and continued entanglements of government and business in China, the intertwined flows of their resources, and the alignments of their interests. It is difficult to see an easy resolution to the underlying conflicts. In the eyes of the developed world, China is a non-market economy. In China's eyes, it is a developing socialist-market economy that needs freedom of action to progress.

Our goal in this chapter is to identify issues of importance to multinational companies operating in China by bridging global and Chinese perspectives on recent developments. We begin with a short list of current opportunities and threats, primarily from the perspective of Multinational Corporations (MNCs) and other foreign investors in China. Then, we follow with a commentary on China's achievements and challenges; with updates on recent government moves to sustain high growth rates and social stability; and an overview of China's strategies moving forward. Finally, we include a discussion of the five major dynamics in contemporary China that we believe will define the future: 1) population dynamics, 2) marketization dynamics, 3) value chain dynamics, 4) institutional dynamics, and 5) environmental dynamics.

Opportunities and Threats for Business

Advocates of ancient yin-yang theory would argue that the opportunities and threats for China over the next several years are one and the same. There are many key indicators for China that could move significantly in either direction, perhaps with collective momentum, and in some cases dependent on external factors. Overall, China's GNP growth has been driven most strongly by exports and fixed asset investment. Employment gains have not been a significant contributor, nor have total factor productivity gains. In contrast to India, China's development has brought an aggregate loss of jobs. Although the standing campaign to rein in fixed asset investment was reiterated as recently as the Spring 2007 National People's Congress, it was clear from the specific plans and budgets presented at the Congress that China's current leadership believes that fixed asset investment and exports remain keys to growth. Externally, there are concerns about adverse trade actions, currency rebalancing, protectionist trade trends, and economic and import slowdowns in China's major markets.

Opportunities

For the better part of a decade, analysts have decried the low consumption figures in China and the fact that GDP growth year after year was driven by exports and infrastructure investment. Now there are signs that consumption is taking off. Starting with the surge in automotive sales in 2003, we have seen large ticket item expenditures at a formidable level. China has joined the U.S. and Japan as a major market for luxury goods producers. But perhaps more importantly, investment-grade private expenditures, such as residential property and related expenditures, are reaching surprisingly high levels in the metropolises of Beijing, Shanghai, and Guangzhou. This leads us to predict the following:

- *Consumption surge*: Consumption in many select sectors will enter a "hockey stick" curve, achieving hyper growth with substantial rewards to all players in the supply chain for the sector.

- *Retail and services*: Both foreign and domestic firms will experience accelerated growth in consumer durables, luxury items, home furnishings, fast foods, and services, such as beauty salons and education. Retailers will benefit from triple leveraging: more regulatory space for services under China's WTO commitments, increased consumer spending, and improved knowledge of Chinese consumer spending patterns. Significant developments are occurring in healthcare services, as private spending increases rapidly, with an aging population driving more utilization and wealthy children mobilizing to provide their parents a better quality of care than previously available.'

• *Mergers and acquisitions (M&A)*: Even as rhetoric in China's domestic media escalates about protecting Chinese state-owned and private enterprises from foreign MNCs, the diversity of interests and fragmented control of M&A activity will create a boom for global strategic and financial investors. High levels of liquidity globally, coupled with excitement about China, have resulted in huge funding capacity now parked on China's shores awaiting the right investment opportunity. Announced M&A resulting in ownership changes of PRC assets increased to 1,945 deals accounting for a total of USD 43.5 billion in 2006, up from 1,757 deals and USD 30.5 billion in 2005.

Threats

A general theme for the next several years is the increased strength of Chinese companies and the outward projection of China's manufacturing, financial, and "soft" power. In a very real sense, we will see systems in conflict as China's socialist market economy, with its hyper-competitive exports, resource acquisition, and intense M&A activity well-financed by the country's surging foreign exchange reserves debuts on the world stage as never before. This is bound to create changes in the global economy.

• *Deflation*: Reforms notwithstanding, major Chinese enterprises in key areas such as steel, aluminum, automotive, pharmaceutical, textiles, and consumer electronics continue to operate according to principles that are not fully marketized. While enjoying subsidies and other benefits that keep them alive, these sectors are willing to operate with little or no margin. Overcapacity in a number of sectors assures Chinese exporters will ship products into the global marketplace at deflationary prices. In sector after sector, Chinese exports dominate major global markets, and margins for everyone—including the Chinese manufacturers—have fallen due to intense competitive pressure.

- *Intellectual Property Rights (IPR) and soft power projection*: IPR issues, which have largely been focused on China's domestic market, will become global, as Chinese exporters increasingly deploy appropriated manufacturing know-how, trade secrets, reverse engineering skills, and work-alike products to build global market share. China's emerging IPR strategy, which is focused on reducing IP costs rather than creating value in IP ownership, will threaten the intangible asset value of global MNCs. While IPR is the headline issue here, China has the potential in the future to export its own style of environmental, labor, safety, quality, and investment processes and protocols into the competitive global marketplace. Firms from other nations may be faced with the prospect of matching Chinese circumstances or facing competitive disadvantages.

- *Volatility*: The scandal surrounding Chinese copper trading on the London Metals Exchange (LME) was the first salvo in an emerging story concerning China and commodity markets. Global media has focused on China's inflationary impact on energy and basic commodity pricing, but in the future we will witness increasing sophistication by China in using undisclosed reserves of strategic commodities and its massive foreign exchange holdings to manage commodity pricing to its benefit in the global marketplace. Some of this maneuvering will be done well, some not so well, but it will change the complexion of global commodity trading.

• *New export pushes*: China has several sector policy studies and plans that converge around the theme of bringing more of the export-driven supply chain on-shore, and driving exports into more lucrative value-added categories. In industries like steel, steel components, automotive, and white goods, highly integrated planning has the potential to generate massive quantities of highly competitive exports.

Overview of China's Achievements and Challenges

In the midst of rapid economic growth, some emerging trends in China can be identified. Economic growth for 2006 registered 10.6%, far surpassing the deceleration goal of 7.5%. Trade continued to expand as a more significant driver of the economy than domestic consumption, and the money supply and fixed asset investment surged. In 2005, China exported more vehicles (a reported 172,800 vehicles) than it imported—the first time since reforms began that auto exports topped imports. In 2006, China exported 340,000 vehicles as the country continued its determined push up the value chain.

Export developments have lead to aggravated trade-related tensions, increased pressure for *renminbi* (RMB) adjustment by major trading partners (especially the U.S.), and protective measures by trading partners against surges in the wake of quota eliminations (especially in textiles). The sheer size of China as a consumer and producer has influenced world energy and steel prices. Trade litigation has begun to address a number of alleged subsidies related to these surges, as well as anticipated rises in exports.

No consensus has yet emerged on the issue of *renminbi* value. The most thorough analysts have argued that a purchasing power parity analysis is the only one supporting the U.S. government calls for a dramatic strengthening of the RMB. Other measures framing the currency value debate, including China's global trade balances and domestic savings and investment ratios, indicated that lesser change was necessary. China agreed in October 2005 to readjust the basic relationship of the *renminbi* to the U.S. dollar by slightly over 2% and changed the method of calculating a daily trading band, basing it on a basket of currencies rather than only the U.S. dollar. By mid-2007, the *renminbi* had appreciated to 7.5 RMB to 1.0 U.S. dollar.

The Chinese leadership has been mildly responsive to repeated visits and pressure from the U.S. Treasury, but there has been no wavering on China's basic principle of "gradualism" in managing its currency. Incremental appreciation and a series of announcements on how the trading bands are to be managed have relieved some diplomatic pressure. But no one expects the *renminbi* appreciation to make a dent in the huge U.S. trade deficit, which has worsened since the first phases of China's currency liberalization. The *renminbi's* "managed float" does not necessarily improve the transparency of the currency management process, as the details of the process being used are not disclosed. Some basic changes in the convertibility regimen have been debated for several years, and there are signs of change. Some early disclosures suggest that a trading zone near Tianjin might be the first to offer occupants free convertibility of the *renminbi*.

In 2006, China racked up a USD 235 billion surplus in trade with the U.S.—the biggest ever—amid renewed calls for an accelerated appreciation of the *renminbi*. Meanwhile, China's huge foreign exchange reserves have become a headache for the central bank. In late 2005, against a background of the U.S. global trade deficit reaching USD 726 billion (it would reach over USD 810 billion in 2006), rising interest rates in the U.S., along with massive government spending deficits, China softly signaled a move to diversify beyond U.S. dollar holdings. But when the potential negative impact on the U.S. dollar became evident, the People's Bank of China (PBoC) quickly retreated, more awakened than before to its crucial role in supporting the U.S. dollar globally.

Globally, China's trade surplus increased from around USD 30 billion in 2004 to USD 100 billion in 2005, and then to USD 178 billion in 2006. The surplus began to surge in the second quarter of 2005 due more to a dramatic slowing of import growth (in part because of import substitution of industrial goods) rather than an increase in exports. In 2006, China's exports took off, growing over 27% over the previous year, fueling the larger surplus.

Current perception of global trade imbalances is not wholly focused on China, and there is increasing discussion about East Asia as a region continuing to depend on export expansion to fuel growth and maintaining a block of undervalued currencies. One argument holds that consumption in Asian economies is very hard to grow because of deeply rooted family savings instincts, weak public social support systems, and demographic profiles. Critics note, however, that artificially undervalued currencies not only drive exports but also depress domestic consumption.

In 2004, China's huge trade surplus with the U.S. was offset by a deficit with Asian trading partners that supplied China's export industries, namely Taiwan, South Korea, Australia, and Japan. This means the values of these other currencies also affect global imbalances and underscores the vulnerability of several Asian economies to impacts from a slowdown in Chinese exports to the West, regardless of whether the slowdown is driven by currency adjustments, global growth slowdowns, natural disasters, pandemics, or other causes. China has been characterized as the engine of Asian growth. It is perhaps more accurately characterized as the gateway of goods from Asia to the rest of the world, and the big channel for the world's wealth back into Asia.

In any case, there is wide recognition that China is now definitely entrenched in the global trade system and the global economy, and it is mounting the stage as a player in global security issues. China is emerging as a global player in capital flows, with Chinese initial public offerings (IPOs) setting records, and a large (USD 200 billion) chunk of its foreign exchange reserves now committed to a huge new investment fund modeled on Singapore's Temasek, along with a significant overseas acquisition capacity in the hands of large state-owned enterprises (SOEs).

With this status, there are risks and issues to be considered in China's rapid growth and, conversely, in China's potential failure to grow rapidly. There are risks and issues to consider in China's continued prosperity under the rigorous hand of the Chinese Communist Party (CCP or Party), and risks and issues to consider in a potential fragmentation or weakening of that hand. There are risks and issues to consider in China's increased engagement in global organizations, causes, communication and information systems, and legal and diplomatic covenants, and risks and issues to consider in China's potential turn toward a new isolation. Below we explore the forces that will drive China one way or another along these paths.

Five Strategies for the Coming Decade

Over the last few years, intense debates over development options in China have helped to redefine or redirect strategies on at least four fronts. To some extent these are on record, with explicit statements from the State Council, the National Development and Reform Commission (NDRC), and other leadership organs. There has been a continuation and refinement of China's critical strategy of "Going Out"; a significant redirection of strategy to address domestic wealth and growth disparities; further direction in the management of national champion companies, brand development, and value chain enhancement; and a formal effort inaugurated to develop consensus among a growing community of IP stakeholders on a coherent IPR strategy.

Does this constitute an industrial policy? In a way it does, but with characteristics suitable to China's goals and current circumstances. It is a kind of "über industrial policy" intended to align the commercial activities of the SOEs, the domestic privately-owned enterprises, and the sundry other ownership models with each other and with the Party's vision. The forceful and public articulation of strategic issues is somewhat new, and arguably the result of a recognition among China's economic leadership of how much economic activity is now outside the direct control of the Party and state. So, even as the state-owned Asset Supervisory and Administration Commission (SASAC) strengthens its direct management of the top 169 SOEs, an entrenched "plan and control" mentality also seeks to reassert significant influence on the non-SASAC players. As is often the case in China, this results as much from competition among potential government players as between government and non-government agents. As talk about changing the holding responsibilities of SASAC continues, emerging competitors include groups like the Huijin Fund (owned by the PBoC). To be sure, as China's overall economic growth has surged, imbalances, stresses, and strains have surged in parallel, and the state alone can no longer cope with them all.

From a commercial standpoint, the strategy developments occur as China confronts an unpleasant reality about its fast growth. In sectors as diverse as home products, consumer electronics, industrial electronics, appliances, automotive, and steel, buoyant revenue growth has been accompanied by sharp margin compression and earnings decline. It appears to be a consequence of the socialist-market model, in which significant capital can easily be concentrated in manufacturing capacity for which there is no discernible market and brief spells of price volatility can lead to a rapid drive to overcapacity in a sector. We have seen examples of this in everything from cabbage to cold-rolled steel.

In several sectors in China, excess capacity has created resilient buyer's markets. Excess capacity in China is notoriously difficult to measure; there are no consistent definitions of what constitutes "capacity." But if retail price trajectories are an indicator, there is more product output pushing against slower growing demand. The prices of automobiles, appliances, consumer electronics, and even housing are deflating at the retail levels. This buyer's market itself stimulates production and export, as bankrupt-proof enterprises sell at or below cost and, under competitive pressure, reduce input costs down the line. Steel prices slid globally as Chinese capacity came online in 2005, even as energy and ore prices escalated, and Chinese mills were global low-price producers throughout 2006. Car sales in China jumped 30% in 2005, but manufacturers' profits dropped by half, according to figures released by the State Passenger Cars Association. From January to November 2005, China's top 100 electronics enterprises posted a total of RMB 812.67 billion in sales, up 16% year-on-year, but their gross profits fell 42% year-on-year, with an anemic 1.93% average profit margin. This is in spite of the fact that China commands over 80% global market share in the key products of these manufacturers. A leading electronics manufacturer, Datang, which has been provided massive support through R&D grants and directed procurement, reported early results for Q1-Q3 of 2005 of losses totaling nearly RMB 200 million. In the course of 2006, several special grants were announced for national champion consumer and industrial electronics makers to address liquidity problems.

In summary, China seeks to address two problems through strategic realignment. First are the high levels of economic growth without a commensurate level of sustainable value creation. Second are the various growth and wealth distribution disparities, from coast to inland, from urban to rural, and from province to province. These problems are the common underpinnings of planning going forward.

The "Going Out" Strategy

There are many facets to this expansive strategy, which intertwine with many of the issues discussed here, including the objective of stretching China's hold on merchandise value chains, and getting control of more IPR, brand names, channels to market, and basic resources. Both for the nation and for individual enterprises, China's foreign currency accumulation and overseas buying power is increasing very fast, through a combination of strong inbound foreign direct investment (FDI), trade surpluses, illicit funds flows, and very successful listings on major capital markets. Acquisition activity is increasing, originally for resources, but increasingly for technology, brands, and market channels. High profile acquisition approaches, like Haier for Maytag, and CNOOC for Unocal, have triggered protectionist countermeasures. We are seeing just the beginning of what will be a prolonged fight over how China can continue to grow its wealth and what China can do with it.

With China's officially-held foreign exchange reserves well in excess of USD 1 trillion, and the PBoC facing a certain decline in the value of the U.S. dollar, the need to use these funds will become more and more acute. In addition, of the USD 6.9 billion China spent on overseas acquisitions in 2005, USD 4 billion was described as retained earnings overseas. Thus, China's official foreign exchange reserves represent a fraction of available buying power. Also, with the recent creation of an over-the-counter hard currency market in China, the process for buying overseas is simplifying. This will impact corporate acquisitions, commodity and resource purchases, and the participation in global equity and futures markets by Chinese firms. Added to the high levels of liquidity already washing across global markets, China's spending capability could prove to be an inflationary force in the coming years.

The End of Protectionism?

The year 2007 marks the end of China's WTO phase-in period. However, China's underlying development goals remain unchanged—create more export value, bring more of the value chain on-shore, and move more total economic activity under the control of domestic private companies or commercialized SOEs. There is a general recognition that on a level playing field many if not most of the SOEs would suffer by comparison to their MNC peers. Thus it would be surprising if protectionism of various sorts does not linger will into the future.

Addressing Domestic Imbalances—Building a Harmonious Society

At the NPC meetings in March 2007, major Chinese leaders continued to stress the importance of "Building a Harmonious Society," along with "Green Growth" and "Building the Socialist Countryside." All three slogans address under-funded, perhaps even damaged components of China's overall reform.

In dealing with an earlier stage of development, Jiang Zemin committed to an ambitious program to redirect investment and development focus on inland and Western China. Not only were State resources dedicated to the undertaking, but incentives were also offered to foreign investors to locate outside their traditional coastal strongholds. The "Go West" campaign targeted disparities in income distribution and massive migration from the inland provinces to the coastal cities. The idea was to create jobs where the people lived, to discourage people from moving to the jobs, and thereby maintain growth and enhance stability.

Travelers to China are stunned by the rapid growth of the coastal cities, a kind of growth that simply does not exist anywhere else in the world—with the possible exception of parts of the petro-dollar soaked Middle East. Foreigners who have traveled in China for decades now are also impressed by the rise of second-tier cities, even some deep in the interior, and the signs of economic development that is not directly linked to the export economy. Nonetheless, from an investment return standpoint, it remains a great challenge to justify investment in the interior, given the relative weakness of consumer spending, the logistical hindrances to export ports, and the relatively undeveloped human capital, not to mention the unwillingness of coastal Chinese to move there.

By the end of 2005, at leadership meetings in China, these realities were recognized, and the "Go West" campaign was effectively ended. Analysis had led to the conclusion that money invested in the interior in an effort to foster development and create jobs was inefficient and ineffective. In its stead, a new strategy of revitalizing Northeast China was set forth. Here, in the home of many of China's oldest steel mills, automakers, industrial manufacturers, power plants, and railroad infrastructure, natural geographic advantages survived, and underutilized production capacity and workforces were already in place.

Nonetheless, China's huge disparities in wealth distribution and its large population living below the poverty line (between 100 million and 200 million, depending on whose definition), remain serious problems. When the leadership change was made in 2003, developments and income disparity were in focus, and hope was raised by the fact that both Hu and Wen had roots and careers in interior provinces, as opposed to Jiang Zemin and Zhu Rongji, both of whom have Shanghai backgrounds. In addition to the new geographic focus of remedial investment, the leadership has increasingly called attention to the risks of letting these issues drift on and on, but to date the resources to address disparities in any serious way are still woefully short. Analyses of the budget figures announced at the 2007 NPC indicated that some wealth redistribution was underway, with a shift in spending to education, healthcare, and other elements of the social infrastructure. But it fell short of levels that would have the kind of impact the leadership rhetoric appeared to indicate.

Building the National Champions

Candidates for national champion enterprises in China have come on various paths. Some were derived from the intersections of institutional interests and powerful support from inside the Party and military elites, like several major industrial electronics companies. Others came from local and once maverick enterprises that succeeded in the marketplace and built name recognition, like some new automotive assemblers and component companies. Others just arose from hundreds of similar enterprises, through the guidance of a visionary SOE manager, and have managed to align with major central objectives, like some home appliance makers.

Clearly, in a society that treasures models for their pedagogical value, national champion enterprises represent best practices, almost across the board, in strategy, product development, human resources, marketing, financial management, and so on. In that regard, they are at the front edge of domestic reform and are widely discussed in the business media and in leadership circles. Chinese business magazines featuring adulating interviews with successful domestic entrepreneurs and SOE managers, articles on management and management gurus, and analytic reports on sectors, trade disputes, or currency and financial matters are now common. The national champion companies are always favorite topics of such reporting, and their successes and growth are chronicled in detail.

National champions are also required to serve as pioneers in the effort to broaden the margins of Chinese manufacturing concerns, and to increase China's benefits from post-manufacture value, especially in overseas markets. Chinese enterprises have looked at potential acquisitions in every link in the overseas value chain and at target markets like the U.S.. Over the last few years, foreign acquisition targets have included primary commodity companies, component makers, final assemblers and manufacturers, logistics companies, and retail chains.

It is fair to call the building of national champions a branding exercise, for both market share and capital acquisition. Great value is perceived in strengthening the name recognition of Chinese companies, IPO fever remains strong in China, and the biggest SOEs, including banks, insurance companies, and basic commodity makers, are well known and get investor support. It is not clear how the third or fourth generation offerings in these large SOE-dominated sectors will do, but so far, big SOE IPOs in Hong Kong and on Shanghai's A-share markets have done extremely well for early underwriters, buyers at the initial offering, and strategic investors who got pre-offering placements. PetroChina shares have soared over 600% since their April 2000 IPO; China Life has also broken 600% since its IPO in December 2003. SinoPec, Chalco, Shenhua Energy, and PICC are among outstanding SOE performers. Other winners in the global equity markets have been Internet companies which have grown astronomically. In fact the IPO process is increasingly critical to in-bound private equity money, and some of the most exciting results for financial investors have been driven by IPO stories.

But many of the Chinese firms in more traditional businesses that seek overseas listings must begin from a very low base of recognition due to a lack of differentiation between products and companies. In the U.S., consumers, the media, and even the

Congress constantly discuss Chinese products, but rarely if ever is there any discussion about a specific Chinese brand. Apart from goods manufactured in China under control or contract of MNCs, there is a flatness to the mass of Chinese-produced goods, and a lack of differentiation as to their provenance. Ironically, even the most recognized Chinese brands abroad, with the exception of Tsingdao Beer, compete almost exclusively by offering prices low enough to offset concerns about the newness of the brand or other consumer concerns about quality, after sales support, and so on. This low-price and cost approach itself is potentially lethal to profit margins of foreign and even Chinese competitors.

This situation may change quickly. It is already clear that some brands that may or may not be Chinese-owned but are completely sourced out of China and are identified as such, are improving their image and developing premium market value. Already, major retail chains overseas are expanding private label products to include Chinese-sourced items, in some cases near the top ends of their model ranges (DVD players and flat screen televisions, for example). There is a very high probability in the coming years that Chinese manufacturers will develop useful product features that differentiate items, especially where demands of the Chinese market have fostered innovation, such as frugal consumption of fuel, electricity, and water as design strengths of Chinese-made home appliances.

The Intellectual Property Rights Strategy

In August 2005, China's State Intellectual Property Office (SIPO) launched a series of meetings explicitly intended to formulate an intellectual property strategy for China. The initiative, which brought together 20 ministries and a range of experts from many walks of life, coincided with a crescendo of discussion in global business media about China's intellectual property practices. The results of the long study and consultations were presented to the 2007 National People's Congress.

China's twin capacities—to reach global quality levels (at least in foreign invested facilities) and to scale manufacturing rapidly—are double-edged from China's perspective. China's qualitative and quantitative achievements focus attention on the role of IP in value creation, and on the apparatus and standard practices of mature economies in IPR protection. Globalization and outsourcing have allowed China to become the factory of the world, even though Chinese enterprises own an extremely small stake in global commercial IP (brands, technologies, patents, know-how, or trade secrets). This combination of manufacturing strength and minimal IP stakes contributes to growing risks to intellectual property owners.

From roughly 1985 to 1995, China's fast growth was fueled by inexpensive labor, as foreign buyers of labor-intensive goods jump-started a huge export boom. From around 1995 to 2005, China's growth was fueled by cheap capital, as capital-intensive industries like automotives, steel, industrial machinery, IT infrastructure, and urban property were driven by massive state infrastructure spending and large scale, low cost bank lending. According to the analysis of the SIPO group, China's growth from 2005 to 2015 will be driven by inexpensive intellectual property.

This view emerged after much discussion in the Chinese media about the high cost of foreign-owned intellectual property, with claims that IP costs often exceeded hardware manufacturing costs, and that the competitiveness of Chinese manufacturers in global markets was being "contained" by what was essentially a tax imposed by less competitive foreign economies. China began to pursue litigation, charging key individual IP owners and patent pools with monopolistic restriction of trade, while concurrently negotiating intensely for relief from high licensing costs for audio and video technologies in DVD players, MP3 storage systems, cell phone technologies, and the like. China ramped up efforts to find alternative standards and technologies that would be locally controlled and priced almost to nothing.

The strategy consensus sought by the SIPO meetings referred to above was pointedly not about improving the collection of foreign IP royalties, or improvement in the identification and enforcement of valuable IP rights within China and globally. It was rather about mapping pathways regarding IP development, funding, protection, and deployment that will best support and facilitate China's growth. In the words of SIPO Commissioner Tian Lipu, it concerns creating "an overall strategy of the whole nation." Indications are that China's IP strategy will be a repositioning of IP in the overall value chain, with the goal of reducing IP cost as a component in manufactured goods, rather than driving IP production with the goal of creating significant value with IP itself.

This is a rational direction for an economy that excels in lean manufacturing, under leadership that believes China will succeed as long as technology containment can be escaped. This is a radical view of IP and its role in the value chain of manufactured goods, a view at odds with what IP-owning MNCs would promote. Put simply, the development of Chinese-owned intellectual property and the apparatus that sustains and employs it (the law and courts, standards organizations and regulations, licensing protocols and practices) are less focused on deriving value from IP and more focused on reducing the cost of IP as a component in manufactured goods. The result will be that IP, like any asset in the global marketplace, will be under significant price pressure from the appearance of low-cost Chinese alternatives.

Five Dynamics that will Define China's Future

Population Dynamics

Although most of us are familiar with a China that is fiercely promoting a one-child policy, the current population dynamics in China are rooted in China's long historical capacity to support large populations successfully. At the core of current demographics is the policy under Mao during the Cultural Revolution encouraging families to have as many children as possible. The resultant baby boom of the 1960s—and its echoes—will drive a steady increase in population until the 2040s, when China's population will peak at 1.6 billion.

Within the gross numbers are trend indicators that underscore challenges to both social security and economic stability. With respect to the former, gender imbalances are growing, with preferences for sons now driving a birth imbalance reported officially as 117 males to 100 females, but probably closer to 120-121 males to 100 females. This is the worst disparity in the world for a large population, as a normal ratio should be between 105-107 males to 100 females. In some Chinese villages, ratios are as high as 300-400 boys to 100 girls. Some provinces are far beyond the national averages, with Hubei at 128.2 to 100, Guangdong at 135.6 to 100, and Hainan at 135.6 to 100.

Villages that still lack water and electricity infrastructure frequently have a generator and a basic ultrasound machine, despite a national law prohibiting the disclosure to prospective parents of a fetus's gender.

In addition to the obvious connection between an emerging shortage of women and an increase in female kidnapping and trafficking in women, sociologists point to deeper problems in social stability that are engendered by such high ratios. Males unable to find a mate are called "bare branches" in China. By 2020, bare branches in the ages between 15 and 35 will number somewhere between 22 million and 30 million men. In the competition for an inadequate number of females, the bare branches that will be unable to find mates to establish a stable relationship and start a family are those without social and economic advantages, and are likely to be primarily migrant, illiterate, and largely disenfranchised males who are already on the margins of society.[1]

A fundamental reality observed by sociologists is that large numbers of bare branches increase the potential for violence and social disorder. Male violence, criminal behavior, and other forms of anti-social behavior drop dramatically as males commit to a mate and establish a family. With over 20 million bare branches from the lower echelons of society expected in the near future, current levels of violence between organized gangs and often-thuggish public security operatives in China will escalate. We have little insight into how highly organized China's underground is, on a local, provincial, or national level. Likewise, we have little insight into how constrained by law and institutions are the armed (but often poorly trained) domestic security personnel. But historically a major source of instability in China has been armed and organized gangs, coalescing into small armies, following orders of local warlords and establishing power in regions where the central government's grasp has weakened.

The counterforce to potential violence emerging from a growing cohort of bare branches is an increasingly authoritarian government willing to use coercion to maintain order. Beneath the surface of President Hu's current campaign for a "harmonious society," we see increasingly violent expressions of discontent, especially by rural populations, and an escalation of government force to control it. No one can predict how this will develop in the complex mix of economic issues, including China's stubborn and growing maldistribution of wealth. But we can say with certainty that gender ratio problems and tens of millions of bare branches will increase the risk of social instability for at least a generation, and with it, decrease the likelihood of political liberalization that theoretically should be enabled by an increasingly stable population.

Another important result of China's population profile is a tidal wave of retirees due in the next fifteen years, even as the social safety systems that were developed for the state-owned economy slip into serious disrepair. China's unfunded pension obligations have been the focus of discussion and research for a decade, and most post-SOE employment models do not provide significant retirement or welfare benefits for workers. In some wealthier urban systems that have substantial foreign-invested enterprises, funds are being created to address part of the need, and civil servants have benefits coverage. Overall, about 25% of China's working population is covered with some sort of retirement fund, and this shortfall is correlated with high savings rates. Basically, Chinese citizens are saving at high rates primarily to prepare for self-funded retirement. A significant advantage of formal employment in a foreign invested or state-owned entity is some level of insurance and social security coverage. But to appreciate the magnitude of the challenge, consider that in 2006, Chinese over 60 years old constituted only 11% of the population. By 2040, that number will rise to 29%, or over 405 million retirees. At the same time, the working age cohort will begin to decline. At present, there are six working age Chinese to support each elder. In 2040 there will be only two.[2]

China's legacy structures for "*laoyang*," or supporting the elderly, were primarily familial, and in the full flowering of Mao's China had become socialist, with social obligations tied to work unit, enterprise, or commune. As the legacy structures of productivity and resource management have faded into a smaller and smaller fraction of China's economy, nothing has been materially implemented on a large scale to take over the burden. It is conservatively estimated that only 25% of China's population has any institutional provisions for retirement, and even for that 25% the provisions are woefully inadequate. Now, as an increasing number of city dwellers are required to reach into their own pockets for healthcare, one unintended consequence of China's one-child policy comes to the forefront. In China, the burden of support, for retirement and healthcare falls on the single child. Direct costs take the form of formal or informal supplements paid to state-supported hospitals, doctors, and support staff, or simply opting for completely privately funded care. Twenty years ago observers were noting the "six pockets"—four grandchildren and two parents—that were devoted to spoiling China's little emperors and empresses. Today, the concern is the burden of six aging parents and grandparents supported by one wage earner.

Healthcare delivery is proving to be an immediate and stubborn problem for both central and provincial leaderships. At the beginning of reforms, there was general access to a basic level of healthcare, with Party and military elites enjoying world-class facilities in a few urban locations. Over the transition period, and accelerating in the most recent decade, the basic healthcare system has deteriorated, certainly in relative if not absolute terms. In the coastal cities, private health provision is a lucrative and fast growing sector. But for the vast majority of urban residents and virtually all rural residents, who cannot afford prices that are approaching private care in mature economies, there is only a low quality and heavily overburdened public healthcare system that has not been significantly refinanced in decades. This, added to high levels of unregistered migrant workers at the bottom of the social ladder in large cities, leaves substantial populations with no formal insurance and little access to any form of healthcare. In response to this void, there is an "under the stairs" social network with minimal support emerging in some cities, and there is the possibility that this shadow network will be more substantially supported, as the central government commits more resources to social infrastructure investment.

The ailing healthcare sector has become a major research topic for the Development Research Center of the State Council, as the search for policy and resource solutions intensifies. Practical issues aside, there is an emotional impact to a trend that is so dramatically counter to China's increasing wealth and power, and such a striking roll back of one of the hallmark achievements of the Mao era, the barefoot doctor and nearly universal healthcare. Of concern are comparisons between today and the beginnings of the reform period. The cooperative healthcare delivery system in the countryside has now essentially collapsed. The number of rural doctors decreased from 1.5 million in 1980 to 1 million in 2001, while that of rural health workers decreased from 2.4 million to less than a quarter million. Across China, 60% of healthcare spending is now out of pocket, which makes people reluctant to see doctors unless in urgent need. On the non-economic front, the central government has even backed away from licensing drugs, which now is a provincial level function, making China a hodge-podge of inconsistent and conflicting pharmaceutical regulations and practices.[3] With the demographic trends discussed above, we can see the burden on the healthcare system growing much faster than the system's ability to accommodate demand.

What are the potential consequences for China and the world of this situation? With the decline in availability of healthcare, massive shifting migrant populations, and a vulnerability to bio-agents, China is facing some dire risks with public health. At the beginning of the reform period, China celebrated the fact that its public health profile was akin to a fully developed country, one in which chronic illness was the focus, with infectious disease essentially conquered. Now, the problems—and the news—are back to infectious diseases, viral as well as bacterial. If the spread of HIV/AIDS, estimated by the UN to affect approximately 1 million in China, is not more effectively addressed than it has been heretofore, estimates are that an additional 20 million Chinese could catch the disease and nearly USD 100 billion in costs could be incurred. Severe Acute Respiratory Syndrome (SARS) was one of a series of viral contagions that have become a part of Chinese life. Cholera, bacterial pneumonia, and other more classic infectious diseases are staging comebacks, and their potential impact on the population is amplified by air and water pollution, food chain contamination, and widespread tobacco smoking.

The common thread linking these risks is the lack of commitment and political will to direct resources to acute needs for social infrastructure that would keep up with China's economic growth. The Fourth Generation of China's leaders, who took power in spring of 2003, rose in part on a commitment to address these issues of lagging social infrastructure, as well as its affiliated risk, the maldistribution of wealth in China. The maldistribution of resources and wealth in China is increasingly a topic in domestic Party discussions and the media. The focus is not only on the obvious disparity between the wealthy seacoast cities and the interior rural villages. There is also glaring disparities within Shanghai, Beijing, Guangzhou, and other prosperous cities, where seriously disenfranchised migrant workers, numbering in the millions, form a massive underclass, and the once aspiring registered residents, now relegated to service jobs, also feel themselves falling behind their aspirations (and even their neighbors) in the excitement of China's economic rise.

December 2005 saw the first use of lethal force against a domestic movement in China since the Tiananmen incident, 16 years earlier. Protests over the confiscation of land to construct a power plant in Dongzhou in Guangdong Province turned violent and several civilians were killed by police (reports vary, listing from three to 20 deaths). This incident, and apparently most of the 70,000-plus officially reported incidents of social unrest in that year were fueled by anger against local Party members, usually over appropriation of land or other resources. It is quite simple. It does not pay to run a rural, rice-growing village in quite the way it pays to manufacture pesticides, or reclaim metal scrap on that same land. The local Party leaders aspire to the wealth they know is being generated by their peers in other parts of China.

The local residents aspire to the same wealth. Unfortunately, the actions of some officials to secure their own positions can put those of others in jeopardy.

The central government is taking steps to address these risks. In the case of Dongzhou, local Party officials have been arrested and punished, as have several villagers who participated in the protests. The government has made good on Wen Jiabao's 2004 promise to abolish the agricultural tax on farmers, which has been touted as the first time in 2,600 years that such an exaction has been abolished. The importance of this tax relief goes beyond the money itself, since farm taxes have long been a symbol of exploitation of the poor by the wealthy. In recent years, such taxes have been the means by which corrupt local officials have squeezed the lifeblood out of their populations. We can surmise that Wen Jiabao's reform timetable, which was originally five years when he announced the planned relief in 2004, was accelerated as a direct result of the growing unrest and turbulence in the rural population. This gives a clear measure of this risk in the eyes of China's leadership, since the government is also in a struggle for the revenue needed to keep physical infrastructure investment strong, and GDP climbing at its current steep pace. In 2006, the number of "mass incidents" in rural settings in China reportedly fell 10%, in part due to greater attention paid by government to the plight of rural residents.

Economy and Marketization Dynamics

The State Council's agent for overseeing the largest SOEs, SASAC, has become increasingly active in recent years. The media has been open, if selective, in reporting on tensions between SASAC and SOE management, in enterprises that had become largely self-managed and self-governed. While the mandate is to assure that the SOEs continue to meet the infrastructure demands of China's rapid growth, that goal is visibly balanced against the state's need to relieve itself of continuous subsidies to them (subsidies through direct grants, through the banks, through asset transfers, through tax relief, through research and development support, or through domestic market listings). SASAC bears major responsibility for maintaining this balance.

SASAC was initially in a somewhat weak position, primarily wielding its power to set a discussion agenda and exercising it through influence on executive appointments. The latter, combined with a major role in restructuring initiatives within sectors and a major role in permitting outbound investment, are SASAC's main levers of power with the SOEs. So in 2005, we saw SASAC rotate the leadership of all of China's major telecoms companies, force restructuring in the electronics-manufacturing sector, and referee a competition between two domestic companies to buy a foreign carmaker. SASAC clearly has influence in the government, and various agencies dealing with regulating and aiding sectors, as well as many associations, are migrating into the SASAC jurisdiction. SASAC not long ago also assumed control of five state investment agencies that can mobilize considerable resources in support of its policies But as more and more SOEs are converted to formal share structures, with or without IPOs, new holding arrangements are being debated that could dilute SASAC's role.

For 2005, SASAC announced excellent results for the 169 SOEs it oversees and declared that only 10% were operating at a loss. While there is some skepticism about this claim, and the accounting is surely not comprehensive, there is little doubt that SOEs are moving forward with the reform agenda, visibly seeking a more diverse management group, purchasing more consulting and development resources, rethinking governance approaches, and improving their comprehension of sector dynamics, large enterprise management systems, and internal controls. Overall, there is a blurring of entities in which the state has an interest. In addition to the SASAC list, companies like communications equipment producers Huawei and ZTE, and even automaker Chery, are increasingly recognized for their potential competitiveness and value creation.

It is too early to determine to what extent we are witnessing a major flex point away from the localization of authority over key industry producers that was launched with the contract responsibility system early in China's reforms. Consolidation of sectors and centralization of industries has never been a perfect solution, but it accomplishes several important goals for the state. First, it creates huge entities in many sectors, which immediately vault into Global 500 slots—and it opens the doors to foreign equity markets. With fewer separate entities, consolidation permits easier oversight for the state, and it can improve the pricing in markets where fierce domestic competition has eroded overall value. Whether it improves competitiveness when Chinese SOEs venture abroad has yet to be determined. Chalco in the aluminum sector, the major steel players, the consolidated automobile makers, and the oil giants—none has really become established in the global marketplace as a serious and mature player. In looking to the future, we are beginning to see differences in industries like aluminum (essentially cast into an enduring monopoly), and steel (in which large regional champions face considerable domestic competition). As a result, China's steel sector appears to be on its way toward intense competitiveness on a global scale.

SASAC appears to be interested in fostering more industry consolidation, and it is worth looking at the potential impact of such consolidation. The decisions to move forward with such consolidation are never made lightly or hastily, and there is sustained discussion and debate. For example, the urgency for a rumored second phase consolidation in the electronics-manufacturing sector, is the result of rapidly growing revenue and rapidly vanishing margins. Put another way, as China becomes the dominant global producer in the sector, the value is concurrently driven further and further down. Overcapacity, what from SASAC's vantage point is redundant investment, creates waves of output that must be liquidated, and will be liquidated at a loss. Consolidation may help, but consolidation nets the bigger players, and sector value is often eroded by small, new entry manufacturers, who have appropriated technology, have competitive local labor and suppliers, and can undercut the mammoth pillar players. SASAC struggles to control the proliferation of investment at the provincial and local levels, where extreme effort or political capital is required. Overall, the process has no provisions for resolution or rationalization, even if grossly uncompetitive entities are created, making SASAC essentially a patron of the enterprises it creates. In many sectors, there has been a cycle of mandated consolidation, then dissolution, and then consolidation again.

Much internal debate surrounds the current approach to the governance, strategies, administration, and even restructuring of the major state-owned industrial and commercial entities. While SASAC's growing power is seen as backtracking by some observers who look for more independent governance and commercialization of these enterprises, the strong role of SASAC has enabled an effective recentralization of governance authority and alignment of major players in sectors, and in some cases has set the stage for a restructuring of sector fragments into large and powerful oligopolistic clusters. Whether these policies will protect the sectors as they improve, or sustain them as they remain as inefficient and cumbersome as in the past is a question that may be answered in the last half of this decade.

Chinese productive enterprises in goods and services cannot accurately be categorized as state-owned, private, and foreign-invested, although these are the groupings that still shape the statistical reporting of the central government. There are dozens of ownership models, and given the complex regulatory and licensing regimens of almost every sector, there are practical adaptations—"*biantong*" methods—that encourage business models with unique and opaque combinations and permutations of licensable entities.

Considering that most economies don't have distinctions like SOE, foreign-invested enterprise (FIE), and private at all, we can appreciate how difficult it is to use ownership structure as a way to measure and analyze what is happening where in the economy.

This is not just a measurement problem, but it is a resource allocation and regulatory challenge for the government. Not surprisingly, innovation, financial efficiency, and agility are found throughout China's developing enterprises, but the private and foreign-invested sector surpass the SOEs significantly by these measures. Commentators have long urged China to address its inefficient systems for capital allocation and regulatory control, to recognize and abet a dynamic private sector that has long been starved for both resources and adequate legal protection for all forms of property, tangible and intangible. Recently, top leaders have issued directives to China's banks and securities regulators to allow more capital to flow to the private sector, and new styles of investment funds are being created that will aggregate domestic capital for such investment. This might be a healthy step toward replacing the unlicensed, informal private banking and lending system that has been the major source of support for entrepreneurs, a system that is not only fragmented and limited, but also costly to the point of being usurious.

The diversity of ownership models has been at the root of China's frustrating efforts to finalize a bankruptcy law and an anti-monopoly law. We have been expecting both legislative initiatives to reach conclusion for years, yet year after year the process has dragged on, until the legislation finally emerged. In an effort to compromise between the acute need for such legislation with anxiety on the part of those responsible for state-owned assets, both laws are riddled with vagaries and odd complexities. These laws are very informative about policy directions and internal debates at the highest levels of government, but, as often happens with new legislation in China, much remains to be clarified through the enabling legislation and circulars that will be forthcoming.

Taking the bankruptcy discussion as an example, not only the SASAC-administered national companies, but 1,500 additional companies (including several other SOEs and private groups) are apparently protected from the courts, creditors, and normal bankruptcy procedures and are to be dealt with through special administrative procedures. In fact, we can see that even diverse groups, like Delong and Worldbest, when they are overwhelmed with debt and are no longer viable, tend to be placed under direct state supervision, if not explicit ownership, for restoration or salvage. Taking the anti-monopoly law as an example, many of the largest and most valuable SOEs operate as monopolies or duopolies. Power and assets are steadily directed to them to support that status, which makes an anti-monopoly law appear to be primarily a way to control private and foreign-invested value creation in the economy.

Finally, a word about one of China's most intractable issues: corruption. Many argue that in a one-party system with no independent regulatory or judicial system, corruption is an inevitable consequence, and corruption as a burden on the system will grow faster than the underlying economy itself. In China, the top leadership appears optimistic that corruption can be controlled—if not eradicated—by severe investigative and punitive measures, combined with saturation ideological training and education. Official media reported that the main Party anti-corruption organ, the Central Commission for Discipline Inspection of the CCP (CCDI), punished 115,143 members in 2005, slightly less than two-tenths of one percent of total Party membership. Over 24,000 members were expelled, and over 15,000 were handed over for criminal prosecution. In 2006, we witnessed the highest level corruption-related purge since reforms began, with a broad investigation of the Shanghai-based Party and government for their use of public money for financing property developments. Shanghai Party Secretary Chen Liangyu, sacked in 2006, was the third highest official to be brought down by corruption charges in China in 20 years. There is little doubt that the Party and central leadership are increasingly concerned about corruption and that serious measures will be taken. The CCDI pledges to improve cadre work style and to undertake "educating leading cadres of the importance of maintaining integrity and fighting corruption through various ways, including publicizing good examples and bad examples."

Corruption is pervasive, and its costs to China's overall growth are inestimable. The ability to reallocate land, direct large state bank loans, and manipulate licensing creates strong supply-side pressure for property development among officials that defies market logic. Not surprisingly in a transitional economy, the biggest victim of corruption is the state itself. We can safely estimate that over USD 1 trillion in assets have been corruptly converted from state to non-state ownership or control. In 2005, China's top auditor reported publicly for the first time on some of the most serious cases, which involved collusion between local Party members and developers to create large multipurpose property developments, displacing farmers or poor rural residents without compensation, and using state capital without prospect of a return

In connection with the anti-monopoly law, there is a tentative provision that addresses administrative monopolies, specifically the corrupt practice by local officials of requiring local companies of all types to buy from designated vendors; submit to special tests, registration, usage fees, and operating conditions; and otherwise be constrained from free market practices. This kind of corrupt practice is among the costliest for foreign investors. Drafters of the anti-monopoly legislation agree that if this controversial provision banning such practices gets through to the final drafts of the legislation it will provide some hope of significant redress for this problem.

China-Global Systems Dynamics

One of the marked changes we anticipate in the last half of this decade is the rapid scaling of China's impact on global systems —trade, financial, standards, and legal. A list of pros and cons that would fairly assess these impacts would be long and controversial, but China's influence would be unquestionable, and this is seen as a threat by many in the G8 economies. Accordingly, in one way or another, a series of visitors to China in recent years have made a point—a condescending point—to exhort China to be a responsible and positive citizen of the world in using its new-found power and wealth.

China's outbound investment expansion has recently been characterized by bold initiatives, clumsy withdrawals, and awkward rebuffs. China's huge foreign exchange accumulation has enabled an aggressive outbound marketing, asset acquisition, and resource acquisition campaign.

China grew its foreign exchange holdings by a staggering 50%, or USD 250 billion from January 2004 to Quarter 1, 2005, with strong inflows of hot money paralleling the modest USD 30 billion in trade surplus and USD 60 billion in FDI. Until 2005 China's leaders had stuck to their legacy of strong, direct management of the RMB exchange rates, resisting intense pressure to readjust the USD-RMB peg, and gaining clout in U.S. capital markets with this huge investment cache. An initial 2.1% appreciation of the RMB against the dollar commenced in 2005, and by October 2006, China's foreign exchange reserves were USD 1 trillion, the largest such figure in the world. In addition, it became clear that China had also accumulated billions in strategic assets, including oil, copper, chromium, and the like.

More recently, China has established a spot market (operated by a set of designated banks) that opens the exchange process but does not liberalize the exchange rate. It will make the supply-demand equilibrium slightly more transparent. Technically, this should be a manageable interface between the RMB and hard currencies, but it remains to be seen how much the PBoC will spend, should a powerful shift in sentiment create intense pressure on the trading band one way or the other. When and if this happens, we will gain valuable indications of the faith China is prepared to place in currency markets.

China's trade relations were not dangerously strained with a single severe crisis in recent years, but an unprecedented number of issues and cases have roiled relationships with major trading partners in North America and Europe. China ended 2006 with a six-fold increase in its trade surplus over 2004, and a USD 235 billion trade imbalance with the U.S., which has added a disputative tone to trade relationships. The U.S. filed an unfair subsidies action against China at the WTO in February 2007 and IPR issues appear to be on their way to the WTO as well. Few observers subscribe to the simplistic argument that the trade imbalances are driven by exchange rate imbalances, and that any possible level of realignment would seriously reduce the U.S. deficit, or, contrarily, that failure to undertake a major realignment would seriously set back the trade relationships. But there are risks, not the least of which is that a Democratic U.S. Congress will be faced with both a weak employment situation and a general perception that China contributes to it. In a key way, both China and her major trading partners are hoping to see a major increase in consumption by China's urban consumers. Signs that this may be happening, discussed above, are good news for both China's domestic economy and its overall trade situation.

U.S. relations with China have been reflected in a series of global public relations stand-offs over U.S. assessment of China's military goals, China's assessment of U.S. containment strategies, abrasive IPR disputes, China's strong advance in East and Southeast Asian leadership initiatives, China's emerging ties with nations the U.S. calls "rogue," and the rising assertiveness of the Shanghai Cooperation Organization against U.S. unilateralism. The U.S.

Department of Defense Quadrennial Defense Review issued in February 2006 was not flattering or comforting to China, and the Pentagon in particular was outspoken about China as a strategic threat to U.S. interests, a position that has influenced the U.S. public's perception of China.

This is against the background of China's vaulting into the top tier of global trade competitors. In fact, some analysts rate China's economy now as the largest in the world, in terms of unit consumption of a range of key materials, dominance of certain key manufacturing and export sectors, and size of key service markets, such as telecommunications. And we need to remind ourselves that China's participation in the global trading system was only reinstituted in 1980.

We are certain to see increased discussion of China as a global investor in the coming years. Already, from Rover to Chrysler, when a major enterprise anywhere in the world is tottering, the conversation always includes the possibility of the Chinese somehow coming with cash for the rescue. But underlying this kind of hopefulness are issues and questions that emerged during the CNOOC Unocal bid that will become more manifest in the next few years. What constitutes fair investment practice for a socialist market economy, where government involvement in large scale investment activity remains a key pillar of policy? How commercial are the transactions from an ownership standpoint? China's government switched the buyer of Ssangyong Motors from BlueStar Chemical to Shanghai Automotive Industry Corporation. The government also switched the buyer of Kazakhstan energy resources from CNOOC to CITIC. As more and more formal, quasi-commercial funds are established with public money, like the Bohai Fund and the Foreign Exchange Fund, how will they balance their commercial goals with their need to align with government policy goals? And as Chinese enterprise buyers shop the world for technologies, how fairly will the owners of these technologies be rewarded and who in China will be beneficiaries of the technology imports? These questions reflect uncharted territory, to be sure, but territory of great significance to the future development of global capital flows.

Institutional Dynamics

China's institutional restructuring as it relates to administrative and political power has been more pendular than linear, depending as much on the leadership succession process and the nature of the leadership powerbase as it does on a planned sequence of reforms. This is in marked distinction to the restructuring of regulators of the economy, such as the central bank, and regulators of banking, equity markets, insurance, and SOEs, for example. The country's top leadership has repeatedly committed to reform of basic political institutions, even as the leaders show more resolve than ever that the CCP shall remain the sole party of significance in China. As in many matters where the top leadership is under some pressure, they have committed to reform but stubbornly refuse to commit to a time frame. Generally, if there is an increase of direct public participation in governance, it will begin at the bottom of the system, with expansion of local elections, which is a move that handily accords with the campaign against corruption.

What is the "harmonious society" of the current campaign in China? This simple and widely touted directive has completely replaced the rather cryptic "Three Represents" of Jiang Zemin. The harmonious society campaign addresses the gap in wealth and living standards across China, the increase in social turbulence resulting from unbalanced growth between coast and inland, between urban and rural populations, the somewhat abrasive and exploitative practices of one class toward another in urban environments, and the exploitation of the people by cadres at the local level. So far, as mentioned above, budgetary reallocation targeting these problems has been unconvincing. Other steps, like the elimination of skyrocketing fees for access to public schools, will take time to play out. The intensity of rhetoric, on the other hand, has increased quickly and markedly. That has impact, and it may presage more significant action at the Party Congress to be held in the autumn of 2007 and at the 2008 National People's Congress.

Judicial reform is another key institutional target. Fundamentally, there is little middle ground between a judicial system that represents the interests of the Party and elite and one that is truly independent, making decisions and building case histories on objective decisions based on statute books. The former reflects "rule by law," the latter reflects "rule of law." Positive developments in certain court outcomes over the last few years have been driven more by a shift in the overall calculus of pros and cons than a basic improvement in judicial independence. Still, for the short term and for issues of primary concern to foreign investors, improvements in both the impartiality and technical capabilities of Chinese courts are meaningful and encouraging. In a sense, a separate branch of the judiciary in major cities is emerging that is committed to a role in the modernizing economy and is dealing with contract issues, IPR issues, labor issues, and other fundamental elements of the investment environment in a positive way.

Judicial reform has focused on improving the efficiency and technical competence of courts, dealing with complex contracts, financial crimes, and intellectual property issues because there is no argument against the benefits that might be derived from these improvements. But the many external factors influencing the courts remain intact. For example, judges are still budgeted at the local level, and the majority of local commercial disputes are likely to involve the economic interests of local Party cadres, governments, and officials. Technical competence is woefully inadequate. Stakeholders in the outcome of a case, outside the courtroom, are often as not given a role in deciding the outcome of the case.

Media and information access and dissemination are major battlegrounds in China. It is one sector where foreign investment and foreign involvement is almost always through compromises and structures that serve little purpose other than to deal with restrictive regulations. The current leadership has signaled in countless ways its intention to maintain tight control over the media and information. The government focus on "healthy content" targets politically challenging content, pornography, and material promoting lifestyle pursuits that are unattractive to the leadership. Strong measures have been taken against editors of newspapers and magazines that have overstepped the bounds and foreign interests have seen less access to key media opportunities in recent years. At the same time, the sector is in desperate need of renewal and commercialization. Consumer appetite for enhanced media and entertainment products is intense in China. The same is true of the appetite for authentic information. China is witnessing a surge of bloggers, and new names reach a high level of popularity on a weekly basis now, with a reported 110 million Internet users across the land. Almost monthly, a website is busted by the authorities for a range of content infractions, including exposing corruption, pollution, epidemics, or the questionable claims of high school textbooks. But in reality the websites are closed because they are flaunting their ability to raise an effective individual voice against the thick walls encircling information that have been a feature of China's political landscape for millennia.

There are few sectors in China's media and information universe that have not been penetrated by foreign investors using popular "*biantong*" methods to circumvent tight regulatory constraints. In some cases, "old friends" of China have had their hands slapped for overstepping regulatory bounds in the media. In other cases, major strategic investors have been publicly embarrassed by activities they have undertaken at the request of the government in exchange for access. For major brands like Yahoo, Google, Microsoft, and Cisco, this risk will only grow in the future, as the push and pull between Internet critics and the CCP intensifies, and technology continues as the weapon of choice. In addition to the major and conflicted players like Google, there are armies of small groups and individuals, working with remote proxy servers, anonymizing software, peer-to-peer networks, and other technology tools to distribute views and news at odds with the state's official stance and the interests of the establishment itself.

China's lagging political, legal, and administrative institutional reforms can only come under increasing stress in the coming years. This is the nature of globalization, where national boundaries are increasingly penetrated by individuals, while they remain, ironically, disabling to governments and their security apparatus. A proxy server in California dispensing real news by Chinese bloggers about avian flu is accessible to any savvy Chinese Internet user, but it cannot be confiscated and shut down by Chinese authorities like one in Tianjin or Wuhan. The instant and essentially free transmissions of ideas and tools around the globe makes the Chinese firewall an indefensible proposition, unless the leadership is willing to take on the huge economic losses of sealing off the IT channels to the outside world—a highly unlikely course of action, barring an unforeseen domestic catastrophe.

Environmental Dynamics

China's environmental challenges receive considerable attention in the world's media, and it appears the largest numbers of NGOs currently operating in China are focused on environmental issues. The problems are acute. There is no question rapid development has been at the expense of the environment, and the confluence of global climate change and the impact of development has resulted in a high level of borrowing against the future in environmental matters.

China's largest urban centers occupy unenviable positions on the list of the world's most polluted cities, with such pollution the result of Mao's industrial infrastructure strategy and the rapid growth of energy and transportation demand. Water is in acute shortage in all of North China, and the desert is encroaching on more and more arable land each year, making its way toward Beijing in particular. Carbon and related pollution from the combustion of China's diverse coal supplies, much of it highly sulphurous, has grown markedly in the last decade, and as China crosses the 1 billion ton per annum mark in coal consumption, there is no easy solution to the challenge of energy demand and the environment.

For transportation, several large cities have converted public transportation fleets to compressed natural gas (CNG), but a massive preponderance of engine-burned fuel is highly polluting. Some cities have reversed a ban from the last decade on automotive engines less than 1 liter in displacement, and are now encouraging the development and sale of 0.8 liter engines and supporting technologies to reduce air pollution.

Less discussed, but of considerable concern, is the distribution in China's environment of bio-factors that potentially have long-term consequences for the population and for agricultural production in particular. Billions of doses of a vaccine developed for humans were delivered to poultry populations in China during the earlier stages of the avian flu development, and many experts expressed fear that this would build resistance in sub-strains of H5N1 that might adapt to human hosts. The vaccine is in the water supply and thus distributed throughout the fowl, human, domestic animal, and vegetation systems. China has taken a protective and somewhat secretive approach to the development of genetically modified crops, parallel to a slow and restrictive market opening to MNC genetically modified crop developers. To what degree the testing and utilization protocols domestically meet international standards is not clear. The same might be said for things as diverse as genetic research and testing in the human healthcare system, where potential economic rewards are huge enough to encourage shortcuts affecting safety.

Environmental enforcement agencies have been gaining strength, but in successive local collisions, the agents of environmental protection lose to the focused economic interests of local Party and government officials and developers. The increased concern over environmental issues and degradation is obvious on the part of citizens and certain media channels that operate on the edge of the official media. The Internet in China is full of discussions about environmental issues, and when a catastrophe occurs, like the nitrobenzene spill near Harbin in 2005, Chinese bloggers are capable of rapid distribution of reliable information in the absence of coverage by the official media. The response to this is ambivalent among empowered individuals in security and propaganda systems at many levels, and there is as much inclination to suppress the information flows as to heed them.

Nonetheless, environmental issues have been a factor in recent social disorders, where local officials not only appropriate land for development purposes, but permit production that is so harmful to the environment that health problems emerge within a few years or even months of launch. In recent months, the number and intensity of these clashes has claimed the attention of the top leadership. The collective impact of NGOs, new channels of information, a more realistic assessment of the risks, and concern over local corruption and destabilization of rural society appear to have elevated environmental issues on the agenda of the central government. Hopefully, over the next several years, we will see China move toward a more serious engagement with its monumental environmental problems, as has been promised in the Eleventh Five Year Program.

Conclusion

China's economic development continues to defy easy categorization and continues to prove naysayers wrong. China is maintaining astonishing growth rates, even as its economy advances to become one of the world's largest. The paradoxes built into China's socialist economic model, as well as the risks inherent in its state-directed bank-administered reallocation system, have not yet had the dire outcomes many outside experts continue to expect.

China is a far more open book than ever before, and information is accessible on most of the policies, practices, and objectives of economic, social, and political development under the current leadership. But there is widespread debate on everything from China's real GDP growth, to China's real capacity, to the ideal value for the *renminbi*, to the real dimensions of China's underinvestment in social infrastructure. Certainly the challenges China faces are constant fare in the world's media, in conferences, and in expert analyses of all aspects of development. Nonetheless, global investors continue to show a resolute and high level of confidence in China's future, with new investors arriving each year. China remains irresistibly inviting although visibly wobbly.

We remain watchful on a number of fronts. Perhaps of greatest significance to foreign companies is the rapid transformation of Chinese enterprises from competitors inside China for China market share into global competitors for market share, assets, and resources around the world. Whether a sustainable trend or not, the impacts in 2004-2006 were pronounced, introducing unnerving instability in commodity prices and resources and, some argue, inflationary bidding practices for corporate assets.

Even as various organizations around the world continue to monitor China's compliance with its WTO commitments, a whole new set of issues outside WTO has arisen with initiatives like the CNOOC bid for Unocal, or the Haier bid for Maytag, or the Shanghai Auto-Nanjing Auto roll-up of Rover's hard and soft assets. What are the ground rules for global acquisitions of China's top 200 firms, which in many cases were created by State Council restructuring orders that instantly de-fragment entire sectors and are funded with subsidized capital? WTO is about trade, not investment, so global mechanisms for addressing issues in global capital flows are relatively undeveloped.

When they assumed office, Hu Jintao and Wen Jiabao were expected to strive for two, somewhat conflicting goals. One goal was to continue and even accelerate growth, by opening up the economy and toughening the commercial environment, moves well-aligned with the WTO compliance process. The second was to redirect growth, driving resources away from the coastal cities and toward the relatively impoverished interior. Internal publications and external analysts are now saying that the regional disparity is proving almost intractable, and in the face of rising discontent with the stubborn maldistribution of resources, the message is being promulgated that such gaps and dislocations are a natural part of fast economic development that must be endured. The focus remains very much on driving economic development, and the most powerful generator of wealth to the direct benefit of the Party and state is not the tax system, but the network of top SOEs.

Increasingly, the giant enterprises, including the oil and gas players, the aluminum players like Chalco, and the electronics players like CEC and Huawei, are gaining strength with domestic market protection and privilege, as well as the benefits of large credit extensions to fuel overseas market expansion and acquisitions. The groundwork is already laid for the extension of this socialist market oligopolistic architecture to sectors like automotive, airlines, pharmaceutical, telecommunications, and semiconductors. It is too early to confirm, but we may be seeing the early signs of a re-balancing toward the socialist half of the socialist-market model.

This difficulty of increasing central control while reining in potential abuse, corruption, and conflicts of interest is part of an even broader balancing act that will determine the future for China. China's high levels of sustained growth have destabilized many internal institutions, processes, and relationships. While this has enabled rapid growth, it has also created substantial risks to the overall commercial eco-system. Taken singly, there appear to be few potentially traumatic risks and adjustments on the horizon. But taken as a whole, it is difficult to see a future in which no significant traumas, some from origins beyond our current vista and view, will not arise and drive sharp turns, if not derailments.

Notes

1. Valerie M. Hudson and Andrea M. Den Boer, *Bare Branches: The Security Implications of Asia's Surplus Male Population*, Cambridge, MA: MIT Press, 2004.
2. Richard Jackson, "Population Aging in China: An Assessment of the Economic, Social, and Political Risks," Paper delivered to a meeting of the CSIS Eurasia Group China Task Force Meeting, October 2005, www.csis.org/media/csis/events/051028_jacksonremarks.pdf. accessed April 2007.
3. *China Development Review*, Supplement (Vol. 7, No. 1, March 2005).

4

China Confronts Globalization: Achievements and Challenges

Robert A. Scalapino
Robson Research Professor of Government Emeritus
University of California, Berkeley

Introduction

Within less than three decades, the People's Republic of China (PRC) has become a global power of significance. Its rapid economic advances have resulted in both major achievements and rising challenges. Trade and investment are expanding at an accelerating rate with such nations as the U.S., resulting in ever-greater economic interdependence and at the same time, heightened tensions relating to imbalance, intellectual property piracy, and protectionism. Competition for resources is also a factor of rapidly rising importance. Indeed, it is the quest for energy security that is a key factor in motivating China's global surge.

Security considerations, however, must not be minimized. Despite increasing military expenditures, China remains far behind the United States in its strategic capacities. Moreover, it is concerned by recent U.S. policies that suggest encirclement. Hence, it has reached out, through both multilateral and bilateral channels to form "strategic partnerships" and participate actively in a variety of organizations. Its improving bilateral relations with Russia and India, moreover, as well as its interaction with the Korean Peninsula, Central Asia, and the nations comprising the Association of Southeast Asian Nations (ASEAN), testify to its desire to achieve a peaceful regional and global environment, enabling concentration on domestic problems and also a balance with the global power of the United States.

Thus, relations with the European Union (E.U.) and the Group of Eight (G8), while troubled by economic problems similar to those afflicting China-U.S. relations, involve on-going dialogues and China's participation in key sessions, although it has not been invited to become a full member of such groups as the G8. Moreover, E.U. hesitation remains regarding several key Chinese requests, notably an end to the arms embargo and status as a market economy.

Meanwhile, relations with Russia have improved measurably in the recent past, both in economic and political-strategic terms, although they remain far from being an alliance in nature. Opposition to terrorism, separatism, and extremism has brought the two nations closer together, with the Central Asian states also included through the Shanghai Cooperation Organization (SCO). Russia, worried on occasion by trends in Eastern Europe and Central Asia as well as by U.S. policies supportive of democracy in the region, finds in China a growing power willing to accept the status quo.

In South Asia, China is reaching out to India without relinquishing its long-existing ties to Pakistan. Both economic and political-strategic considerations are again involved. While China and India will remain competitive in certain respects, and wary of each other's strategic goals, a more compatible relationship has much merit from China's perspective, given the instability in the region. China's expansion in the Middle East, Africa, and Latin America betokens first and foremost the quest for resources, notably oil and gas. However, reaching out to the nations of these regions also provides a means of strengthening China's global influence. Thus, Chinese assistance is given to a number of states, especially in Africa, and high level visits have increased in frequency. It is in this manner that China increasingly warrants consideration as a global power of rising importance.

Globalization, however, poses problems as well as opportunities with respect to the PRC domestic scene. At present, the penetration of external technology and culture are having a noticeable influence upon the Chinese citizenry, especially the younger generations. The propensity for widening differences, based in part upon external stimuli coupled with the expanding class differences (a product of economic growth), pose a growing challenge to the Chinese leadership. In this context, moreover, the power of ideology to effect unity has significantly declined, and the dependence upon nationalism has risen. Yet when nationalism is manifested too forcefully, it can damage China's international relations, as has happened on certain occasions. Thus, a critical challenge is that of coping with the domestic impact of rapid economic growth at home and simultaneously an expanding openness to external influences of diverse types.

China Key Political Issues

In a period of less than three decades, China has gone from being a reclusive nation, increasingly conflicted internally and largely isolated from the external world, to becoming first a regional power, and now occupying an increasingly prominent global position while maintaining, despite rising challenges, a relatively stable home front. Although the forces driving China's internationalization have been largely economic, they also involve political and strategic considerations. The Fourth Generation of Chinese leaders has been mainly trained as engineers and in other technical fields although they have had lengthy party experience. They have generally chosen to concentrate on handling China's complex domestic problems, and hence prefer a stable regional and global environment.

At the same time, with ideology declining as a unifying force, nationalism has risen with ever-greater potency, sometimes seriously complicating PRC international relations. In addition, the strategic landscape has greatly broadened. In addition to the Asia-Pacific theater including the United States, China's relations with such regions as Europe, Central Asia, the Middle East, Africa, and Latin America are taking on ever-greater significance. Moreover, economic and political-strategic factors are increasingly interwoven at the regional and global levels.

China's primary political concerns, however, remain largely domestic, and its strategic policies focus foremost on Northeast Asia, the region of which it is an integral part, as well as on the United States, an omnipresent force. Nevertheless, since China's reach now encompasses the globe, the achievement of a unified, coordinated set of policies has been further complicated.

The following analysis centers upon six critical aspects of international relations confronting China in its quest for an effective global status. Each is in some degree interrelated as will be indicated. Together, they reveal China's achievements and challenges as they are currently manifested.

China's Interaction with the Foremost Global Power

The U.S. is likely to remain the leading global power for many decades, although precisely how it plays that role is subject to a number of uncertainties. Will the heavy costs of past unilateralism induce a propensity for withdrawal from certain commitments? Or will the trend be toward greater emphasis on multilateral and bilateral ties, as has recently been manifest in East Asia?

Meanwhile, American domestic politics are relatively stable despite incessant cross-party quarrels. Ideological or policy differences between the two major political parties are modest, with the political center in a dominant position. Within each party, there are "rightist" or "leftist" elements but while these may color policies in certain instances, they are not sufficiently strong to be commanding.

The U.S. economic scene is more complex. While GDP annual increases recently have been satisfactory, being in the 3-3.5% range, many observers worry about the rising budget and current account deficits. In fiscal 2006, the U.S. budget deficit was USD 248 billion and its current account deficit reached USD 879 billion. Clearly, a constructive approach to this problem cannot be postponed indefinitely. Meanwhile, the importance of the U.S. economy to other nations, especially the major global powers—the E.U., Japan, and China—is vital.

In terms of Sino-American economic relations, what is the current situation? First, trade continues to advance rapidly, and so does America's trade deficit with China. According to U.S. figures, that deficit reached on the order of USD 235 billion in 2006. Chinese authorities dispute this figure, and also point out that nearly one-half of China's exports to the U.S. are produced by foreign owned companies, many of them American. Yet the U.S. demand that China take measures to alleviate the deficit continues.

Another troublesome economic issue has been that of intellectual property theft. This matter is highly complex. About 150,000 Chinese students are currently studying in the United States, and some 700,000 Chinese tourists and businessmen visit the country yearly. Some Chinese are working for major U.S. defense contractors. It is not surprising that the unauthorized transfer of technology occurs despite U.S. regulations restricting such transfers.

The fact that the *yuan* has been fixed to the dollar thereby maintaining the Chinese currency significantly undervalued has constituted another American grievance. The 2.1% revaluation of the *yuan* against the dollar in July 2005, coupled with the subsequent Chinese pledge to attach the yuan to a basket of currencies (primarily the dollar, euro, *yen*, and South Korean *won*), reduced tension temporarily, but the results of these actions remain to be seen. Despite a gradual *yuan* appreciation in 2005 and 2006, many Americans (and Europeans) assert that much more is required.

Certain economic tensions will be difficult to resolve, but the leaders of both China and the U.S. realize the importance of a positive economic relationship, given the stake that both countries have in promoting continued growth in trade and investment. Thus, regular channels of communication have been created, reaching up to top leadership levels. The visit of President Hu Jintao to Washington, originally scheduled for early September 2005, but subsequently postponed until April 2006, and the disagreements over protocol arrangements, illustrates both the desire for comprehensive agreements and the scope of the problems to be resolved.

Exchanges have also raised the crucial issue of resources, an issue certain to grow in significance in the years ahead. The U.S. Department of Energy has opened a Beijing office to promote cooperation in energy efficiency, energy supply, and the use of clean energy technologies. Since it is anticipated that by the year 2025, China will need 12.8 million barrels of oil daily and the U.S. will require 28.3 million barrels, no economic issue is of greater consequence.

Hope lies in the fact that both China and the United States need each other economically and that this need will become ever more critical. To maintain its economic momentum, China requires

U.S. investment, technological expertise, and trade. The United States needs China to continue to invest in U.S. Treasury bonds to aid in covering the U.S. debt, and also seeks maximum access to the China market as living standards there continue to rise. Moreover, the two nations will become increasingly intertwined economically through purchases or extensive investment in each other's companies as well as in other respects. These developments will require constant consultation and dialogue at both official and private levels, and as noted, the appropriate channels are now being set up.

Turning to the political front, China's evolution in recent decades might be defined as the movement from a hard authoritarianism to authoritarian pluralism. Its leadership at present is more collective. With no Mao or Deng on the scene, one-man dominance does not exist. Thus, one critical need is to retain policy coherence and stability under collective leadership. Moreover, relations between Beijing and the provinces and localities currently represent a greater distribution of power, which is a product of economic growth. Federalism, *de facto* or *de jure*, is an evolving reality.

Further, rights with respect to speech and publication have expanded, with actions such as demonstrations by angry farmers, unemployed workers, and students also taking place on a greatly enlarged scale. China is not a democracy as the West would define that term, nor is it likely to become one in the foreseeable future. Both authorities and many citizens fear that the risk of instability in this vast, heterogeneous society, still in its early developmental stages, would be too great. Yet in a variety of ways, openness has grown, posing complex problems for political leaders.

Despite the domestic changes underway in China, political issues remain a factor in China-U.S. relations. On occasion, the United States accuses China of violating human rights and operating in a dictatorial fashion toward its people. Chinese accusations are usually more general. The U.S. is charged with arrogance, interference in the domestic affairs of other nations, and seeking to maintain global hegemony. Despite the continuance of political controversies between the two nations, however, they are usually more subdued than in earlier times, and from an American standpoint, they clearly take second place to the economic concerns set forth earlier.

It is on the strategic front that the impact of globalization upon Sino-American relations is most clearly revealed. As indicated, China often asserts that the U.S. aspires to be a global hegemon. In response, China has not only taken an increasingly active role in such regional organizations as ASEAN Plus Three, the Asia-Europe Meeting (ASEM), and the ASEAN Regional Forum (ARF), but it has reached out to the E.U., Central Asia via SCO, and to two other major powers in its vicinity, Russia and India.

China's current relations with Japan, however, constitute a problem that impinges directly upon its relations with the U.S. Sino-Japanese relations have been more negative in recent times than at any time since World War II. Despite steadily expanding economic relations with Japan, China fiercely attacked the Japanese government over Prime Minister Junichiro Koizumi's visits to the Yasukuni Shrine, textbooks that allegedly minimize Japan's wartime crimes, and the rise of a "right wing nationalism" that seeks to restore Japan's military strength. Although repeated apologies by Japanese leaders for wartime actions have been made—the most recent being Koizumi's remarks at the time of the 60th anniversary of the end of World War II in August, 2005—these are rejected as inadequate. Despite the olive branches offered by China to Koizumi's successor, Shinzo Abe, fundamental differences remain.

At an earlier point, China accepted the U.S.-Japan security relationship with minimal complaint, primarily because it was viewed as a means of keeping Japan under control. Recently, however, the alliance has been broadened to encompass cooperation on such programs as missile defense. Japan has been reaching out, expanding the scope of its security concerns, with U.S. approval. Moreover, Prime Minister Abe supports constitutional revision to give full legitimacy to Japan's expanded defense program. China has become ever more critical of these developments, and naturally, this impacts upon Sino-American relations in the strategic realm. Among other consequences, it stimulates an expanded Chinese effort to achieve "strategic partnerships" with most of its other neighbors.

Meanwhile, Taiwan continues to pose a more immediate issue in China-U.S. relations. Beijing consistently proclaims that Taiwan is its most pressing concern, and the issue by which it will measure its relations with others. Chinese policy towards Taiwan has recently shifted from one solely marked by intimidation and threat to efforts to cultivate the Taiwan parties opposing the Democratic Progressive Party (DPP) government, and to influence the Taiwanese people by economic and cultural actions, even through the proffered gift of two pandas. In this manner, China has entered Taiwan politics in a more direct manner than at any point in the past. Yet the results remain uncertain. Beijing insists that "One China" be recognized as a non-negotiable principle, and further, that the formula for reunification be "One Country, Two Systems." To date, poll results show that a strong majority of Taiwan's citizens have rejected that formula, and that, for now, they support neither a formal declaration of independence nor unification, preferring the status quo.

The United States stands by its somewhat ambiguous policy. It opposes both any formal declaration of independence and any attempt to resolve the issue by force. While applying various pressures upon the government of President Chen Shui-bian to avoid provocations, the U.S. has continued to offer military weaponry for defense purposes, and some U.S. officials have even complained that the Taiwan Government is not responding sufficiently to its defense needs.

This issue is not likely to be resolved in the near future, even if the more moderate Chinese policy has some positive effect. Meanwhile, Chinese military strength with respect to cross-Straits defense will continue to grow. Hence, Taiwan will constitute a serious impediment to removing the "threat" thesis on both the U.S. and Chinese sides.

Meanwhile, China's efforts to improve relations with other neighbors have produced generally favorable results. In part, the gains have been through multilateral channels. The Shanghai Cooperation Organization's cooperation on border issues and opposition to separatism and terrorism are one example. The free trade agreements being negotiated with ASEAN as well as efforts to reduce or compromise territorial disputes are another. Bilateral channels have also been utilized effectively. The "security partnership" with Russia has resulted in joint military exercises in mid-2005, and high-level visits with India have produced an easing of earlier tensions. Relations with North Korea were strained by the test of a nuclear device by Pyongyang in October 2006, while dealings with South Korea have been reasonably positive, as have relations with Mongolia.

In addition to the economic advantages, through its recent policies, China has acquired a *de facto* buffer against perceived American encirclement. However, one important fact should not be overlooked. Almost without exception, while China's neighbors want favorable relations with this massive nation, they have varying degrees of apprehension regarding its rising economic and strategic power. Hence, most want a continuing American presence in the region.

As will be noted shortly, China has also reached out to regions beyond its perimeters, seeking to improve relations with the G8 and in the Middle East, Africa, and Latin America. While its reasons have been primarily economic, political and strategic considerations play some role. China wants to be respected as a major global power, equal to all others.

What has been the American response to China's revised strategic policies? In broad terms, the United States has maintained its global alliances while initiating new strategic policies. It has also shifted to some extent from unilateralism and "an alliance with the willing" to multilateralism and greater flexibility, especially in East Asia. The costs of unilateralism have had an impact on American thinking and policy.

U.S. military strategy is also undergoing a significant change, as noted. The new emphasis is upon ultra-modern weaponry, long-range deployments, and bases kept in readiness by allies. Troops and bases abroad are being reduced, and allies like Japan and South Korea are being requested to play a greater role in their own defense.

The "China threat" thesis remains a factor in American politics and policies. A 2005 Pentagon report asserted for the first time that China's military expansion could pose a threat to U.S. allies in Asia and could disturb the balance of power. A separate assessment claimed that Chinese military expenditures were in the neighborhood of USD 90 billion per year, three times greater than the official figures. This was vigorously contested by Chinese authorities, who also noted that China's defense capacity was vastly inferior to that of the U.S., where 2005 military expenditures were approximately USD 400 billion. Meanwhile, the U.S. applied pressure upon both the E.U. and Israel to maintain an embargo or cease sales of high tech weaponry to China.

In sum, China's current relations with the United States are characterized by one word—complexity. The leaders of both nations realize the importance of this relationship in terms of their respective national interests. Thus, they are attempting to resolve or contain issues of contention. Moreover, on a number of fronts, from the battle against terrorism to the North Korean issue, varying degrees of cooperation are taking place between the U.S. and China—yet the contentious issues will not disappear or be easily resolved.

China's Expanding Relations with the E.U. and the G8

The presence of Prime Minister Wen Jiabao at the 6th ASEM Finance Ministers' Meeting in Tianjin on June 26, 2005, and the attendance of President Hu Jintao at the G8 Outreach Session in Gleneagles, Scotland a few days later, on July 7th, testify to the importance assigned to China's relations with Europe by its leaders.

In the speeches delivered, both men placed emphasis on economic ties, as might have been expected. Wen spoke of the importance of exploring strategies for ASEM economic and financial cooperation, as well as opening the major issues in the world economy to intensive examination. Hu set forth four steps to be taken in advancing cooperation between "North and South," primarily involving intensified economic interaction.

Trade and investment between China and Europe have been steadily rising. Chinese exports to the E.U. rose 26% in 2006 from the previous year, though they remained well behind those to the United States. However, as with the U.S., the E.U. was having problems with respect to China trade. An E.U.-China agreement was reached on June 11, 2005 regarding textiles. By assigning growth quotas, the intention was to give China the opportunity for reasonable growth while providing a respite for European manufacturers. Shortly thereafter, however, China began to exceed its quota in various categories, and stockpiles accumulated in various locations of goods shipped before the June agreement, causing an escalating crisis. Divisions within the E.U. on how to handle the matter also mounted. Some E.U. leaders argued that protectionism, including the quotas imposed on textiles, threatened domestic economies. In early September, an agreement to allow goods which had been temporarily held from the market to be counted against the future quota was reached. The E.U. also imposed tariffs on shoes made in China, claiming Chinese producers were being unfairly subsidized. An E.U. Policy Paper on trade with China issued in October 2006 focused on a range of tariff and non-tariff barriers that have blocked E.U. access to China. All of these indicate that the trade issue is likely to remain a difficult one.

Meanwhile, China's attractiveness for E.U. banks as an investment prospect has grown. The Royal Bank of Scotland and the UBS of Zurich both acquired stakes in the Bank of China in 2005, in advance of Bank of China's 2006 IPO. Under pledges made to the WTO, China has opened its corporate lending and consumer banking market to foreign banks from the end of 2006.

Despite the rapid growth of trade and investment, however, as noted earlier, China's two key demands have thus far not been accepted by the E.U. These demands are the removal of the arms sale embargo and the application of market economy status to China. The arms embargo was applied after the June 1989 Tiananmen clash. Beijing's subsequent human rights record (and U.S. pressure) remains the major obstacle to removal. Various E.U. economic officials also assert that given the extensive governmental involvement in the economy and the weak enforcement of laws, China does not warrant market economy status at this point.

Political differences between China and Europe have been largely relegated to NGO discussions. China has urged a dialogue with the G8 encompassing a wide range of security issues, including those relating to human security, but movement on this front has been minimal. Nevertheless, with its involvement in Central Asia and more extensive relationships developing in the Middle East and Africa as well as with the Russian Federation, China's global strategic presence is likely to be of increasing interest to the members of NATO and the larger G8 community. While its full membership in the latter body is unlikely in the near term, nevertheless its interaction is certain to continue.

Sino-Russian Relations—Recent History and Current Trends

From an early point in its history, the PRC has had a complex relationship with Russia and its predecessor, the Soviet Union. Initially a protégé of Moscow, the Chinese Communist Party came to power with significant Soviet aid during the Chinese Civil War. Russia also provided assistance during the Korean War, albeit not to the extent desired by China. By the beginning of the 1960s, however, troubles between China and the Soviet Union had emerged, ranging from Beijing's objections to Russian dominance of the international Communist movement and Khrushchev's "revisionist" policies to Russian dismay over the rash PRC economic policies and its rival territorial claims. The Sino-Soviet division reached a climax with the bloody conflict on China's northern border in 1969. Subsequently, Mao set ideology aside to reach an accommodation with the U.S. in response to the perceived Soviet threat.

Significant improvement in Sino-Russian relations did not commence until after the collapse of the Soviet order at the beginning of the 1990s. Slowly at first, the two nations began to seek the re-establishment of a positive relationship. Progress was erratic partly because the new Russia struggled with serious economic problems, and therefore presented limited opportunities for trade and investment. In addition, it was experimenting with a new political system, one substantially different from that of China.

In the recent past, however, substantial changes have begun to take place. While the Russian economy still presents severe limitations, China-Russia trade has expanded rapidly, reaching USD 33.4 billion in 2006. Russia has been a key source of military supplies, nuclear technology, and energy. China's goal is to achieve a trade volume of USD 60 billion to 80 billion by 2010, with the emphasis on oil and natural gas, mineral resources, and timber processing. Investment thus far has been limited, totaling only USD 1 billion for the two nations in 2004. Like others, Chinese have been complaining about the lack of market standardization, the various restrictions on business activities, corruption, and the inefficiency of local officials in Russia. Nonetheless, business firms in the three provinces of Northeast China have been moving into the Russian Far East (notably Primorsky province) in increasing numbers. Moreover, during President Hu's visit to Moscow at the end of June 2005, bilateral agreements on energy, electricity, and finance were signed. In 2006, the two governments agreed to a target of USD 12 billion in Chinese investment in Russia by 2020.

During President Putin's visit to China in March, 2006, moreover, a memorandum was signed pledging long-term contracts between the two nations for the delivery of Russian gas, oil, and electricity, with Russia building two gas pipelines to China. Also discussed was a possible connection with the East Siberia-Pacific oil pipeline, bringing a branch into China. These developments would be in addition to the earlier Russian commitment of oil deliveries to China by rail totaling no less than 15 million tons per year.

At the same time, China's increasing economic involvement in Russia, and especially in the Russian Far East, evokes apprehension on the part of many Russians. Bold economic advances such as China's bid for PetroKazakhstan, a leading oil producer, and the influx of Chinese into Primorsky, where the indigenous population has declined in recent years due to adverse economic conditions, creates worries in certain circles.

Nonetheless, in its political-strategic dimensions, the Sino-Russian relationship has generally advanced. The positive course has been abetted by the resolution of the final territorial issues. Moreover, a number of high-level meetings have taken place between leaders of the two nations, with statements of accord, including a pledge of "strategic partnership," ensuing. Naturally, Beijing, in contrast to Washington, has not complained about

Putin's alleged lapses from democracy. China has been quite willing to let the Russian domestic political scene develop without comment or involvement. In Central Asia also, where political trends have often revealed serious instability, China has generally remained aloof. This has no doubt pleased Putin who has been deeply perturbed on occasion by American support for elements considered more democratic. Indeed, while it is not expressed openly, both Moscow and Beijing are concerned by what has been regarded as a deepening American political intrusion into Central Asia. This sentiment no doubt prominently influenced the SCO request that a deadline be fixed for the withdrawal of American bases from the region.

The joint Sino-Russian military exercises at Vladivostok and the Shandong Peninsula which began on August 18, 2005, represented the culmination of efforts to build a closer strategic relationship. These exercises were officially based on the principles of "non-alliance, non-confrontation and non-targeting of third countries," thereby representing a desire to avoid being labeled a response to U.S. power. Moreover, Russia has had similar exercises with the U.S., India, Japan, and some of the NATO states. However, to many observers, the exercises signaled a desire to achieve a greater strategic balance in the region.

The Sino-Russian relationship is far from an all-encompassing alliance and it is likely to remain so. Putin's desire is to restore Russia to the status of a global power, and in this effort, he must achieve balanced relations with the West, (including both the E.U. and the U.S.), and the East (including not only China but also India, nations in the Middle East, and elsewhere). Nonetheless, latent suspicions between China and Russia will remain as a product, in part, of history and of rival nationalist impulses. Yet China's present relations with the Russian Federation are vastly better than was the case a few decades ago.

China's Expanding Outreach in South Asia

In the years following the creation of the People's Republic of China, relations with South Asia, centering upon Pakistan and India, were in sharp contradiction. Pakistan was treated as a quasi-ally despite its limited economic potential and substantial socio-political differences. Such treatment was due entirely to Beijing's desire to have a counteractive force to the emerging India-Soviet relationship. China's relations with India steadily worsened in the late 1950s, with territorial disputes centering upon the Himalayan region and Indian acceptance of the Dalai Lama as a refugee being central causes. Thus, it was not surprising that a bloody conflict took place along the Sino-Indian border in 1962, a conflict won by China, but kept limited to avoid greater costs.

India aligned itself with the Soviet Union largely to balance the China threat. It also made certain positive gestures to the West, including the United States. While its political system remained democratic, however, with even the Indian Communists supportive of competitive politics, the economy was largely inward-oriented due to Congress Party policies.

In recent years, events have produced major changes, both in terms of India's economic policies and its international relations. India has begun the process of economic reform and is seeking to operate on the global stage, despite the urgent need for further economic reforms. It has become a major force in terms of technology and services. It is training a large number of engineers and other technicians, with various American giants turning to Indian teams to devise technological programs that will set the pace for the years ahead. Together with China, India will soon witness a massive upsurge in productivity, and as consumer markets, producers, investors, and users of energy, these two nations are already becoming global actors of major proportions, meanwhile interacting both cooperatively and competitively. In the past two decades, India's GDP growth has averaged 6%, lower than China's

10% but significantly higher than most economies. It is estimated that in the years immediately ahead, both nations will advance at a 7-8% growth rate, and by mid-century, China and India will represent the first and third largest economies in the world, with only the United States as a competitor.

There are challenges, however, that cannot be ignored. Those relating to China have already been set forth. At this point, the two nations combined represent only 6% of global GDP. Rapid growth must continue if poverty is to be reduced and unemployment is to decline. Whereas China is destined to face the problem of aging in the years ahead, with a decline in the number of its younger generations, India will be faced with a rising population, reaching 1.6 billion by 2050, with the difficulties attending this condition. India must also meet the problems of bureaucratic dominance, rigid labor laws, and inadequate infrastructure. Both nations, moreover, face the serious problem of environmental degradation and the wasteful use of key resources.

Under these conditions, China and India have good reasons for increasing economic cooperation despite the prospect of rising competition in certain areas. In 2006, bilateral trade was only some USD 20 billion, but there are good prospects for substantial increases, with both countries opening their markets and reducing obstacles to trade and investment. President Hu signed 12 trade agreements with India on his November 2006 visit. At the same time, in the effort to obtain such resources as oil, competition will grow, as was indicated by rival bids by China and India in Kazakhstan.

Meanwhile, efforts to improve political relations are now underway, with high level visits taking place, and various statements pledging friendship and cooperation having been issued. The territorial controversy has been set aside, and China no longer voices public displeasure over the Dalai Lama's residence in India.

The latest moves by China to create a more favorable relationship with India have been abetted by recent advances in India-Pakistan talks aimed at removing economic barriers and easing decades of hostility over Kashmir. While progress has been modest, the level of India-Pakistan tension is lower than at any time in the recent past. Thus, China can pursue more easily a policy pioneered by the United States, namely, the effort to maintain good relations with Pakistan for strategic reasons while improving overall relations with India. In the case of the U.S., the reasons for the latter course are political as well as economic. India is the world's largest democracy, and as such, a model for other developing nations, especially in its vicinity. Further, India remains part of a potential balance against the rising power of China. Thus, the U.S. and India reached an accord on India's nuclear energy program, an accord based on the principle that U.S. security strategy hinges on the nature of the regime, and its threat or non-threat to the United States rather than the weapons possessed that determine Washington's attitude.

China has also sought to improve its relations with the small states that are India's neighbors, including Bangladesh, Sri Lanka, and Nepal, as well as with Myanmar, a Southeast Asian nation on India's periphery. The Nepali terrorists, despite labeling themselves "Maoist" do not appear to receive any Chinese support. In certain cases, such as Myanmar, however, Chinese economic penetration has been significant, and the cause for some concern.

On balance, China's position in South Asia is more positive and more stable than at any time since the founding of the PRC. In China's quest for both protection on its peripheries and increased global influence, this is of significant benefit.

China's Expansion in the Middle East, Africa, and Latin America

Increasingly, China has been dispatching a variety of individuals from government officials to technicians and businessmen to the Middle East, Africa, and Latin America. While strategic considerations are sometimes involved, the primary motive is economic, specifically, to expand China's access to resources, especially oil and gas, and to widen the market for its consumer goods. In exchange, various forms of assistance have been proffered as well as personal rewards. On the whole, the policies have been successful, with China increasingly playing a significant role, especially in the economic realm, in the countries of these regions. It should be noted that China's oil consumption has been growing at the rate of 7.5% per annum; hence, the acute need for new supply sources.

In the Middle East, attention has been focused on Iran, Saudi Arabia, Qatar, and Yemen. With respect to Iran, China has opposed the U.S. attempt to impose UN sanctions on Tehran for pursuing uranium enrichment, and has sold military weapons to that nation. In return, it received a USD 70 billion agreement giving a Chinese company a large stake in one of Iran's biggest oil fields. In Saudi Arabia, which President Hu visited in 2006, China has reached citizens through satellite TV and an expanding consumer market, while drilling for oil in certain sectors of the country. In the Middle East as elsewhere, Beijing has not been disturbed by the existence of political authoritarianism, or reports of government-launched massacres. In this respect, it has had certain advantages over the United States, although American policies are by no means consistent with respect to the call for democracy and protection of human rights.

In Africa, China has frequently gained access and support by providing assistance. For example, it advanced a program providing for continent-wide debt forgiveness totaling some USD 1.2 billion. Chinese engineers constructed a plant generating electricity for the Angolan capital, along with an additional USD 2 billion infrastructure loan to that nation in exchange for oil. President Hu's visit to Gabon in February 2004 aided a Chinese company in obtaining exploration rights for onshore oil. And in the case of Zimbabwe, when President Mugabe visited China, he was named an honorary professor by the Chinese, and commended for his "brilliant contributions" to diplomacy and international relations. President Hu's visits to Morocco, Nigeria, and Kenya in 2006 and an eight country visit to Africa in early 2007 were widely seen as efforts to cement existing ties and to create new ones. Thus, through a combination of economic aid and the cultivation of friendly personal relations, China has made important advances in the African continent.

In Latin America also, gains have been registered. When President Hu visited this region in November 2004, a series of economic agreements were signed. Another high level delegation led by Vice President Zeng Qinghong visited the region in 2005. Subsequently, China was able to take advantage of the tensions between Venezuela and the United States to advance its oil purchases in Venezuela. In some cases, however, after initial hopes on the part of Latin American states, disappointment has ensued. Brazil hoped that China would become a major economic partner, but Chinese investment has been limited. Recently, Brazil's leaders charged that China wants merely to obtain raw materials with no value added, and export its consumer goods. Probably China's opposition to the effort of Brazil (along with Japan, Germany, and India) to acquire permanent membership in the UN Security Council has fueled recent resentment.

Nonetheless, China's advances in the developing world have been significant, and add to its augmented strength in Southeast and Central Asia.

The Impact of Globalization on China's Domestic Politics

Today, China stands in dramatic contrast to its socialist neighbor, the Democratic People's Republic of Korea (DPRK). North Korea, still impoverished despite belated and very cautious economic reforms, remains a largely closed society, keeping its ordinary citizens isolated, notwithstanding certain advances in economic and cultural relations with the Republic of Korea (ROK). China, on the other hand, has combined major economic reforms that have dramatically altered the old socialist order with an open receptivity to external interaction on a steadily expanded scale.

Today, millions of Chinese are acquiring cell-phones. TV sets have been commonplace for a decade. The inroads of western music, Japanese and Korean entertainment, and foreign literature of a widely varying nature are now having an influence on both Chinese thought and behavior, especially among urbanites and the younger generations.

At present, tourism is a major industry in China, with millions of foreigners pouring into the country over the course of a few years, and some 31 million Chinese going outside the PRC in 2005. Further, foreign entrepreneurs, teachers, and workers are making China their home, at least on a temporary basis. The age when the outsider was viewed with wonderment is largely over.

It is not surprising that ideology has lost much of its appeal. Mao Thought, along with Marxism-Leninism, is for ceremonial purposes, duly recited at the proper time and place, but rarely having serious emotional or intellectual impact. The truly potent political force in contemporary China, as noted earlier, is nationalism. The most appealing slogan is "Make China rich and strong," and the effort for China to be respected as a major regional and global force is also enthusiastically embraced. Indeed, like all other nations, China at present must deal with three semi-conflictual forces: internationalism, nationalism, and communalism. The latter term refers to the appeal of religion, especially fundamentalism, ethnicity, or one's local community for individuals seeking a more meaningful or psychologically satisfying identity in this revolutionary age.

Thus, the present era presents new or enhanced challenges to China's political leaders. Citizens who are subject to a variety of external as well as domestic influences are more likely to express their desires—and their grievances—openly. To be sure, China's explosive economic growth in itself creates greater class divisions and a new range of problems. But the intrusion of the external world onto the domestic scene can only complicate the matter. The fact that China is experiencing tens of thousands of public demonstrations—small, medium, and large—is not surprising. Further, in institutions of higher learning, the issues of what should be taught, and what sources should be used, have increasingly come to the fore.

In sum, major issues that are products of a combination of stimuli are now posed. What degree of freedom, what degree of control should exist? How can nationalism be used as a force for unity, yet still be controlled when it threatens to damage relations with important nations? And how can the growing generational cleavages be prevented from creating serious instability? In these as well as in other respects, China confronts modernity as the price of its success.

Milestones—Looking To The Future

In assessing China's future prospects in this age of globalization, only one prediction can be made with assurance: the future—as has been the case with the past—will be dominated by complexity. Sino-American relations will be troubled by continuing unresolved economic issues. Recent events have illustrated how difficult it is to achieve and maintain agreement on such matters as Chinese textile imports and, in broader terms, the massive U.S. trade deficit with China. Moreover, competition for resources, especially oil and gas, is likely to grow. On the other hand, China and the United States are going to become ever more closely intertwined economically, with both trade and investment continuing to expand. Thus, the health of each nation's economy will be a critical variable. Fortunately, despite the deficit problems, the U.S. economy does not seem in imminent danger and China's economy appears likely to grow at a 7-8% rate or higher in the years immediately ahead. In this scenario, economic problems can be resolved or contained.

On the political front, substantial systemic differences will remain. Despite its shift toward greater openness, for the foreseeable future, China will retain an authoritarian system which will result in periodic American criticism. In turn, U.S. international policies will be defined by Beijing as authoritarian. It is likely, however, that political criticisms by both parties will be relatively muted to permit attention to be directed elsewhere, as has been the case in the recent past.

Strategic issues are likely to be more prominent. Among these, Taiwan is of primary importance. Fortunately, as noted, China has shifted its policy from one of threat to one of appeal, with efforts to win support from the Taiwanese people via expanded economic and cultural interaction, and contacts with political leaders other than Chen Shui-bian. Thus, in the near term, China is likely to gamble on a policy aimed at gradual absorption rather than one focused on militancy. However, there is little likelihood that the fundamental issues blocking reunification will be resolved. With China's military strength rising, moreover, the Taiwan issue will remain of critical importance to Sino-American bilateral relations. Basic U.S. policies are unlikely to change, but Washington will continue to make it clear to all parties that a peaceful resolution is the only rational route. In any case, China's resort to force seems most unlikely, at least in the near future.

On a broader front, a "China threat" as well as an "America threat" will be voiced by certain groups. With both nations increasing and modernizing their military forces, and apprehension present over such problems as Sino-Japanese relations, recurrent tensions are likely. Yet relations between China and the U.S. in all probability will remain positive on balance in the years immediately ahead. The reason is simple: positive relations are clearly in the interest of both nations, as well as that of the region and world. Whether the problem at issue is economic, political, or strategic, settling or containing it through dialogue is vastly more fruitful than allowing it to reach a boiling point. Whatever extremists in either state seek to promote, national leaders will almost certainly be motivated to curb rising tension, and the use of leaders' visits, official dialogues, and NGO interaction to achieve this will almost certainly expand.

As has been noted, China's relations with the E.U. and the G8 have some of the same challenges as those with the U.S. Reaching agreements on trade has not been easy, and such difficulties are likely to remain or reoccur in the years ahead, with protectionism a continuing threat. If the key problems can be resolved, however, the E.U. is likely to give China the market economy status it seeks in the not too distant future. Much will hinge on whether the E.U. itself can undertake the internal reforms (such as those concerning voting rules) necessary and whether the current political divisions within it can be satisfactorily resolved. A positive scenario on these fronts would provide greater confidence vis-à-vis others such as China—but it is by no means guaranteed at this point. It is possible, but unlikely that China will be admitted to full membership in the G8 or OECD, but it is virtually certain that it will continue to be invited to the meetings of such organizations as a participant.

Security issues will remain generally secondary, but lifting the E.U. arms embargo is likely to depend on China's policies toward Taiwan and such regions as Central Asia, where the E.U. has an expanding interest.

Meanwhile, Sino-Russian relations are likely to continue on an upward course, but will remain far from an alliance. On the economic front, much will depend on whether the promises regarding Russian economic growth materialize, as well as progress in the sale of its key resources to China.

The SCO appears likely to operate effectively, and with their border issues resolved, China and Russia have no strategic problems of a serious nature. However, as noted, concern in the Russian Far East regarding an expanding Chinese economic and physical presence will continue to cast some clouds over the relationship. Russia's interests, moreover, lie in pursuing a balance with the West and Asia, as well as with India and China. Nor is Russia likely to abandon its insistence upon having precedence in Central Asia. Thus, China must be careful to keep its nationalism under control, avoiding any restoration of old imperial territorial designs. On balance, however, the prospects for a favorable Sino-Russian relationship in the coming years are good.

Meanwhile, in looking at the road ahead for China in South Asia, a number of variables must be considered. If, as expected, China and India continue to move rapidly ahead economically, the bilateral relationship will benefit on balance, despite areas of rising competition. Almost certainly, the Sino-Indian rivalry over resources (especially oil), will intensify, centering upon the Middle East and Central Asia. However, if both nations advance, the benefits of progressive economic interaction through expanded trade and investment will outweigh the negative factors. If on the other hand, either nation falls into an economic recession, tensions will certainly rise. However, this course seems unlikely, at least in the immediate future.

The political-strategic scene is also complicated. China and India are not likely to be close allies, and India will probably continue to look to both Russia and the United States as balancing forces. Indeed, certain Indian leaders have called for a strong strategic and economic "partnership" with the United States, terming it "a natural ally." At the same time, on issues like terrorism, separatism, and extremism—the issues that have strengthened SCO—China and India may well find common cause.

China's relations with other South Asian nations—and particularly Pakistan—are not likely to be sacrificed for the sake of India, and Beijing's position that India, along with Australia and New Zealand, should be excluded from the first East Asian Summit held in Malaysia in December, 2005, indicated that China does not want to see India expand its influence into areas where China seeks a key presence. Nor is China soon likely to change its position on India's admission to permanent membership in the U.N. Security Council. Thus, China will probably seek a balanced relationship with the nations of South Asia, with no specific nation given clear priority.

Meanwhile, China will continue to extend its reach to the Middle East, Africa, and Latin America. The primary motive will be economic, and assuming that China continues its rapid economic growth, its role as a global power will be strengthened. At the same time, with a few exceptions, its relations with the vast array of nations in these three regions will probably have limited strategic significance. As it gains economic leverage, to be sure, China can put pressure on a given nation with respect to certain political or strategic issues. However, in all probability, it will remain committed to non-involvement in the internal affairs of these countries or their international relations. This practice is vastly different from the era when China promoted socialist revolutions on an international scale, and no reversion to those policies is in sight.

Finally, as we have noted, China's domestic politics are being increasingly influenced by the combination of rapid domestic growth and expanding international intercourse. Almost certainly, this will continue in the years immediately ahead, constituting rising challenges to China's leaders. The thesis that China is at risk of collapse or monumental chaos seems greatly inflated, but relations between the government and the citizenry are almost certain to become more complex in the years immediately ahead. Thus, the premium will be upon making those reforms—both economic and political—that are essential in this revolutionary age, and making them in a timely fashion. That is the price for becoming a global power.

Bibliography

Berger, Suzanne and Richard K. Lester (eds) 2004, *Global Taiwan*, Armonk, NY: M.E. Sharpe.

Black, J.L. 2004, *Vladimir Putin and the New World Order – Looking East, Looking West?*, Lanham, MD: Rowman and Littlefield.

Bonnell, Victoria and George Breslauer (eds) 2001, *Russia in the New Century*, Boulder, CO: Westview.

Broedsgaard, Kjeld and Bertel Heurlin (eds) 2004, *China's Place in Global Geopolitics*, London: Routledge.

Buszynski, Leszek 2004, *Asia Pacific Security – Values and Identity*, London: Routledge.

Keith, Ronald C. 2005, *China as a Rising World Power and its Response to "Globalization,"* London: Routledge.

Lee, Kyung Tae, Justin Yifu Lin, and Si Joong Kim (eds) 2001. *China's Integration with the World Economy: Repercussions of China's Accession to the WTO*, Seoul: Korean Institute for International Economic Policy.

Liu, Ling 2005, *China's Industrial Policies and the Global Business Revolution*, London: Routledge.

Mahbubani, Kishore 2005, "Understanding China," *Foreign Affairs*, September-October, pp. 49-60.

Mandelbaum, Michael (ed.) 1998, *The New Russian Foreign Policy*, New York: Council on Foreign Relations.

Park, Bokyeong and Kang-Kook Lee 2005, *Natural Resources, Governance, and Economic Growth in Africa*, Seoul: Korea Institute for International Economic Policy.

Shams-Ud-Din (ed.) 1999, *Nationalism in Russia and Central Asian Republics*, New Delhi: Lancers.

Yoo, Tae Hwan and V. Balaji Venkatachalam 2005, *A Brief Appraisal of India's Economic and Political Relations with China, Japan, ASEAN, the E.U. and the U.S.*, Seoul: Korea Institute for International Economic Policy.

Wang, Jisi 2005, "China's Search for Stability with America," *Foreign Affairs*, September-October, pp. 39-48.

Zheng, Bijian 2005, "'Peacefully Rising' to Great-Power Status," *Foreign Affairs*, September-October, pp. 18-24.

Zweig, David and Bi Jianhai 2005, "China's Global Hunt for Energy," *Foreign Affairs*, September-October, pp. 25-38.

Articles from *Financial Times*, *The New York Times*, *The Wall Street Journal*, and the *China Daily*.

5

China: Socio-Political Issues

Tony Saich

Daewoo Professor of International Affairs, Kennedy School of Government;

Director, Harvard University Asia Center

Introduction

In recent years, the policy contours of the Hu Jintao–Wen Jiabao leadership have become clear. The main thrust is a form of populist authoritarianism, with policy gestures to those who have not benefited as much as others from China's reforms to date combined with attempts to tighten control over state and society, in the name of preserving social stability as the key foundation for continued economic growth. There is no evidence to suggest that President Hu intends to introduce the kinds of political liberalization that some had hoped for before his appointment. From the outset, the new leadership has strived to show that they were leaders of a different stripe, concerned about the rural and urban poor and determined to get to grips with the inequalities that have accompanied reforms. It was noticeable that Hu and Premier Wen's pre-and post-promotion visits were not to the glitzy cities of Shanghai and Shenzhen, but to the poorer parts of China, including the rural base areas where the CCP built its pre-1949 support and which provided the launch pad for it to take national power.

There are three significant discontinuities and one continuity in the Hu-Wen policy emphasis compared with the previous leadership of Jiang Zemin. First, current policy is more people-centered and populist. There has been a noticeable shift in the discussion of economic policy, with a greater emphasis on sustainability, the quality of growth, and dealing with the significant inequalities. Second, Hu is more orthodox in the political realm than Jiang. There is no doubt that the atmosphere has become tighter under his leadership. Hu has emerged to date as a strong Leninist leader who has sought to clamp down on dissent and to limit the range of ideas expressed in the public sphere. A more optimistic interpretation might be that this stance is necessary for Hu to consolidate power by showing his conservative credentials—before adopting more liberal reforms once his power is consolidated after the next CCP Congress. Both Deng Xiaoping and Jiang Zemin moved to the left on occasion to shore up their position, and after Jiang consolidated his position he became more sympathetic to loosening control over society and talking about political reform. However, there is a general sentiment among reformers that Jiang often mouthed "leftist" sentiments out of necessity; he did not really believe them, whereas Hu does and is a strong believer in Leninism. Third, Hu does not share Jiang's pro-U.S. disposition in foreign affairs. Essentially whenever it was politically feasible, Jiang tried to move China to a position of accommodation with U.S. interests and established his foreign policy in terms of the relationship with the U.S. By contrast, Hu seems much more suspicious of the U.S. and its intentions and has tried to build alliances with other countries and to build linkages with countries that are not close to the U.S.

One continuity with the past is the belief in the paramount position of the Party in the system and the idea that only the Party can be trusted to carry out reforms. Hu has continued Jiang's policy to reassert Party control over as much of state and society as is feasible. The reforms of the late-1980s to separate Party and state were rolled back after 1989 and have not been seriously discussed since then. Hu clearly does not trust the state to carry out effectively Party policy (and in this he might be correct).

Thus, in the absence of external shocks, policy direction is liable to follow along these lines, until a new generation of leaders can consolidate their power in a decade or so. However, the key question is whether simply trying to crack down on dissent, eradicating political alternatives, and placing primacy on maintaining social stability will be sufficient to deal with the issues confronting the Party over the medium-term. It is clear that unrest is increasing, particularly among those who have had their land seized in the countryside, or have been charged exorbitant illegal fees, or have not received their pay, or who have been deceived by employers defaulting on pension obligations. Incidents of unrest have been responses to corrupt and illegal actions by authorities, and this combined with significant government corruption have fuelled social unrest. The central leadership is aware of this, and has responded with calls for better and more transparent government and for the Party to monitor itself and the government more effectively. However, without allowing any external monitoring, the effect will be limited. The key question is whether the Party can develop the governing capacity to deal with these multiple challenges or whether the disturbances will reach such a level that the politico-administrative system will be overwhelmed.

Key Socio-Political Issues

First, we outline four social issues that have evolved into acute policy challenges in China. Second, we look at leadership responses and constraints on political reform, before concluding with three scenarios for future developments.

Social Developments and Issues

During the reform period, China has undergone four sets of transitions that have shaped socio-economic evolution. First, it has moved its workforce from low-productivity agriculture to higher-productivity manufacturing and service work, following the pattern of universal development, including that of its neighbors in East Asia. Thus, there is nothing magical about the economic development of China other than it was retarded for so long by faulty Maoist policies. Second, unlike its East Asian neighbors, China has undergone a second economic transition from a planned economy to a more market influenced economy. This has brought enormous benefits, but also has created new problems of unemployment, as inefficient state-owned enterprises have closed down or shed workers. Third, during these double economic transitions, China has undergone a demographic transition from a very young population to a quickly aging population. This has major consequences for dependency ratios and the number of elderly who will have to be supported in the future. Fourth, there has been a transition from reliance on the collective to a belief in the individual. Socialism rests on the principle that the individual can derive more from the collective than he/she can by working alone. Markets place individual choices and their regulation at the center. China's reforms have seen a shift from the collective as the organizing focus to one based on individual choice. This creates a problem for the Party as its ideology is based on the former premise and it cannot offer effective guidance in the new society. The resultant conflicted morality—a raw capitalist outlook with the rhetoric of an existing socialist system—presents a problem for future leaders, as there is no civil society that might provide a bond in the event of CCP collapse.

For the individual, this contradiction creates confusion as official rhetoric bares little resemblance to reality as lived on the streets. The result is distrust of government, an attitude of putting oneself first, and a subsequent moral vacuum.

Out of these transitions four pressing issues have arisen.

Demographics

With China's rate of population growth declining significantly, the population is aging rapidly, presenting rising pension and medical obligations and severe problems for care of the elderly. In some rural areas, there are serious gender imbalances that will lead to a high number of unmarried males (see also Chapter 3). The future population will be increasingly urbanized, as surplus labor is moved off the land, leading to the question as to whether employment can be generated sufficiently quickly to prevent unrest.

China's stringent family planning policy has been geared to limiting population to 1.6 billion by 2050. The birth rate dropped dramatically from 33.43 per 1,000 in 1970 to 12.40 in 2005, with a corresponding drop in the natural growth rate from 25.83 per 1,000 to 5.89 per 1000 in 2005. Mortality rates have also been dropping and stood at 6.51 per 1000 in 2005. The overall trend will not significantly impact on aggregate economic growth, but there will be other important effects due to the changing structure of China's demographics.

First, the population will age significantly. Research has shown that, for example, there are links between aging populations and savings rates. Overall, China's median age will increase 13.8 years during the first half of this century. With a lower fertility rate there will be a lower domestic savings rate, but there will also be a higher return to labor because of its relative scarcity and a lower return to capital. China will be the first society to grow old before it grows rich. At the end of the twentieth century, China officially entered the aging stage in terms of internationally recognized criteria, with 10% of its population over 60 years of age. By the end of 2005, there were almost 144 million people over 60, accounting for 11% of the population. A total of 16 million were aged over 80.

Second, China will grow old while continuing to industrialize and urbanize with the consequence that there will be an even greater need to maintain rapid and sustainable economic growth. According to the China National Committee on Aging, those over 60 years of age will account for an estimated 16% of China's population in 2020 (248 million) and 31% (437 million) in 2050. The population over 80 years old is expected to reach 22 million in 2020 and 83 million in 2050. The rise in the number of aged will put tremendous pressure on medical expenditures. An aging population will also bring serious consequences in terms of dependency ratios and pension obligations that the state will have to meet. In 2000 there were 15.60 people over 60 years old for each 100 at work and this is predicted to rise to 29.46 in 2025 and 48.49 in 2050. The ratio of the working to non-working population is also dropping fast, from 6:1 in 1991 to a projected 2:1 by 2020. Thus, whereas pension contribution rates for workers were only 3% of payroll when China began this system in 1951, they had risen to 20% by the mid-1990s. Unless something is done (and certainly policy will change), by 2033 Chinese estimates suggest that payroll rates of around 40% will be needed to fund pensions. Pension non-payment has been a key cause of urban protest and the image of the new leadership as a "caring" government, which Hu Jintao and Wen Jiabao have sought to project, will be severely damaged by not looking after the nation's pensioners.

In addition to aging, another adverse consequence of the one-child policy has been a distortion of male-female ratios. The 2000 census reported the ratio of males to females as 106.74:100, or 41.27 million more men than women. However, at birth the ratio was 119.92:100 and by age four it was 120.17:100. In some counties the reported discrepancy between female and male children was alarmingly large. Jiangxi and Guangdong had ratios of 138.01:100 and 137.76:100 respectively with rural Guangdong at a rate of 143.7:100. This clearly indicates a strong trend to further imbalance in the ratio over the next 10 to 15 years and beyond. Ratios like these mean that at least 1 million men per year will not be able to find a marriage partner, while the *South China Morning Post* (25 August 2003) suggested that there could be as many as 100 million Chinese bachelors by the year 2020. This will drive up the bride price in the rural areas and will result in increased illegal trade in women and in prostitution. The thought of large numbers of males who cannot find a bride and drifting into cities looking for work is a potential cause for unrest, and the increase in clientele for commercial sex workers will increase the potential for the spread of HIV/AIDS.

Over the next decade, urbanization will proceed apace with an estimated 300 million to 500 million people expected to migrate from the rural areas to towns and cities by 2020, providing an urban population of around 800 million. Urbanization is seen as the best way to provide a long-term solution to the problems of inequality that stem primarily from urban-rural differences. In world terms, China is "under-urbanized" as a result of controlled urbanization and the household registration system. In rate of urbanization, China lags behind several transitional societies, such as Hungary (64%) and Russia (73%), as well as the remaining socialist countries Cuba (75%) and North Korea (59%). Meeting the urbanization goals of shifting at least 300 million to the cities and suburbs will present major challenges for the government in terms of investment in urban infrastructure and planning. It will also present significant challenges for job creation. The programs for infrastructure will provide employment opportunity, but whether the manufacturing and service sectors can be expanded sufficiently to deal with this expanded urbanization and accommodate the estimated 150 million to 200 million surplus rural laborers remains to be seen.

Employment

The future employment trend for China will be to boost the underdeveloped service sector of the economy as a part of the process of urbanization. Yet, a recent World Bank study suggests that China needs to maintain a 10% growth rate in order to provide sufficient employment opportunities. This is above the Chinese government's stated desire to regulate GDP growth at around 8%, a target it has failed to meet in recent years as growth has repeatedly topped 10%.

There is a range of estimates of unemployment in China. Official figures show registered urban unemployment rising from 3% (6 million) in the mid-1990s to only 4.2% (8.4 million) by 2005, despite employment in the state-owned enterprises (SOEs) sector dropping by around 40 million. These figures exclude those who have not registered as unemployed, including the large number of workers "laid off" (*xiagang*) by still functioning SOEs. Thus, a more realistic estimate for the real urban unemployment rate was 9.36% for 1997 and 12.3%[1] for 2002. Even this does not take into account the 150 million to 200 million more surplus rural workers acknowledged by China's leaders.[2] Scholars at the Rand Corporation estimated an open and disguised unemployment rate (urban and rural) of around 23% or 170 million.[3] In any case, unemployment is a more important issue than the official figures suggest.

Not surprisingly the unemployment is worse in the Northeast and the West, homes to much heavy and manufacturing industry.

It is clear that the state sector will never again be the main engine for urban employment, either for those laid off or for the estimated 11 million to 12 million new entrants each year on the job market. Even with an improved growth rate, increases in employment generation have been dropping as enterprises have been forced to become more efficient. Employment growth over the next decade is projected at 1.4% per annum, slightly up from the 1.1% in the 1990s, but well below the annual employment growth of 4.2% in the 1980s.

There is a clear policy priority to expand other avenues for employment growth, but producing sufficient jobs will remain a major headache for China's leadership over the next decade. According to official accounts, SOEs shed 3 million jobs a year until 2006. Tian Chengping, Minister for Labor and Social Security, reported in a September 14, 2006 speech that China needed to create 24 million urban jobs per year to absorb the new labor force, including migrants and college graduates, but was creating only around 11 million jobs per annum. Lu Zhongyuan of the Development Research Center of the State Council does not see the employment pressure alleviating for 20 to 30 years. Yet while the former major sectors of the economy have been shedding jobs, the more vibrant sectors of the economy are prevented from sufficiently rapid expansion because of the lingering state bias against the non-state sector of the economy. How destabilizing these trends will be depends in part on the continued growth in the economy, the ability of the non-state sector to generate sufficient employment, and the capacity of the authorities to keep unrest in check.

The best option for employment growth is the service sector, which in China employs a smaller percentage of employees than other countries at a similar level of development. Allowing effective foreign investment into this sector could generate a boom of 40 million to 50 million jobs. The other main option for employment expansion is enhanced development of the private sector. Geographically, private enterprises are heavily concentrated in the coastal areas with Jiangsu, Guangdong, Zhejiang, Shanghai, and Beijing home to 54% of the national total, and the Western provinces with only 14%. It is clear that those cities and provinces with a higher growth rate and standard of living are also those with a higher level of private enterprise. For example, in Wenzhou and Taizhou, where the private economy is dominant, there is little unemployment, in contrast with towns like Mudanjiang in the Northeast that are dominated by old SOEs.

Inequality

Such employment and demographic trends have inevitably fed into increasing inequality in China and to the creation of new pockets of poverty. China's post-Mao development strategy has consciously eschewed social equity and sought to use inequality as a stimulant for economic activity and growth. There is a clear urban bias to development, as well as a coastal bias, and a conscious exclusion of migrants from integration into many urban services.

Inequality has been rising under the reforms, with the Gini coefficient rising from 0.33 to around 0.49. This means that China has shifted from being one of the more egalitarian countries in Asia to becoming one of the least. Not surprisingly, wealth has become more concentrated. In June 2005, the National Statistics Bureau noted that the 10% most affluent households in the country enjoyed 45% of the country's wealth, while the poorest 10% shared only 1.4%. The disposable income of the richest group was 11.8 times greater than that of the lowest 10%, up from 10.9 times a year before. For a country that still describes itself as socialist, these trends are difficult to justify and could provide an easy rallying point for the opposition. The Ministry of Labor and Social Security even stated that the growing income gap was likely to cause instability by 2010 if no effective solutions were found.

Inequality in China goes beyond just income to include access to public goods and services. Access to health and education services was still widely available in the 1980s, but became more dependent on income in the 1990s. For example, in 1998, 22.2% of those in high-income areas were covered by cooperative medical facilities, but only one to three percent of residents in poorer areas were covered. With rising health costs, it is not surprising that illness is one of the most cited reasons for poverty among the poor, something exacerbated by the collapse of the pre-paid collective medical system with the disbanding of the communes in the early 1980s. As a result, some 90% of rural households have to pay directly for almost all of the health services used. Thus, not surprisingly, illness has a close correlation with poverty.

Given such problems, it is not surprising that poverty is another major issue for China. The Asian Development Bank (2001), using the norm of USD 1 per day in purchasing power parity (instead of China's figure of USD 0.66) and the preferred consumption norm, suggested China had about 230 million poor residents, some 18.5% of the population. If one applied a norm of USD 2 per day, the number was 53.7% of total population. This put China roughly on a par with Indonesia (15.2% and 66.1%, respectively) and considerably better off than India (44.2% and 86.2%, respectively). Despite rapid economic growth, Chinese officials acknowledged in May 2004 that 56.17 million residents were living on below USD 1 per day and officially some 23.6 million were living on below USD 0.85 per day at the end of 2005. On the other hand, the World Bank estimated that some 135 million people, nearly 10% of China's population, were living on USD 1 per day in 2004. Official Chinese poverty statistics do not cover urban China, but the number of urban residents who received the minimum subsistence support was 22.34 million in March 2005. Such figures clearly underestimate urban poverty and do not include the migrant population.

What such figures reveal is that despite tremendous progress, China still confronts a number of policy challenges moving forward. First, there is a significant group of rural poor who have not responded to policy measures, market openings, and the benefits of "trickle down." Second, there is a very large group that is vulnerable to economic downturn and liable to recidivism. Third, there is a smaller but rising number of urban poor whose poverty is the product rather than beneficiary of reform.

Does the inequality matter? Yes, for both economic and political reasons—and while a certain rise in inequality is inevitable, some has been the result of concrete policy choices. There is a general consensus among economists that rising inequality can be detrimental to long-term economic growth. In China, a major focus of future development strategy will have to be consumption-driven growth and this will require better integrated domestic markets and a more equitable spread of purchasing capacity. The lack of access to adequate education and health facilities will also retard growth by denying effective opportunities to many of China's young. Last but not least, there is political risk associated with this strategy as the Chinese leadership still claim to be socialist and to represent all sections of the population. The inequality, particularly if it becomes a major cause for unrest, could be a rallying point for opposition. The current leadership has tried to address these concerns through populist measures to raise rural incomes, provide free rural education, and to provide support to those badly affected by lay-offs in the West and Northeast. However, these rising pressures for redistribution can heighten inefficient allocations of scarce resources through the state sector in order to provide what can only be short-term benefits at the expense of sound long-term growth. Jiang Zemin's plans to develop the West and Wen Jiabao's strategy to revive the Northeast largely through transfer payments and state support are good examples of this.

Social Unrest

Given the trends outlined above and the tremendous scale of transition that China is undergoing, it is not surprising that social unrest is on the rise. In fact, the government's stance encourages people to be unruly when they have a grievance. Since the political system lacks effective channels to express genuine grievances, citizens are driven to extra-legal means such as demonstrations and strikes. The overwhelming concern for the central leadership to maintain social stability makes the situation worse. Given that the origins of most social unrest lie with the illegal actions of local governments or those with powerful connections, citizens are unlikely to receive redress through official channels that are controlled by the local Party bureaucracy. This reduces options to either sitting at home peacefully waiting for redress that is unlikely to come, or taking to the streets and creating a public disturbance that will get the attention of government at higher levels. If the disturbances receive sufficient attention, then the higher levels are liable to direct their subordinates to resolve the issue swiftly in order to maintain public order. This resolution could be repression, buying people off, or actually solving the problem. The chance of achieving a result through civil disorder is higher than simply waiting at home for an enlightened leader to come by.

At present, the protests are not a threat to regime survival as the vast majority are not overtly political, and derive from economic grievances that are a product of the reforms. Major causes of unrest are industrial restructuring, financial pressures on local governments that lead to illegal levies, manifest increases in inequality, and high-handed behavior of local officials. Respondents' attitudes in a national survey conducted across China by the Kennedy School of Government in the Fall of 2003 about the way policy is implemented by local governments should raise concern. Irrespective of place of residence, the general view among respondents was that, when implementing policy, local officials and governments are mainly concerned with their own interests, are more receptive to the views of their superiors rather than those of ordinary people, favor those with money, and are formalistic in implementing policy rather than dealing with actual problems. These feelings are held even more strongly by those living in villages than those with an urban household registration. For example, in our sample, only 19.7% who live in villages think that local governments bring benefits to ordinary people when implementing policy, while 52.6% see them as mainly concerned with their own interests. In major cities, 41.4% felt that policy execution favored those with money, while only 39.3% thought that it took care of individuals in difficulty. By contrast, in the villages these percentages were 54.7 and 23.6 respectively. Clear majorities also felt that when implementing policy, local officials sought to move closer to their superiors rather than thinking about looking after ordinary people.

In the urban areas, most collective protests have come from the forced demolition of homes for redevelopment, the failure to meet payments either for salary or pensions, or from lay-offs. In the countryside, the main bones of contention have been the imposition of illegal fees, land seizures, and resistance to unpopular policies such as family planning. What has been interesting in the recent period has been the rise in protests because of environmental issues.

The levels of unrest have been increasing and have created concern among China's leadership. According to the Ministry of Public Security, there were 58,000 recorded protests, or "mass incidents" in China in 2003, 74,000 in 2004 (involving 3.76 million people), and 87,000 in 2005.[4] This increase of discontent was not restricted to protest alone. In the first quarter of 2005, the State Council Petitions Bureau in Beijing reported an increase of over 90% in the number of letters and visits requesting government redress of grievances compared to the same period the previous year. However, it is apparent that the senior leadership does not know how to respond effectively. The leadership has recognized that, on the whole, the protests are not political and do not deserve a harsh response. For example, Minister Zhou, while calling for vigilance, noted that "extreme measures" should be avoided and that the problems were "internal conflicts among the people." Even more remarkably, Chen Xiwen (who oversees agricultural policy), while criticizing violent protest, saw the rural protests as a sign that farmers were recognizing how to protect their rights and interests. That said, there is no doubt that the leadership remains concerned about the possibility of unrest getting out of hand and will seek to repress such incidents. This was forced home by a *People's Daily* commentary on July 28, 2005 that warned that no illegal attempts to disrupt social stability would be tolerated, and that the protection of stability comes before all else. Also, the leadership has curtailed the right of citizens to petition the central government directly. Combined with the message that conflicts should be resolved through the existing system, this is not encouraging and puts considerable power in the hands of the local authorities—who have been responsible for much of the disturbance in the first place.

Developments and Milestones

Prospects for the Future

These issues have caused the central authorities to respond through the kind of populist authoritarianism noted above. Without external shocks there is no reason to believe that this policy approach will change. It will affect, however, the general attitude to economic development and policy choices. As noted, the leadership has tried to introduce policies that benefit those who have not benefited as much as others from reform, such as dropping the agricultural tax on farmers and subsidizing agricultural production. This is a major policy shift, but it is leaving local governments strapped for cash and they will resort to other measures to raise funding, which may well increase social unrest. Thus the problem of funding local governments will be exacerbated by measures that have been introduced to alleviate rural poverty. In March 2005, Premier Wen announced that school fees would be abolished for 14 million students in the poorest counties and by 2007 all rural students would receive free primary education. In August 2005, the central government decided to expand the pilot program to provide subsidized healthcare to rural residents. The central government was to expand its subsidy to 20 per *yuan* per person per annum and local governments were to increase their contributions similarly. In the same month, the State Council announced that the threshold for individual tax payment would be raised to 1,500 *yuan* from 800 *yuan*.

Unfortunately, the system needs more extensive structural reform and better representation for disadvantaged groups to make such measures effective and sustainable. Stopgap measures that are introduced should not be at the cost of productive investment. China's investment patterns and preferential fiscal policies have favored the coastal regions at the expense of the interior, while formal credit access is highly biased to capital intensive SOEs, and rural net taxes remain highly regressive. To change this situation would require a major reallocation of resources that, in turn, would require a significant shift in political sentiment. Despite the campaign to establish a "comfortable" (*xiaokang*) society since the Sixteenth Party Congress (November 2002), and Hu Jintao's and Wen Jiabao's populist disposition, a major reorientation is unlikely, given the structure of political power. The 16th Politburo, like its predecessor, has a strong provincial representation, but essentially represents the richer, coastal areas of China. Upon its election, it looked as if there was a limited attempt to appoint some leaders from the inland areas, but subsequent personnel shifts have taken away that illusion. Despite the campaign to develop the West,

Sichuan, the most important province in the west of China still enjoys no representation at the highest levels. The Party Secretary of Xinjiang does have a place on the Politburo, but this has more to do with the center's intent to maintain its territorial integrity and to resist any moves for autonomy rather than to address issues of poverty and inequality. This means that for all intents and purposes the current Politburo resembles its predecessor, with major municipalities (Beijing, Tianjin, and Shanghai—at least until the ouster of Shanghai Party Secretary Chen Liangyu over corruption charges in late 2006), and the wealthy coastal province of Guangdong enjoying representation, while the inland and poorer areas of China are excluded. This is unlikely to change in the future. Given this, one may presume that policy will continue to be biased in favor of the "haves" while rhetoric will continue to be paid to the needs of the "have-nots."

Is meaningful political reform likely under Hu? While hope springs eternal and observers both inside and outside China expected significant political reforms to be introduced at the last two Party Congresses, they have been disappointed and are likely to remain so. It should not be forgotten that the primary purpose of the CCP is to remain in power for as long as possible and its leaders are not going to introduce any changes that might threaten their position and foment instability. This viewpoint has been strengthened not only by their own domestic challenges in 1989 (and the split that these caused within the Party elite), but also by their observations of post-Soviet Russia and the problems that they feel market economics and democratic politics have brought. In particular, the fall of Suharto in Indonesia and the "color revolutions" in former Soviet satellites have caused many in the elite to re-think any significant political opening. The message seems clear—keep economic growth booming and a tight lid on any potential dissent.

Despite long-term benefits that would come from significant political reform in terms of ameliorating corruption, providing institutionalized outlets for dissent and protest, and increasing transparency, there are strong countervailing pressures. First, China's leaders interpret democratic reforms as essentially destabilizing, undermining both social stability and economic growth. It is important to remember that the bottom line of CCP legitimacy is its capacity to deliver the economic goods. It has sought to buttress this with a strident nationalism that is popular with urban elites and through reliance on reviving traditional Confucian views toward benevolent authority.

Second, the Party's monopoly on power allows it to dispense patronage, fuelling the corruption that is a feature of contemporary Chinese political culture. Gradualism in reform has brought significant economic benefits, but has allowed the Party to co-opt new elites into the power structure, thus reducing external pressure for political change. The Party is now seen by many as a bastion of privilege that represents the new haves over the have-nots.

Third, the Chinese system is extremely decentralized and it is often difficult for the center to control activities of local officials even if they should wish to. The theft of state assets, the corruption, and the use of official position to pursue private wealth are all most marked at the local levels of government. Thus local governments have little incentive to make their activities more transparent or accountable to the public at large.

Fourth, with rapid economic growth continuing, the new urban elites appear to have little interest in more democratic reform. Not surprisingly, as they have fared well under the existing system, they see no compelling reason to change it. There is no strong constituency that favors political change. Private entrepreneurs benefit from connections to the Party, or indeed may be former Party officials themselves. The laid-off workers are politically marginalized and while there has been an upsurge in farmer protest there is no evidence that the protests have gone beyond the local realm. Indeed, most evidence supports the view that the protestors retain trust in the national leaders and see the problems as purely local aberrations rather than systemic flaws. Our 2003 survey showed continued high levels of support for national leadership, but this dropped dramatically as government got closer to the people. Of the respondents, 86.1% expressed the view that they were relatively or extremely satisfied with the government work and the level of service of the central government. This dropped to 75% for the provincial level, 52% for the district and county, and to only 43.6% for the township, village, or neighborhood committee. This is important as it is distinct from many developed economies, where satisfaction levels tend to rise as government gets closer to the people, indicating that people feel that they have greater control over the decisions of local government and may be able to influence local policy and resource allocation.

Future Scenarios

Future scenarios for China depend to a large extent on the capacity for the economy to keep developing smoothly. While economic growth will slow eventually, over the next five to ten years there is no reason why rapid growth cannot be maintained if correct policy choices are made. Growth should come down to around 6% by 2015 and between 4% and 5% by 2025. However, the Chinese economy is more integrated into the world trading system than ever before and this makes it more vulnerable to general trends within the global economy: a major slowdown in the U.S. economy or rapidly rising prices for natural resources could cause problems for the Chinese economy.

Domestically, the unrest that is local and isolated at the moment could always boil over into a major conflict between state and society. It should be noted that the Chinese economy does not need to slow by too much before the state will lose its capacity to dispense largesse to its followers and for the costs of buying social peace to become problematic. There are a number of potential scenarios for China's political future and one cannot rule out systemic collapse, even though this seems least likely. History does not offer much comfort for a peaceful transition as communist regimes, unlike some other authoritarian systems, have only changed with the collapse of the *ancien regime*. There are two potential causes that could trigger systemic collapse and while both are possible they are not probable in the foreseeable future. The first would stem from economic collapse. While there are systemic distortions in the economy and an extremely vulnerable banking system, wise policy choices should ensure continued high levels of economic growth over the next decade. The second catalyst would be if the social tensions and inequalities led to sufficient unrest to force the leadership to undertake significant political reforms in order to retain control. Here we shall just sketch three possible scenarios.

1. The most likely scenario over the short to medium term is a continuation of the politics of muddling through. Bold initiatives are unlikely. An essentially technocratic approach will prevail, while the leadership tries to maintain an authoritarian political structure combined with growing economic liberalization. Minimal reform is likely in the political system, with a continued focus on strengthening the legal system and building capacity and skills within public administration. The main potential for promoting reform would lie with the ability of people and organizations to exploit the deliberate vagaries of official pronouncements to experiment with cautious reform initiatives. Here the national consensus will be weak, and the corruption will continue, as will the lack of social cohesion. The Party would still flirt with a strident form of nationalism in order to bolster the national consensus. This will mean that frictions with the U.S. and Japan will

continue and any genuine rapprochement is unlikely. Policy will continue to balance the tensions between appeasing the new economic elites and trying to provide support for those who have been left behind by the reforms.

2. This scenario would see the leadership responding to the increasing diversity in society and the rising protests by moving to accommodate with society and to try to form a new social compact. Instrumental in this process would be a re-evaluation of the events of 1989 and a return to the reform agenda put forward by Zhao Ziyang in 1987. Optimists would like to see China following in the footsteps of its East Asian neighbors with a transition to "soft-authoritarianism" followed by a democratic breakthrough ensuing as a natural corollary from economic growth. This would be a beneficial scenario not only for many in China but also for the international community, as the new leadership would adopt a much more friendly posture to the U.S. and Japan, and it would lead to considerably reduced tensions over Taiwan, providing a potential route to reunification.

For the reasons outlined above, this does not seem likely. It would require a segment of the ruling elite to be willing to break with the old system and to form a new compact with progressive forces in society. One could argue that there was such an opportunity in 1989 but that it was rejected by orthodox Party members. Some argue that economic growth is creating a middle class that will support change and that the increase of marketization will cause the rule of law to be taken more seriously. However, it is hard to see what would cause the current elite willingly to reject the current system.

3. A third scenario would see the current leadership becoming sufficiently disturbed by the potential for unrest and by what it interprets as U.S. attempts to isolate it internationally that it would adopt a more xenophobic nationalism combined with an inefficient authoritarianism domestically. In this case, the Party would be dominated by the new elites who would read any opening up of the political system as leading to an erosion of their privileges and benefits. The CCP maintains that without it chaos would ensue. By consistently cracking down on alternatives and restricting the growth of a vibrant civil society that could form the basis for a new system, the CCP has created the possibility that an "uncivil society" might take power—the most probable outcome would be rule by the new economic elites backed by the military, in the name of preserving social stability and national sovereignty. A strident nationalism might provide a minimal level of social glue to give the new regime a residue of support. A more likely variant would be the emergence of a pre-democratic Latin American-style political system. Under this scenario the inequalities would continue to rise, with the Party becoming the preserve of the elites and with their power backed up by the military. The lack of political reform would produce a permanent underclass in both urban and rural China that would be portrayed as a threat to stability and continued economic progress. The Party-dominated State would be in continual friction with society.

Milestones in the Political Calendar

A number of milestones in the political calendar will provide some indications of where China is going in the future. The 17th Party Congress in September 2007 will mark the expected mid-point of the Hu-Wen leadership and will be the CCP Congress where they can have the most impact over the future direction of China. Most important will be the leadership promotions that take place, as these will give a good indication of both policy direction and also who the successors to Hu and Wen are likely to be. However, we should not look for all the promotions to be from the Fifth Generation of leaders as there are still those in Hu's own generation who could be promoted into the Politburo at this time.

The 10th National People's Congress will be held in March 2008. This Congress will introduce the next five-year development strategy and will provide an opportunity to assess how ingrained Hu and Wen's emphasis on equitable and sustainable growth has become. Traditionally in China, the lead up to the formation of a new Five-Year Plan has been a time when leadership tensions have come to the fore and have spilled out into the public arena. While policy differences can be papered over in normal times, when it comes to setting economic priorities into the new plan, the stakes become higher.

The Summer Olympic Games will be in Beijing in 2008. How the games come off will be crucial for China's future development and for how the international community views China. How the games are managed is entirely in the hands of Hu and Wen, and the approach China takes will reflect their attitudes and predisposition. While China wants to use the games to build national pride and to show off its new international status to the world, hosting the games contains many risks and will reveal much about just how far China has come in terms of integrating with international norms. If the leadership put security to the forefront because of their fears of unrest or actions by groups such as *Falungong*, the Olympics will be a public relations disaster for China and will set back reforms and damage its international prestige. If China is able to provide a secure but relaxed environment for the games where the international press enjoys a hospitable environment, it will bode well for further reforms. At the moment the betting is on the former.

In addition to these major events, the direction of future policy will be gauged by a number of other specific events. For example, China will pass new regulations both for its domestic non-governmental organizations and also for international non-governmental organizations working in China. The kind of control that the Party wishes to retain over society will be indicated by these regulations. It is likely that the regulations will retain the need for each organization to find a sponsoring agency and they are likely to introduce more stringent financial and organizational requirements than currently exist.

Premier Wen has raised the possibility that, in the future, elections might be possible at the township level. Currently, elections operate at the village level. Raising elections to the township level would be a significant step forward and is important because unlike the village, the township forms an official part of the governing structure in China. The PRC Constitution recognizes national, provincial, and township governments. Villages are practical administrative divisions under the authority of townships for purposes such as the census and postal services, but without political decision making or administrative authority. Townships, on the other hand, have some real authority.

One thing that is certain is that the Fifth Generation of leaders, who will consolidate their power around 2015, will adopt different priorities to the current leadership. Each new leadership cohort has sought to stamp its mark on policy and they will be no different. They will take power at the time when demographics begin to sour, when the economy will start slowing, and when the pressures for more substantial political reform will mount. As described in Chapter 7, the educational background of the Fifth Generation is significantly different from its predecessor's and its training in politics, law, management, and economics will stand them in better stead to deal with these challenges than the current leadership of trained engineers.

Notes

1. *Urban Poverty in the PRC*, Asian Development Bank, Project No. TAR PRC 33448, 2002.
2. Tian Chengping, "Labor and Social Security Development in China," speech at the Brookings Institute, September 14, 2006.
3. Charles Wolf, Jr., K. C. Yeh, Benjamin Zycher, Nicholas Eberstadt, Sungho Lee, *Fault Lines in China's Economic Terrain*, Santa Monica, CA: Rand, 2003.
4. *Washington Post*, August 10, 2005; *Financial Times*, January 19, 2006.

Bibliography

Asian Development Bank 2001, *Country Economic Review: People's Republic of China*.

Asian Development Bank 2002, *Urban Poverty in the PRC*, Asian Development Bank, Project No. TAR PRC 33448.

Horizon 2003 and 2004. *Zhongguo jumin pingjia zhengfu ji zhengfu gonggong fuwu yanjiu baogao (Research Report on Citizens' Attitudes to Government and Government Provision of Public Goods)*, Beijing: Horizon.

Saich, Tony 2004, "The Changing Role of Government," Background Note for the World Bank Report on China's 11th Five Year Plan.

Saich, Tony 2005, "Development and Choice," in Edward Friedman and Bruce Gilley (eds), *Asia's Giants*, New York: Palgrave Macmillan, pp. 227-241.

Wolf, Jr., Charles, K. C. Yeh, Benjamin Zycher, Nicholas Eberstadt, and Sungho Lee 2003, *Fault Lines in China's Economic Terrain*, Santa Monica, CA: Rand.

Articles in the *China Daily*, *People's Daily*, *Xinhua*, *The Economist*, *Financial Times*, *New York Times*, and *South China Morning Post*.

6

China's New Banking System

Jonathan Anderson
Managing Director and Chief Economist, Asia, UBS

Introduction

We can't think of a single topic that raises more questions, misconceptions and debate than the state of the Chinese banking system. For most of the 1990s and into the 2000s, Mainland banks were commonly painted as unreconstructed "basket cases" without any real credit culture, continuing to pour huge sums into value-destroying activities, and raising the risk of a financial crisis. However, since the initial recapitalization and subsequent public listing of large state-owned institutions such as the Bank of Communications, the China Construction Bank, and the Bank of China in Hong Kong beginning in 2005, Mainland commercial banks have enjoyed an unprecedented renaissance in popularity, with global retail investor demand often bordering on euphoria. If equity market valuations as of mid-2007 are to be believed, these banks are on par with some of the best-managed global majors such as HSBC or Standard Chartered.

Needless to say, this sudden and wrenching turnaround has left many observers confused. Have we really seen a fundamental change in the behavior of the Chinese banking system? Do state-owned financial institutions really deserve the hype they have been receiving? Or are banks at risk of yet another bout of sharply rising non-performing loan (NPL) ratios and deteriorating balance sheets, particularly after macro overheating and overinvestment in recent years? How should we think about the longer-term prospects?

Our answer is that the "bad old days" of massive resource misallocation and flagrant disregard for economic realities are well and truly over, and we don't foresee a return to anything close to the bad debt levels of the past decade. On the other hand, the coming liberalization of the Mainland financial system will present new challenges for Chinese banks–challenges that still leave the medium-term outlook for the commercial banking system in question.

We are left with the following conclusions, which will be developed in turn:

1. ***China's bank cleanup is real.*** At the end of the bubble in the mid-1990s, financial system NPL ratios were as high as 60% of outstanding loan assets, and as late as 2001 analysts still routinely put the ratio at 35% or higher. However, since 2003 the Chinese government has embarked on a cleanup program of historic proportions, and by the end of 2007 the share of bad loans in the banking system should fall below 10%, an acceptable figure by emerging market standards. And despite the fact that much of the debt removed from banks' balance sheets has simply been transferred to state-owned holding vehicles, we don't

expect any serious macroeconomic repercussions from the eventual workout.

2. *Bank performance has improved significantly.* Many observers point to the excessive credit growth figures during 2002-2004 as evidence that nothing changed in the commercial banking system; the government has simply thrown in an enormous pool of money without carrying out underlying reforms. However, this bout of overlending can't even begin to compare with the length and virulence of the 1991-1995 bubble, and whether we look at macroeconomic regulation, banking supervision, internal operational controls, or the quality of borrowers in the system, we find strong improvement in every area.

3. *Foreign entry is a "red herring."* The end-2006 deadline for full opening of the banking system to foreign competition was one of the most touted and closely watched events in China, but as of this writing in April 2007, there is no evidence whatsoever of a looming foreign onslaught. The reason is simple: the Mainland is already one of the most overbanked economies in the world, and outside of niche markets in major cities there's not much room for new greenfield entrants. As a result, foreign banks are much more interested in acquisitions strategies, buying into established players with further growth potential, and over the next decade China's large state banks will most likely face competition from exactly the same players that are contending markets today.

4. *Privatization comes at the right time.* Despite the widespread improvements in macro- and microeconomic regulation as well as the recent bailout, commercial banks remain severely hampered in one key area, and

that is ownership. With all large institutions fully owned by the state until 2005, and civil service appointees in top positions, banks have had an extremely difficult time escaping a culture of lending based on government pressure. In this sense, the landmark decision to begin privatizing financial institutions came at the right time; in the 2005-2007 period, the Chinese government has sold nearly 25% of its interest in major state banks to foreigners, with sizeable domestic public listings also undertaken. By the end of the decade, we expect the state to be reduced to a minority shareholder in the commercial banking system, and this is perhaps the single best guarantee of more market-oriented lending practices going forward.

5. *However, Chinese banks now face new challenges.* Taken by themselves, the above findings tend to paint a very optimistic picture for Mainland banks. However, we still see significant challenges coming from another direction: the liberalization of the domestic financial system. For more than a decade balance sheets and profitability have been artificially supported by administratively controlled lending and deposit rates, as well as a state-mandated monopoly on financial intermediation. Over the 2007-2012 period we expect liberalization of interest rates, the creation of more vibrant domestic equity and bond markets, and further opening of the external account—all of which threaten to push Chinese banks from a "high-growth, high-margin" status into a "low-growth, low-margin" future.

The Old Days are Gone

Perhaps the biggest surprise to many observers of China's banking system is that the system has only existed at all since the mid-1980s.

As late as the mid-1980s, China didn't really have banks per se; for most of the post-war era, the few existing financial institutions were little more than treasury arms of the Ministry of Finance, allocating funds to productive enterprises as part of the budgetary plan and holding deposits for accounting purposes.

During the 1980s, China began the first serious steps towards creating a modern financial system. From a virtual monobank serving much of the economy, the People's Bank of China (PBoC) was gradually stripped of its corporate finance functions and began operating as the country's central bank. The government removed enterprise expenditures from the state budget and forced firms to deal with commercial banks for working capital and investment financing. The "big four" state-owned commercial banks—the Bank of China, the Industrial and Commercial Bank, the Construction Bank, and the Agricultural Bank—began their gradual evolution from sectoral financing agencies to full-service national banking institutions. The authorities also encouraged the development of small-scale credit cooperatives to serve the needs of farmers and small businesses.

The 1990s saw a virtual explosion of banking activity, particularly during the rush for growth in the "bubble" years 1991-1995. A host of smaller new commercial banks joined the fray to compete for deposits and loans, mostly with state-controlled backing, and the credit cooperatives also became an aggressive source of credit growth. As of end-2005, in addition to the big four state-owned commercial banks and the three state policy banks (Agricultural Development Bank, Export and Import Bank, and the State Development Bank), China had 12 major joint-stock commercial banks, 108 city commercial banks, over 400 foreign banking institutions with either branch operations or representative offices, and more than 30,000 credit cooperatives (see Table 6.1).

Table 6.1. Who Are the Players?

(RMB billion, end-December 2005)	Assets	Loans	Deposits
Monetary institutions	**35,528**	**18,914**	**28,179**
State-owned commercial and policy banks	**22,429**	**10,772**	**16,630**
Bank of China [1]	4,077	1,508	3,053
Industrial and Commercial Bank [1]	6,804	3,129	5,746
China Construction Bank [1]	4,615	1,984	3,737
Agricultural Bank of China [1]	4,537	2,121	3,770
Agricultural Development Bank	850	787	94
Other depository institutions [2]	1,546	1,243	229
Other commercial banks	**8,562**	**4,459**	**6,450**
Joint-stock and regional banks	5,900	3,129	4,577
Joint-venture and foreign banks	635	318	179
City-level banks	2,027	1,011	1,693
Rural and urban credit cooperatives	**3,380**	**1,967**	**2,951**
Finance companies/other	**1,156**	**1,717**	**2,149**

Notes: Loan data include claims on non-financial sector, excluding government.

Deposit data include liabilities to non-financial sector.

[1] UBS estimate for end-2005, adjusted for consistency with PBoC banking survey.

[2] Including the State Development Bank, China Export and Import Bank, trust and investment companies, and leasing companies.

Sources: CEIC, UBS estimates

To give an idea of the scale of 1990s credit expansion in China, in 1989 the total outstanding money stock was only 70% of GDP, whereas by 2000 the ratio was already more than 140%. Against the backdrop of breakneck credit growth, a massive financial bubble, an environment of state-dominated borrowers, no experience with risk management, and almost no autonomy to decline requests for funds, it should come as no surprise that a large share of the loans extended in this period went bad.

How big was the problem? We may never know for sure. China didn't publish official non-performing loan figures for the banking system until 2000, after the first major balance sheet carve-out and recapitalization had already taken place, and even then market estimates still suggested a figure twice as high as the official ratio. This is hardly unusual for emerging markets, of course, where market NPL estimates are generally above official levels, but in China the situation is exacerbated by two additional factors. First, although accounting practices have improved considerably, banks are heavily dependent on implementation at the branch level, where there are serious concerns about the quality and reliability of local audits. In particular, local bank managers are still under strong pressure to show "good" and "improving" bad loan figures, which biases the number downwards.

Second, the heavy traditional indebtedness of the state-enterprise (SOE) sector meant that many firms could afford to pay nominal amounts of interest, but may have had no hope of repaying the principal amount. This put the true "impaired asset" figure well above the reported value of non-performing loans, as the latter only reflected loans on which interest was overdue. "Evergreening" of loans (i.e., automatically rolling over principal payments into a new loan) has been so prevalent in China that it is virtually impossible to gauge the state of impaired assets.

Having said that, we can nonetheless give a round figure for the Chinese banking system's bad loans. Based on market estimates (published and unpublished) from ratings agencies, the International Monetary Fund, and investment bank analysts, we estimate a peak impaired asset ratio of 50% to 60% of all loans outstanding in 1997-1998. This makes China a record-holder for bad debt in the Asian region, on a par with Indonesia at the height

Figure 6.1. Historical Peak NPL Ratios in Asia

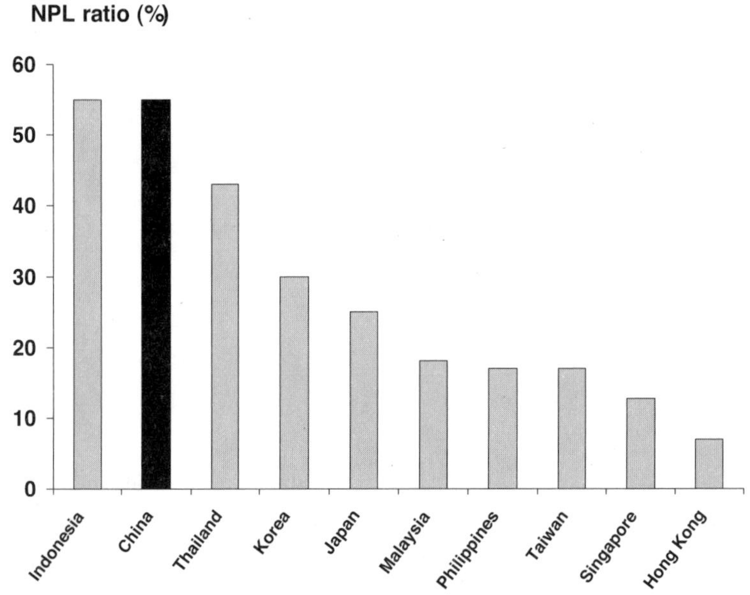

NPL ratio (%)

Sources: CEIC, UBS, and IMF estimates

of the Asian crisis, and well above peak ratios in other neighboring economies (see Figure 6.1).

As we will show below, the period from 1998-2001 was a relatively quiet one for the commercial banking system, with slower economic growth and more cautious lending practices—but in 2002-2004 China erupted into another period of overinvestment and excessive lending, with property developers and infrastructure projects pushing credit growth rates up into strong double-digit levels. By our calculations, perhaps 25% of loans given in these years should be counted as non-performing.

If we consider an NPL ratio of 5% or even slightly higher as "normal" for a fast-growing emerging economy like China, this still implies a cumulative figure for "excessive" NPLs of roughly USD 850 billion, or one-third of all net credit extended over the 1991-2006 period. Whether measured in nominal terms or as a share of the economy, this once again makes the mainland an absolute record-holder among major countries for bad debt creation.

China's Historic Bank Cleanup

Now let's turn to a key question: Of that estimated USD 850 billion figure, how much is still on the books of the banking system as of mid-2007? The answer may come as a surprise to casual observers; by our best estimates, more than USD 500 billion has already been written off commercial bank and non-bank balance sheets, with another USD 150 billion or so expected to leave by end-2007.

In other words, by the end of 2007, China should have a financial system NPL ratio of just over 10% (by our estimates, compared to an official NPL ratio for commercial banks of under 6%, see Figure 6.2). This is still somewhat on the high side by

Figure 6.2. Stock NPL Ratios in China

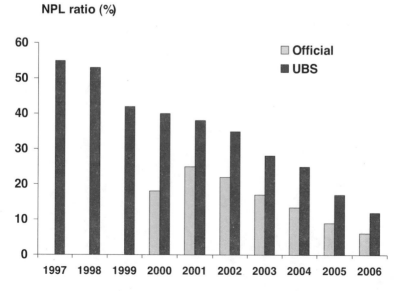

NPL ratio (%)

Source: CEIC, UBS estimates

current Asian standards (see Figure 6.3), but is far from the levels of the "bad old days," and taken at face value essentially means that the Mainland banking system should be free and clear of the worries of systemic instability of the past by the end of 2007. In line with the above findings on the size of China's NPL problem, this also marks what is certainly the largest cumulative cleanup in banking history.

How did it happen? The first round came in 1998, when the Chinese government decided to carry out what it saw as a "first and final" recapitalization of China's big four state banks with roughly USD 200 billion of financing. As Table 6.2 shows, this was a relatively standard package by international standards, funded through quasi-fiscal bond issuance by state-owned asset management companies (AMCs) and direct injections by the Ministry of Finance with limited support by the central bank. This

Figure 6.3. Where China Fits In, April 2007

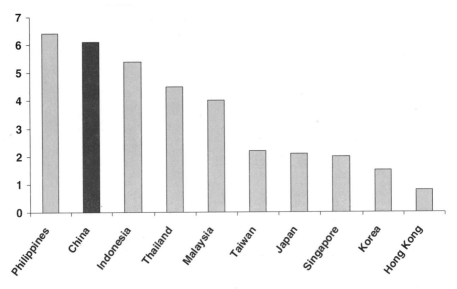

Official NPL ratio (net of provisions, %)

Source: UBS Equity Research

Table 6.2. Official Support to the Financial System Since 1998

Item	Date	Amount (USD billion)	Source
Recapitalization injection - "big four"	1998	34	Ministry of Finance
AMC carve-out	1999	5	Ministry of Finance
AMC carve-out	1999	48	PBoC
AMC carve-out	1999	120	State AMCs
Refinance credit to RCCs	2002-06	25	PBoC
Recapitalization of "big four"	2003-06	75	PBoC
Subsidized NPL carve-outs	2004-06	100	PBoC
Tax relief for NPL write-down	2004-06	20	Ministry of Finance
Banks own funds	2003-06	75	Commercial banks
Estimated additional support in 2007	2007	100	PBoC/ Banks

Source: UBS estimates

package was successful in reducing the financial system NPL ratio from 55%-60% to under 40% by our estimates—but of course still left commercial banks with a substantial bad loan burden on their balance sheets, a burden that was not sufficiently recognized by either the banks themselves or the government at the time. For the next five years the authorities were silent on the issue of further support, as then-Premier Zhu Rongji remained personally adamant that the state banking system should "grow out of the problem" on its own.

However, with the new administration of President Hu Jintao and Premier Wen Jiabao in 2003, things changed both suddenly and drastically. For reasons to be discussed below, the government decided to begin the privatization process for large state banks by listing shares on overseas exchanges. And with the requirement of improved transparency and better information on the state of commercial bank balance sheets, it was clear that this meant having to clean up the outstanding bad loan problem first.

In the event, the authorities acted anything but gingerly, embarking instead on a rapid new program of new recapitalization and write-offs. Between end-2003 and end-2007, our estimates show as much as USD 400 billion was allocated in support for the state banking system. Moreover, compared to the previous program in 1998, this round was far more unorthodox in terms of instruments and financing. The Ministry of Finance still played a significant role by providing direct resources and tax relief, but this time the lion's share of funding came from the PBoC in the form of outright transfer of official foreign exchange reserves and domestic currency refinance credit, as well as flow earnings of the banks themselves.

In many countries, this might have been the end of the story: banks got into serious trouble, whereupon the government fixed the problem by cleaning up the loans and repairing balance sheets. However, given China's socialist background as well as the rapid structural changes since the mid-1980s, the case of the Mainland banking system is much more complicated. The 2003-2007 bank bailout raises a host of sticky issues including potential moral hazard, the macroeconomic costs of the cleanup, and the very future of the banking system itself. And it is these issues to which we now turn in the remainder of this chapter.

Moral Hazard and Financial System Reform

Perhaps the most common argument among outside observers today is that nothing has really changed in the Chinese banking system, i.e., that despite a new coat or two of paint, banks are still the unreconstructed relics of a decade ago. If this is the case, then recapitalizing financial institutions at best means throwing good money after bad, as the next wave of bad loans will inevitably wipe out any new capital the state puts in. At worst, the very act of subsidizing a balance sheet cleanup makes banks even more inclined to disregard market signals and take excessive risks, leading to an even bigger problem down the road. And sure enough, many analysts already see the seeds of future destruction in the current macro cycle: once again, China has erupted in a bout of bank-led overinvestment and overlending; once again, the economy is facing capital misallocation and rising excess capacity; once again, banks are likely to be left "holding the bag" with rising NPLs as a result. Surely it would have been better to take far stronger measures to improve bank performance first before committing state funds — and critically, before selling shares to the hapless domestic and overseas public?

However, in our view these arguments fail wholesale on two counts. To begin with, both the banking system and the Chinese economy have seen very significant changes since the early 1990s, changes that make it very unlikely that financial institutions will ever see high double-digit NPL ratios again. And second, it turns out that bank cleanup and recapitalization are themselves the key to further progress in financial system restructuring.

Factors Determining the Success and Failure of Banking Systems

To see why, consider the five factors that historically determine success or failure in any banking system around the world:

- The level of government interference
- The quality of macroeconomic management
- Deregulation and structural change
- The quality of internal controls
- Ownership and privatization

Government Interference

State control of resource allocation and the use of banks for quasi-fiscal lending almost always results in poor asset quality. Nowhere has this been more true than in China. After all, the commercial banking system got its start in the 1980s when the Chinese government began to route direct state budgetary allocations to productive enterprises through the banking system, with very little change in the administrative process. Again, at that time, state banks acted as little more than treasury agents. And even as quasi-private collectives and non-state enterprises sprang up through the 1980s and the first half of the 1990s, banks continued to focus on funding the state sector in line with government planning policies.

However, things have changed considerably since the mid-1990s. To begin with, the state sector accounts for a much lower share of total bank borrowing today in 2007 than it did in the mid-1990s. On a stock basis, we estimate that Chinese SOEs still account for nearly half of all outstanding loans in 2007 (and close to two-thirds of commercial non-agricultural credit)—but remember that these numbers are for stocks, not flows. In the mid-1990s, the total stock share would not have been half but rather 75% or more, and this implies a continued decline on a flow basis, perhaps to as low as 30% to 35% in 2007.

Why the difference? In part because of the rising share of non-state firms, including privatized former SOEs; in part because of the introduction of mortgage lending and consumer finance; and in part because of market share gains by smaller, more aggressive commercial banks less susceptible to government pressure.

This does not automatically mean that the quality of lending has improved, as the recent ill-fated experience with consumer auto finance amply demonstrates. Indeed, as we will show below, a sharp change in the competitive environment can actually harm banks. But the point remains that the state no longer dictates where the majority of bank loans go.

Second, when the state does dictate it now does so in a very different way. Of course both local and central governments still put direct pressure on financial institutions to lend to favored projects and sectors, but commercial banks are no longer treated like treasury arms of the State Planning Commission or the Ministry of Finance. In fact, the State Planning Commission no longer exists in its original form, and China's much-vaunted Five Year Plan is now little more than a set of official macroeconomic forecasts and policy targets. Moreover, central management of the banking system has been passed to regulatory agencies like the PBoC and the China Bank Regulatory Commission (CBRC, the mainland bank regulator), which have a vested interest in improving bank performance and stabilizing the economy. As a result, banks now face a more balanced set of state pressures—on the one hand, (mostly) local governments pushing for higher lending to "their" commercial projects, and on the other key central government agencies pushing for better credit practices and transparency—that would not be so unfamiliar to city-level banks in the U.S. or Europe.

Finally, and equally important, the quality of state borrowers themselves has improved in leaps and bounds. After the bursting of the economic bubble in the mid-1990s, the Chinese government undertook the historically unprecedented task of downsizing the state sector by closing unprofitable SOEs–and not just through cosmetic changes, but rather tens of thousands of enterprises were dissolved, putting more than 25 million state workers out of a job. As a result, profitability in the remaining state industrial sector jumped sharply between 1997 and 2000, and has remained high ever since (see Figures 6.4 and 6.5).

Once again, this does not guarantee that everything is fine, as state banks still find themselves under pressure from local governments to help pay unemployment benefits and pensions, support housing and education expenditures, and, as discussed below, to lend to duplicative and unviable new projects. But it does mean that Mainland banks are mostly spared the painful task

178   *China Into the Future*

Figure 6.4. The State Share of Chinese Industry

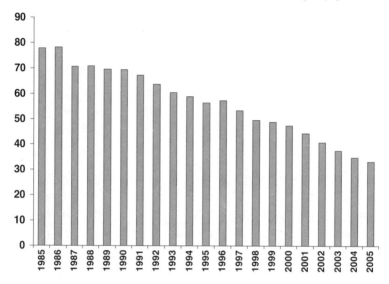

Source: *CEIC, UBS estimates*

Figure 6.5. Industrial Profit Margins in China

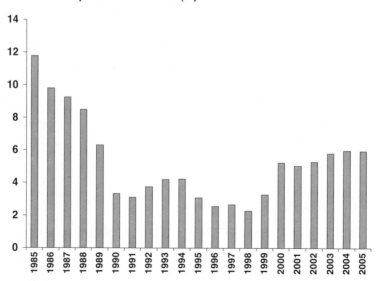

Source: *CEIC, UBS estimates*

faced by so many of their emerging market counterparts, i.e., of throwing away enormous sums year after year to subsidize large, loss-making state companies. When a Chinese SOE comes to borrow from a bank today, the borrower is generally profitable on a current cashflow basis.

Macro Control and Liquidity Growth

Indeed, since the early 1990s, Mainland banking system losses haven't come from ordinary quasi-fiscal lending to industrial enterprises during normal years, but rather from explosive boom-bust cycles where state banks throw credit indiscriminately at new, wasteful projects and sectors. We call this China's "white elephant syndrome," the chronic tendency to overlend in good times when the economy is buoyant and profits are high.

This could not be more visible at the macroeconomic level, as China has been the most volatile economy in the region over the past three decades. Even if we account for the enormous swings in Asian performance during the late 1980s bubbles, the 1997 financial crisis, and the 2001 global IT downturn, the variance in China's nominal GDP growth rates has been nonetheless as high or higher than any of its neighbors (see Figure 6.6).

In part, this is because of China's inflationary past. As the government liberalized prices in the 1980s and early 1990s, the consumer price index tended to shoot upwards, reaching as much as 25% year on year in the 1991-1995 bubble before receding into deflation only a few years later. However, the real story lies in China's enormous real growth swings. Figure 6.7 below shows our estimates for real GDP and domestic demand growth rates since 1980. As you can see, the Chinese economy has resembled nothing so much as a rollercoaster ride, careening from nearly 15% year-on-year growth in 1984-1985 to outright recession by the end of the decade, then back to strong double-digit growth

Figure 6.6. Economic Volatility in Asia, 1980-2004

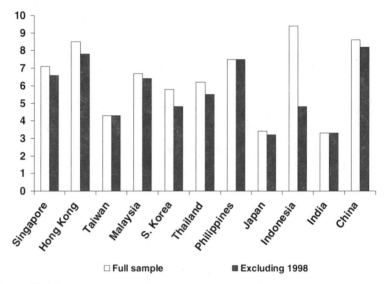

Standard deviation of nominal GDP growth (%)

□ Full sample   ■ Excluding 1998

Source: CEIC, UBS estimates

Figure 6.7. China's Boom-Bust Economy

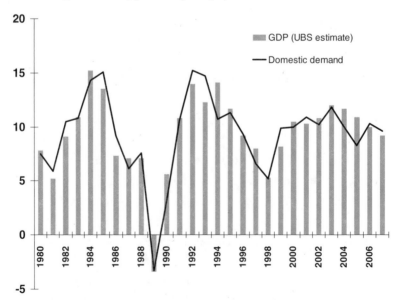

Real growth rate, year on year (%)

Source: CEIC, UBS estimates

followed by another sharp downturn in the 1990s. Needless to say, the upturns were accompanied by rampant overinvestment and euphoric financial market outperformance—and the subsequent downturns saw widespread overcapacity, disappearing profits, unemployment, and in some cases political turmoil.

Looking back at the chart above, however, it is clear that the economy has visibly "settled down" since the beginning of the decade of the 2000s. This may come as a surprise to many outside investors, who generally assume that Chinese volatility has been increasing since 2000, but in fact nothing could be further from the truth. If we focus on the line showing domestic demand trends, it's clear that by far the biggest boom-bust swings came during the 1980s, when growth dropped from 15% year-on-year to -5% year-on-year in the space of just a few years. By the 1990s, the amplitude had moderated to a range from 15% year-on-year to positive 5% year-on-year, already a significant improvement. And the cycle post-2000 has been even more moderate, with domestic demand growth peaking at around 12% year-on-year in 2003 and troughing at around 7.5% year-on-year in 2005; the pace has since stabilized at 9.5% in 2007.

You can see the same thing in Figure 6.8 below. In previous cycles, money and credit growth rose to 30% year-on-year, and remained at that pace for a number of years before coming off hard in the subsequent downturn. By contrast, in the latest round, loan growth barely spiked above 15% year-on-year and has quickly settled back into a more stable range.

Even more important, the downturns in the 1980s and 1990s were always marked by a sharp drop in profitability as well as a sizeable buildup of industrial inventories. This time around, as we saw above, industrial margins have stayed at much higher levels than at any time in the 1990s, and the level of inventory buildup has fallen to historic lows as a share of GDP.

Nor does China face a looming contraction around the corner. As of mid-2007, Mainland data consistently show *rising* corporate

Figure 6.8. Money and Credit Growth

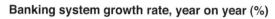

Banking system growth rate, year on year (%)

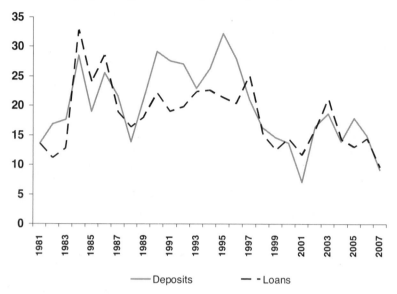

Source: CEIC, UBS estimates

earnings growth over the past few quarters, particularly in over-invested heavy industrial sectors, and well-behaved industrial inventories. According to nearly every macro indicator, the bottom of the current cycle was in 2005... and not 2007 or 2008.

What changed? How did the Chinese economy escape the massive swings that characterized previous decades? The first factor, as discussed above, is the decline in the state economy, as state institutions have only limited incentives to control costs and maximize profits. China's so-called collective and private firms face real, binding capital constraints and are not prone to "boom-bust" overinvestment cycles—but 20 years ago they were still a very small part of overall non-farm activity.

Even more important, however, is the establishment of viable macroeconomic regulation. During the 1980s and 1990s, the government removed most of its traditional socialist planning levers, but did not have functioning market institutions in place. For example, one reason the massive credit bubble of 1991-1995 was able to last so long was the effective absence of a modern central bank or regulatory agency; even after it was clear that investment and asset price growth was hugely unsustainable, it still took years for the policy authorities to coordinate a cohesive response. By contrast, during the latest overheating round the PBoC began tightening in mid-2003, only 12 months after the cyclical upturn began. This helps explain why industrial profits have held up so well in the mid-2000s—and why we have not seen even remotely the same kind of inventory buildup as in the 1990s. And this, in turn, implies that the subsequent flow of new bad loans should be orders of magnitude less in ratio terms than it was a decade ago.

Another key difference is that this time around China has a more globalized economy with a higher trade to GDP ratio, and as a result the Mainland has had much more success in "exporting" its cyclical volatility abroad. At the peak of overheating in 2003, booming Chinese demand spilled over into import spending at a record pace, nearly 50% year-on-year in real volume terms, thereby dampening the upward pressure on domestic GDP growth. And when China woke up in 2005 with weaker demand and a looming excess capacity overhang, it was overseas suppliers who took a disproportionate hit, as domestic heavy industrial firms shored up margins by taking market share at home, pushing down imports, and driving up the trade surplus. As troublesome as this may sound for the rest of the world, remember that the Mainland economy is still only 5% of global GDP; the global economy as a whole has a much easier time weathering "China shocks" than does China alone.

Deregulation and Structural Change

Economic studies consistently find that periods of financial deregulation and structural change in the banking industry give rise to bank troubles, in both emerging and developed economies, and China has been no exception. Financial deregulation contributed significantly to overheating in the "bubble" years, with a virtual explosion of new institutions coming on the scene. As can be seen from Figure 6.9, cooperatives, smaller commercial banks, and finance companies contributed disproportionately to liquidity growth between 1992 and 1996; their share of total loans nearly doubled, from 12% to 22%, in the first half of the 1990s, before stabilizing over the next five years.

Now fast forward by a decade; the period 2002-2005 was also one of rapid lending, and sure enough, smaller banks and cooperatives once again led the charge. Between end-2001 and end-2005, their share of total loans outstanding rose by another 10 percentage points, from 24% to 34%. However, there are also two important structural differences between the 2000s lending boom and the 1990s bubble. First of all, the big story of the 1990s was the emergence of new institutions; much of the credit growth came from joint-stock banks, cooperatives, and finance companies with little knowledge of the business and no track record to speak of. By contrast, the main trend of the mid-2000s has been consolidation. The government has been slowly closing or consolidating insolvent rural credit cooperatives; most urban cooperatives have now been folded into city banks; and the trust and investment companies that gave rise to repeated market scandals in the 1990s have subsequently seen their lending functions curtailed and regulated. The only truly new market entrants today are foreign banks, following the liberalization of foreign competition after China's WTO entry—and in our view the so-called "foreign threat" is likely to prove nothing more than a red herring.

Figure 6.9. The Rising Competition

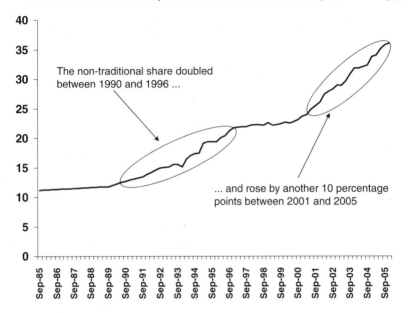

Other commercial bank/cooperative share of total financial system lending (%)

Source: CEIC, UBS estimates

No "Foreign Threat"

This is an important point, and given the attention paid to foreign entry in 2006 and 2007 we believe it's worth a detour to discuss the issue in detail. According to the terms of China's WTO accession agreements, as of January 1, 2007 foreign commercial banks gained the right to carry out a full range of domestic and foreign currency financial services on an equal footing with their domestic counterparts, without restriction. And looking at the financial press over 24 months running up to this date, this change has been billed as the greatest challenge yet to the Mainland banking system, with the specter of foreign entry on a massive scale pushing creaky domestic institutions out of business.

In fact, however, January 2007 came and went … and so far there is no evidence whatsoever of a foreign onslaught. In fact, when we ask foreign banks how they feel about the recent opening, we generally find a striking lack of enthusiasm for a grand greenfield push into China, i.e., setting up new flagship branches in every city and township across the nation. Virtually no one is planning this now, and we suspect no one will be planning this five years after the opening as well.

One reason, of course, is that "competing on an equal footing with domestic institutions" isn't the most appealing prospect. The government maintains fairly onerous restrictions on new expansion for most banks in the system, foreign or not, in the form of high capital requirements, branch-by-branch licensing, and approvals, which make it difficult to expand sharply in a short period of time. Considering that foreign banks' market share in total assets stood at a paltry 1.7% of the banking system total at end-2006, even in the most optimistic scenario it's difficult to imagine the foreign market share increasing past 5% over the next half-decade; this is hardly a massive threat to the health of domestic incumbents.

Even more telling is the source of that projected increase; according to our estimates most of the foreign gains would come from non-traditional areas such as wealth management, non-interest income, and payments systems. Notably missing from this list are bread-and-butter corporate lending and retail deposit-taking, where most Chinese banks spend their time operating today.

Why? Because in a very fundamental sense, the Mainland economy is already overbanked. Look at Figure 6.10 below; broad money M2 (the sum of cash, and demand and time deposits in the banking system) is nearly 200% of GDP in China, twice as high as the Asian average, three or four times the average level in the U.S. and the E.U., and a higher ratio still of other emerging markets like Mexico and Brazil.

What's more, most of these deposits are held in the provinces, where state banks have a branch network numbering tens of

Figure 6.10. China's Overbanked Economy

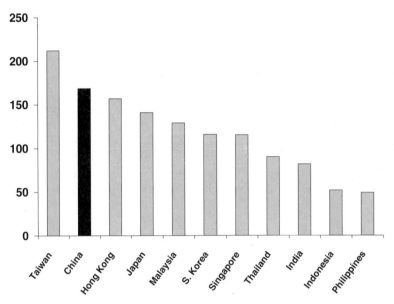

Banking system deposits as a share of GDP (%)

Source: CEIC, UBS estimates

thousands already in place, making it very difficult for foreign institutions to consider pursuing a national strategy. And even in the major urban areas, where foreign banks are already making inroads into trade and international services, core banking markets are very crowded indeed; every large city has not only the big four plus joint-stock commercial banks, but also a host of city-level credit institutions, all of which are very aggressive in competing for market share.

In this environment, the optimal strategy is not to depend on greenfield new branch openings, but rather to buy into existing players, and this is precisely what we see major foreign banks doing in the mid-2000s. Of course foreign players are putting up flagship branches in a few major cities, but in dollar terms the amount of funds spent on mergers and acquisitions in 2005-2007 is already much greater than capital inflows into new branches. How much additional pressure does this put on the Chinese banking system? The short answer is none at all. Foreign strategic stakes in domestic institutions don't add to competitive pressures in any meaningful way; rather, they simply represent existing capacity changing hands. One could argue that large state banks are at greater risk than before because of the threat of smaller players increasing market share gains through foreign capital backing. However, even this argument looks tenuous since the "big four" state commercial banks themselves have been quite successful in attracting foreign partners. It's true that overseas investment has raised hackles about foreign ownership of banking assets, but the fact remains that WTO liberalization doesn't really imply any significant change in the structure of the financial system in China.

Internal Governance and External Supervision

One of the most common criticisms of Chinese banks is that "they don't know how to lend." From a historical point of view, this is a fair statement; Mainland banks have only been operating as independent commercial entities for two decades, and the experience of the early- to mid-1990s certainly puts their performance in an unfavorable light.

However, it's not true that nothing has changed. Since the mid-1990s, both the government and banks themselves have been working hard to restructure, upgrading controls and procedures in nearly every area. Table 6.3 shows the traditional governance and regulatory system in China, as well as changes to date. At the beginning of the 1990s, Mainland banks had only very rudimentary internal governance structures in place, and almost no formal risk supervision from the monetary authorities. Since then there has been significant progress, and in a formal sense banks today are much better equipped to act as market-based, commercial institutions: China has an aggressive regulatory agency in place; quarter and annual audits are now a routine practice; large banks have adopted international accounting and formal risk management practices; credit histories and credit databases are coming into use; bank staff are much better trained than in the past; and financial statistics are orders of magnitude more reliable than they were only two decades ago.

Table 6.3. Institutional Progress in the Banking System

	Traditional situation	Current status
Corporate structure	The traditional state-owned enterprise structure has a dual-track authority structure, with state-appointed management and a powerful Communist Party committee. Ownership of assets is by "the people," i.e., unclear which agency within the government exercises ownership rights.	All large state banks have been converted into joint-stock entities with a formal board structure, and government shares have been transferred to a unified financial holding company (Central Huijin Investment). Three of the "big four" have already listed shares publicly, with average 20% foreign ownership.
Internal governance	Regional and local governments appointed branch management directly, and influenced lending decisions.	Personnel decisions have been centralized, and large loans are cleared through the head office as well.
Accounting systems	State banks had rudimentary accounting and loan classification systems.	Banks have adopted new accounting standards and the international five-tier classification system, and have broadly computerized and centralized databases. All large state banks have done international audits; for others, audits are still done internally through local auditors.

Table 6.3. Institutional Progress in the Banking System (cont'd)

	Traditional situation	Current status
Risk management	Very little formal knowledge.	Banks have undergone significant risk management training, but in a controlled interest-rate environment there is little scope for serious implementation.
State interference	Banks were subject to strict overall credit controls, and lending decisions were made according to plan approvals, with significant lobby and interference at all levels of government.	Policy lending functions were split off into the state policy banks in 1994-1995, and credit quotas were abolished in 1998. Some large investment plans are still subject to governmental approval, but loans are to be made on a commercial basis, with management responsible for asset quality and profitability. Local government pressure for quasi-fiscal lending is still significant.
Supervisory environment	Bank supervision and regulation were carried out by individual departments within the People's Bank of China, as well as the Ministry of Finance.	Supervisory and regulatory functions have been passed to the independent China Bank Regulatory Commission, which has been very active over the past few years.

Source: UBS

This does not mean that Chinese institutions are now on par with their developed market counterparts. Far from it; the fundamental problems of state ownership, state influence, and a civil-service lending mentality are still entrenched in the financial system, and until we see strong outside ownership and a better management structure, banks will still face difficulties in improving risk management and fully resisting policy pressures. And this brings us to the final and perhaps most crucial issue: that of ownership.

Ownership and Privatization

It's difficult to exaggerate the important of market-based ownership and management on banking system performance. After all, you can change internal management systems, improve outside regulation, and adopt better macroeconomic controls, but it is difficult to fundamentally reform the way banks do business if top bank managers are appointed civil servants with close ties to central and local governments. In the Chinese context, this has clearly been an important driver of the repeated "boom-bust" cycles of the past few decades.

As of 2000, the question of the ownership structure of Chinese banks didn't even merit serious discussion. Large state banks were 100% state-owned; second-tier institutions were almost completely held by state-owned entities; and local credit cooperatives were exactly that: cooperatives. The financial system was already very competitive, but there was virtually no outside private ownership. Not a single bank was listed on domestic or foreign exchanges, and while foreign banks could open a few branches in major cities, they were effectively prohibited from buying into Chinese institutions. Official policy was guided by the spirit of the 15th Communist Party Congress in 1997, which listed the financial system as a priority sector where the state should continue to hold the reins. In this environment, the very news in 2001 that Newbridge Capital, a foreign private equity firm, was negotiating a nearly 20% stake with management rights in second-tier player Shenzhen Development Bank came as an unexpected shock to investors, grabbing financial headlines for months.

Half a decade later, the landscape had changed radically. Not only did the Newbridge deal go through, but so have others like it. By mid-2007, foreign banks and other overseas investors have purchased equity stakes in nearly two dozen Chinese financial institutions, with further deals under discussion. And the 2005-2007 period has seen a veritable flood of public listings on domestic and overseas markets—including, crucially, three of the "big four" state-owned commercial banks. In fact, adding in strategic equity stakes, the Bank of China and the China Construction Bank by early 2007 were nearly 25% foreign-owned, with the Industrial and Commercial Bank of China not far behind at 18%, something that would have been unthinkable only a few years before. And the final large state bank (the Agricultural Bank of China) is preparing for restructuring as we write, including public listing plans as well. The government still imposes a 25% foreign ownership cap in any Chinese bank, with no more than 20% by a single outside investor, but looking at current trends we expect these ceilings will be relaxed significantly over the next few years. Throw in subsequent domestic A-share IPOs, and we believe the state will become an outright minority shareholder in the "big four" by the end of the decade.

Why the sudden change? One thing is clear: it's not about the money. Most smaller Chinese banks have very strong liquidity positions and high capital adequacy ratios, and the large state banks essentially received a clean bill of health following the massive write-off and recapitalization effort outlined above. As a result, Mainland financial institutions simply didn't have any need of domestic or foreign equity capital to develop and expand their operations.

What China's banks do need, however, are stronger outside governance and oversight, together with modern management practices. In this sense, the Chinese authorities are now following what we might call the "PetroChina model." PetroChina was one of the first large flagship state enterprises to list in Hong Kong and New York in 2000, and the decision to list the company was an extremely controversial one at the time. After all, the firm's structure was very complex and (just like the state-owned commercial banks) they hardly needed the money. What the Chinese government found, however, was that an overseas listing provided a "one-stop shop" for SOE reform. Instead of civil servants, global management, human resources, and investment banking firms took the reins of the restructuring process, identifying and stripping off unproductive assets, clarifying pension liabilities, carrying out full audits, and redefining governance responsibilities. Once the listing was completed, PetroChina also inherited a professional investor base intent on scrutinizing accounts and management decisions. As a result, the company has generally won respect as a well-run, transparent organization, and the Chinese authorities probably have more (and better) information on its activities than they did under the old regime. Fast forward a few years to 2003-2006, and this is precisely the government's logic in pushing large state banks to list overseas.

One very common criticism of the recent rash of listings and strategic stakes is that the authorities are essentially dumping China's banking system problem onto the backs of private and foreign shareholders. Wouldn't it have been better to carry out a full and fundamental reform first, and then sell off ownership share only when it was clear that banks' behavior has changed?

Reading the earlier sections above, however, it should be clear that we don't agree with this logic. China has already downsized the state sector, liberalized its economy, improved macro regulation, reformed internal operating procedures, restructured bank governance, and introduced greater competition in the financial sector. At this point, the sole (and crucial) remaining problem has been precisely that banks are state-owned and state-run, and in our view none of the other reform and restructuring measures will "stick" until the state finally gets out of the business of running these institutions. Seen in this light, privatization is not a premature miscalculation but rather the final effective guarantee that banks will not turn around and repeat the mistakes of the past. Needless to say, it will still take years for the introduction of new investors and owners to bring about a substantial change in state bank behavior patterns—but the authorities are clearly on the right path.

Why No Macro Repercussions?

Could the Cure be Worse than the Disease?

The huge sums of money spent to clean up balance sheets have certainly resolved the lion's share of China's commercial banks' financial problems. However, this is not the entire story, as there is more to a debt cleanup than just moving bad loans out of banks; in addition, you have to deal with the borrower that defaulted on the loan in the first place. This means foreclosure, asset disposal, corporate restructuring, and, in some cases, outright bankruptcy. And according to many observers, this is where China falls short. The common argument runs as follows: Of the nearly USD 500bn in NPLs removed from commercial banks as of end-2006, the vast majority were simply handed over to government-owned special purpose vehicles (the four so-called state asset management companies, or AMCs: Great Wall, Cinda, Huarong, and China Orient); only a small fraction were actually sold to domestic or foreign asset recovery specialists. And the state AMCs have done little with the assets; for the most part, they are still languishing on the AMC accounts, which in turn means that nothing has been done to restructure loss-making SOEs, which remained saddled with a crushing bad debt burden. In this view, the government has simply moved the bad debt problem from one part of the state financial balance sheet to another, without addressing any of the underlying issues.

Moreover, if Chinese banks have been supporting a critical mass of loss-making enterprises, then moving to foreclose on outstanding debts—not to mention freeing up lending decisions and moving to market-based resource allocation—could result in a big round of closures, redundancies, and social unrest. In short, the concern is that cleanup efforts to date have been mostly "sleight of hand," and the eventual real costs of bank restructuring could be very high indeed.

Fortunately for the economy, these concerns are highly exaggerated. As we saw above, state banks are not primarily in the business of propping up unprofitable SOEs year after year; instead, most NPLs come from what we call the "white elephant" syndrome, of throwing excessive resources at new, inefficient, and often fully redundant projects that often never make it to completion. Making better loan decisions would avoid overheating cycles, but not bankrupt the economy.

Nor does China have much to fear from a debt workout, as the authorities have been anything but slow in enterprise restructuring. Remember that the broad bulk of banking system NPLs came from the great mainland bubble of the early and mid-1990s; no sooner had that bubble burst than the Chinese government undertook one of the largest retrenchment programs in history, laying off tens of millions of workers and shutting down tens of thousands of state enterprises. However, even if the company was shut down, the lack of a working bankruptcy infrastructure and formal commercial property rights meant that outstanding debts were often never resolved and assets were never foreclosed. And this presents a fascinating paradox: In most countries, a large stock of bad debt is a harbinger of economic pain to come. In China, by contrast, bad debts are more a residual reminder of economic pain already incurred.

And this helps explain why AMCs have taken so long to dispose of non-performing loan assets. It's certainly not true that AMCs have done nothing, but it did take more than half a decade for them to "resolve" the initial USD 170 billion carve-out tranche (in part through direct recovery and sales and in part through debt-equity swaps), and it may be many more years before they can clear the remaining amounts currently on their books, not to mention future inflows.

The key point is that these large unresolved sums are not a sign of slow progress in economic restructuring, and therefore, from a macro point of view it doesn't necessarily matter how long it takes to clear them up, as long as they are no longer sitting with banks. And in this sense, moving NPLs off banks' balance sheets is far from "sleight of hand"; rather, it is one of the important steps in guaranteeing financial system stability. The crucial difference between a bank and a state AMC is that the latter is not a depository institution. Systemic crises arise when banks' financial position deteriorates to the point where they cannot meet current market liabilities; AMCs do not face this problem, so by shifting bad loans away from banks, the government has vastly reduced the financial risk to the economy.

Who Will Pay the Bill?

This still leaves the question of who will pay the bill for the financial balance sheet cleanup. After all, the arguments in the previous section imply that Chinese recovery rates on impaired debt assets should be very low, and experience so far points to a range between 10% and 20%, far below the emerging market average of 35% to 45%. Doing the math, if the authorities are committed to removing USD 850 billion in NPLs from the banking system, then someone needs to bear the USD 700 billion ex-recovery cost, or roughly 30% of 2006 Chinese GDP.

The answer is that the costs have been split between the fiscal authorities, the central bank, and commercial banks themselves—

and the biggest surprise here is how little negative impact this has had on any of the players involved.

Consider first that the real value of China's bad debt stock has been eroding sharply over time. In the middle of the 1990s, when the bulk of the outstanding NPLs appeared on commercial banks' balance sheets, the total would have been close to 60% of GDP; however, since average nominal GDP growth over the past decade far exceeded the implicit nominal "carrying cost" of keeping NPLs on the book, the cumulative amount fell to the 30% figure we arrived at above.

Now, of the USD 700 billion in total costs, the Ministry of Finance has so far borne an estimated USD 180 billion, of which USD 60 billion are direct fiscal transfers and tax incentives and the remainder are the implied guarantee on the state-owned AMC bonds given to commercial banks in 1998. The budgetary amounts already paid total 7% of 2006 GDP (or 15% of GDP at the time they were borne), but have clearly failed to make so much as a dent in budgetary finances; just look at Figure 6.11, which shows the path of China's fiscal indicators over time (note the different scale in the figure for the budget balance given its smaller size). The mild funds paid out so far have been absolutely overwhelmed by a sharp structural rise in tax revenues, which allowed for a reduction in the annual budget deficit even as spending on all categories has increased. And the principal on outstanding AMC bonds now represent only 5% of GDP, a sum which, if it were paid in full tomorrow, would increase China's gross government debt to only 30% of GDP. This is an extremely low figure by international standards, even before we account for the asset positions that make China one of the world's largest official creditor nations on a net basis.

Next up are the banks themselves. Between 2002 and end-2007 we put total NPL provisioning at nearly USD 100 billion for the banking system as a whole, but this stands against estimated pre-tax operating profits of USD 400 billion for the same six-year

Figure 6.11. The Fiscal Recovery

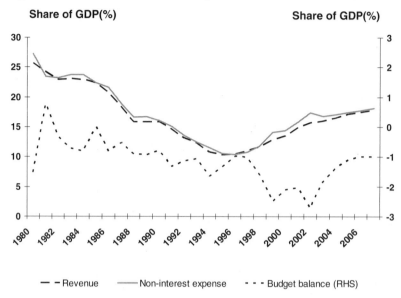

Source: *CEIC, UBS estimates*

period. And net profit margins for recapitalized institutions have gone up steadily during the same period, despite banks' increased efforts on provisioning and write-downs. This situation won't last forever, for reasons we'll discuss further below, but to date banks have clearly had little trouble footing the share they've been asked to pay.

Finally, we turn to the role of the central bank, which is easily the most controversial and misunderstood part of China's bank restructuring effort. By our count, about half of the total recapitalization burden to date, or some USD 250 billion, has been borne by the PBoC; this includes refinance credit both to financial institutions and to AMCs, subsidized NPL write-downs, and the direct transfer of official foreign exchange reserves. Moreover, we expect the monetary authorities to continue to play a sizeable role in the remaining cleanup over the next year or two. With the exception of the transfer of USD 60 billion from the foreign exchange reserve account, all of this has come in the form of monetary expansion—a highly unorthodox policy according to international practice.

Essentially, this is "costless" financing for a bank bailout, in that it doesn't affect formal government finances now and is unlikely to in the future. If this sounds too good to be true, it's not; central banks all around the globe print money every day, (so-called "base" or "reserve" money), and to the extent that real demand for money is rising and base money creation is non-inflationary, this creates what economists call seignorage: a new claim on real resources in the economy.

In most economies, the possibilities for seignorage are small because base money is a small fraction of GDP and real money demand grows at a very slow pace. However, in China, where base money is more than 40% of GDP and real money demand grows at an average pace of 12% per year, the PBoC can effectively print and distribute some USD 80 billion per year without having to worry about the inflationary consequences. And this means that in principle, the PBC could have funded the entire bank bailout tab simply by writing cheques on itself over six or seven years— perhaps the only country in the world where we can make such a claim. This won't be the case, of course, as much of the actual finance has come from other sources as well, but this explains why we believe effective monetization by the Chinese central bank will continue to play a role going forward.

The New Challenges for Chinese Banks

Reading the previous section, it can easily appear that we are giving a glowing bill of health for the Chinese financial system—and indeed, compared to the situation in the late 1980s and mid-1990s we conclude that the outlook is much more stable and optimistic today. However, just because the common perceptions of a "dual threat" of massive bad debts and a looming foreign invasion turns out to be misguided doesn't mean that banks are fully out of the woods. In fact, there are other strong challenges waiting around the corner, as the government begins to withdraw a wide range of artificial supports for the financial system.

Why No Banking Crisis in China?

Begin with the following lead-in question: If Chinese banks lived with extremely high NPL levels for most of the last decade, then why didn't we see a banking crisis similar to those in Indonesia, Thailand, or Korea, not to mention dozens of other emerging economies around the globe? The Mainland has had its share of trouble in smaller institutions such as trust, investment, and securities companies, and even city banks, but despite numerous scandals and personnel changes in the major commercial banks over the past years, there has never been a hint of systemic stress. How could this be? The answer is that state banks were able to survive these past 10 years in a high-NPL, bad balance sheet environment because the Chinese authorities put strong policies in place to ensure their survival. Among others, we would highlight the following four key support pillars:

First, Controls on External Capital Flows

Unlike most of its neighbors, and in sharp contrast to the Asian crisis economies of 1997-1998, China has a very restrictive capital account regime with strong controls on portfolio inflows and outflows. There are leakages as in any economy, but in China's case

Figure 6.12. No External Margin Call

Non-FDI portfolio capital flows (share of GDP, %)

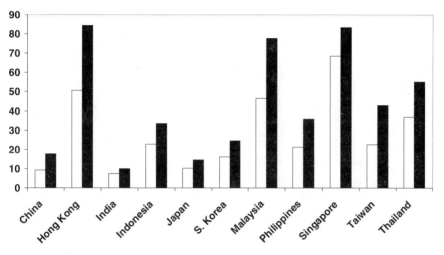

Source: CEIC, UBS estimates

these have always been relatively minor (as seen in Figure 6.12, which shows the historical magnitude of non-FDI portfolio capital flows as a share of GDP for Asian economies). With ordinary depositors' access to foreign exchange blocked, and the *renminbi* exchange rate generally under appreciation pressure to boot, Chinese banks have never been susceptible to an "external margin call."

Second, Limited Alternative Financing Channels

In part in order to ensure that China's structurally high savings are intermediated through the banking system, the authorities employ a variety of formal and informal restrictions on other financing channels. *De facto* limitations on corporate equity and bond issuance mean that the savings flow directed to these instruments has never

Figure 6.13. Where are the Equities and Bonds?

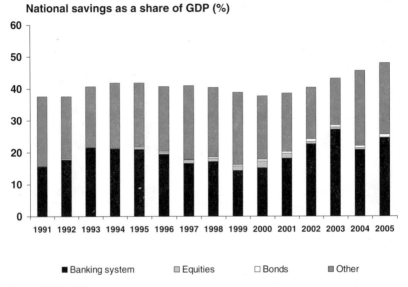

National savings as a share of GDP (%)

■ Banking system   ▨ Equities   □ Bonds   ▨ Other

Source: CEIC, UBS estimates

exceeded 2% of GDP; as a result, banks have enjoyed a virtual monopoly on funds flows, routinely attracting around 20% of GDP in new savings year after year (see Figure 6.13). China also actively manages market access within the banking system, limiting the operating scale of smaller commercial banks through licensing requirements and restrictions on funding sources, not to mention the historical ban on foreign bank operations.

Third, Direct Interest Rate Controls

Alone among major Asian economies, China's central bank directly controls commercial bank interest rates. Up until 2004, lending and deposit rates were set at fixed levels with almost no room for fluctuation. As of January 2004, the ceiling on bank lending rates was removed, but banks are not allowed to lend below prescribed reference rates, or increase deposit rates above the mandated ceiling.

In practice, this means that Chinese banks have enjoyed an effective guarantee that lending rates would remain high and deposit rates would remain low. Since the mid-1990s, the PBoC has made a number of adjustments to administratively fixed lending and deposit rates, but in all that time has never reduced the loan/deposit spread. In fact, with the sharp worsening of loan quality following the mid-1990s bubble, the central bank consciously moved to widen spreads in order to shore up banks' profitability and stave off possible financial instability (see Figure 6.14).

With a historical gross return on assets of some 5.3% per annum, Chinese banks may not look particularly wealthy by Asian standards (the regional average was 6.11%), and Mainland

Figure 6.14. Lending/Deposit Spreads in China

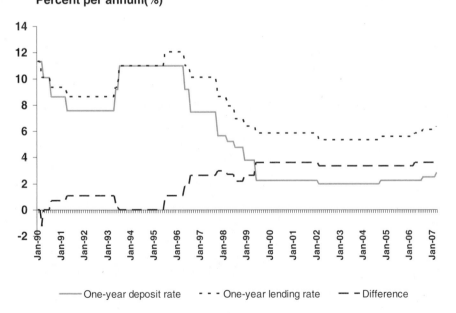

Percent per annum(%)

Source: CEIC, UBS estimates

lending-deposit rate spreads are only slightly above the Asian norm. However, what really matters for bank liquidity is the *ratio* of lending rates to deposit rates. To see why, consider the following two hypothetical banks: Bank A earns 10% on loan assets and pays 5% for deposits, while Bank B earns 6% on loan assets and pays 2% for deposits. Bank A's lending rates are twice as high as deposit rates, which means that a 50% NPL ratio is enough to drive net interest earnings to zero. Meanwhile, Bank B's lending rates are three times as high as deposit rates, so Bank B can live with an NPL ratio as high as 66% without running out of net interest cash flow. In other words, Bank B is less susceptible to liquidity problems than Bank A—despite the fact that Bank A has a higher headline interest spread than Bank B.

Looking at average loan/deposit spreads and ratios for Asia, it turns out that China's spread is at the higher end of Asian experience—and the loan/deposit interest ratio is by far the highest in the region, nearly 3.5 times the average by our calculations. This helps explain why Chinese banks have been able to avoid a liquidity crisis even with historical NPL ratios which likely peaked above 50%. This also explains the sharp jump in state commercial banks' reported profits following the NPL cleanup and market listings; with high spreads, banks have a virtual license to print money.

The above example is obviously oversimplified, and should not be interpreted to imply that Chinese banks are more profitable than elsewhere. Even when relieved of their historical NPL burden, Chinese state banks have a very costly payroll structure, with far more branches and personnel per dollar of income than in other Asian economies; Mainland banks are also far behind their regional counterparts in generating non-interest income from fees, etc. Nonetheless, the logic is clear: the higher the ratio of lending to deposit rates, the better positioned banks are to withstand a large proportion of non-performing loans.

Finally, An Implicit State Guarantee

China does not have a formal deposit insurance scheme, but given the sheer size and state-owned status of the four large commercial banks, depositors have always been very comfortable leaving funds in these institutions, and state banks continue to attract the majority of new flow household and corporate deposits. This is not simply because of an abstract state guarantee for these institution; rather, China has a very concrete 15-year history of stepping in to provide liquidity at the very hint of possible instability, beginning with the wave of small non-bank collapses in the early and mid-1990s and ending with the massive NPL writedowns and recapitalization of the early and mid-2000s. In every case, both the government and the PBoC have been very quick to respond with the needed injection of funds.

The New Challenge

As the reader will have already surmised, our view is that each of these "pillars" will be gradually weakened and in some cases even removed over the next five years—and in large part precisely because of the authorities' success in cleaning up bank balance sheets, restructuring their operations, and stabilizing the economy. Of course we're not looking for the rug to be pulled out suddenly from under banks, i.e., we still see plenty of support for the financial system at a macro level. However, going forward, Chinese banks will inevitably face lower balance sheet growth, rising competition from other financing sources, and lower interest rate margins—all of which will have their influence on the profitability and attractiveness of these institutions. Let's look at each of the expected policy changes in turn.

Capital Account Liberalization

For more than ten years the government has repeated time and again that opening its capital account and achieving full currency convertibility are key long-term policy goals, but until recently had done very little to realize its intentions. In the 2006-2007 period, however, the situation has changed considerably. With a record-high trade surplus and a clearly undervalued currency putting pressure on monetary policy at home, and rising trade frictions with neighbors, China now has a strong vested interest in generating capital outflows in order to reduce the size of the overall balance of payments.

As of this writing, we have already seen a number of measures aimed at opening external capital markets. To begin with, the government has loosened individual restrictions on purchasing foreign exchange and transferring funds abroad in limited amounts. The securities regulator has already adopted a QDII (qualified domestic institutional investor) scheme allowing financial institutions to remit funds offshore for fixed income investments and we expect a similar decision in favor of retail equity flows in short order. Chinese companies are now actively encouraged to find overseas direct investment projects. And the new State Foreign Exchange Investment Corporation (SFXIC) should soon begin issuing *renminbi* bonds in order to remit funds offshore for official portfolio diversification purposes.

All of these decisions represent a more or less direct loss of traditional business and balance sheet growth for domestic banks. Of course the scale of opening is currently very small, i.e., the government is not exactly throwing open the doors to massive outflows from the banking system, and our guess is that even a decade hence we will still be talking about a major capital account liberalization in the future tense. On the other hand the SFXIC in particular could soon be raising as much as USD 100 billion per year in new capital for outward investment, which represents a steady if gradual potential drain on funding resources.

Opening of Alternative Financing Channels

We already saw in Figure 6.13 above what a large portion of Chinese domestic household and corporate savings is intermediated through the banking system in the form of monetary assets—and how little goes through other financing channels such as equities and bonds. You can see the same point in Figure 6.15 below, which shows the composition of financial wealth in China compared to other emerging and developed countries.

However, this is not a result of natural market preferences, e.g., that somehow Chinese firms and individuals happen to like monetary assets to a much greater degree than the rest of the world. Rather, as we noted above, this reflects an effective historical

Figure 6.15. China: The Odd Man Out

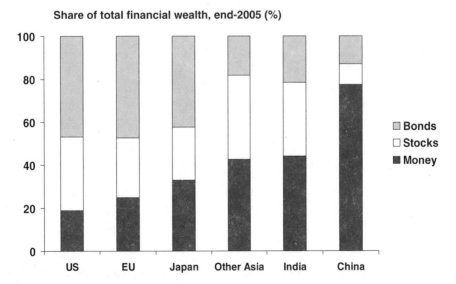

Source: CEIC, UBS estimates

moratorium on alternative financial instruments. In the case of bonds this is more or less stated official policy; since the collapse of the financial bubble in the mid-1990s, China's planning agency has taken a very dim view of companies entering debt markets, and the virtual explosion in tax revenues in the 2000s has obviated the need for strong government issuance. On the equity side, the Chinese government has been a booster of new public offerings in theory, but in practice the securities regulator was forced to restrict listings to a trickle in view of the falling stock market from 2001 through 2006.

Once again, however, in 2006-2007 the government's stance has changed substantially. After the 2006 rally sent domestic stock market indices up nearly 150%, the securities regulator is now encouraging as much new issuance as possible as a means of soaking up excess liquidity, and companies have been quick to jump on board. From 2001 to 2006 average new domestic issuance was RMB 75 billion per year, with the 2005 figure only half that amount. In 2006, by contrast, companies raised RMB 250 billion in the stock market, and expected new issuance in 2007 is much higher still.

A similar boom is occurring in corporate debt markets. Between 2000 and 2004 firms raised a paltry RMB 25 billion a year through bond issuance, but in 2005 alone the number increased to RMB 200 billion, and then doubled again to RMB 400 billion in 2006. At the beginning of this year, China's senior leadership took the decision to shift oversight and approval authority for corporate bonds from the former planning agency over to the securities regulator, a move that is widely expected to yield further rapid expansion in the size of the market.

In other words, savings are starting to leak out of the banking system and borrowers are starting to turn to direct capital market finance. How important are these trends? Again, we're not looking for any significant derating in the near term—but look at the potential changes over the next decade or two. Since 1990, China's nominal economic activity has increased at an average pace of 15% year on year, while bank balance sheets have expanded at a rate more like 22% year on year; not only have Mainland financial institutions been "keeping up" with the rest of the economy, they have actually outperformed by a very wide margin. However, if we assume that households and firms "re-align" the composition of financial wealth balances into line with international standards by, say, 2025, and that average nominal GDP growth will be 11% to 12% over the period, we get—average bank balance sheet growth of only 6% to 7% year on year for the next 20 years, i.e., still strongly positive, but a far cry from the current double-digit rates of expansion.

Interest Rate Liberalization

Perhaps the most sensitive issue of all for Chinese commercial banks is that of interest rates. You can see why, as even small adjustments in administered rates can have a significant impact on profits. According to official statistics, operating profits of the "big four" state banks were RMB 263 billion in 2006, compared to total end-year deposits of RMB 18.8 trillion in those institutions. Doing the math, a 100 basis-point increase in deposit rates (leaving all other factors unchanged) would have been enough to wipe out a full three-quarters of state bank profits in 2006. Now, we clearly expect profit levels to increase further in 2007 following recapitalization and equity listings, and we don't expect the government to take precipitous interest rate moves any time soon. But in our view this remains the most significant macro risk to banks' profit outlook going forward.

Why would banks be at risk? Because in our view, any move to liberalize interest rates would result in a potentially significant narrowing of loan/deposit spreads. We say this for four reasons. To begin with, as we showed above, Chinese spreads in 2006-2007 are at historical highs when looking at the past 20 years. They are also quite high by Asian standards, and even higher still if we compare with the historical level in other high-growth, lower-inflation regional economies. Third, the fact that the PBoC maintains a binding ceiling (but not a floor) on deposit rates and a binding floor (but no ceiling) on lending rates clearly suggests where the pressure points are for each rate category. And finally, we actually observe spreads narrowing in the banking system; smaller, more nimble commercial banks very commonly undercut their larger competitors by offering higher "under the table" deposit rates and, similarly, lower lending rates through various schemes in order to increase market share. It's very difficult to estimate the free-market equilibrium level of the interest spread, but our guess is perhaps only half the current level.

This situation distorts incentives to improve commercial performance; as long as margins on "plain vanilla" lending operations are high, banks have a strong incentive to expand their traditional loan book, and very little incentive to find alternative non-interest sources of income. This, in turn, helps explain why Chinese banks' share of fee and other income is the lowest in the region.

The PBoC has long discussed its intention to move toward a market-based interest rate system over the medium term. As discussed earlier, the authorities had a strong incentive not to liberalize rates when state banks were loaded with non-performing loans—but the expected bailout and recapitalization of the Agricultural Bank of China in 2007 would effectively remove the last barrier to market reforms. Once the clean-up is completed, we see no reason for the government to keep interest rates controls, and would expect major steps toward liberalization soon thereafter.

Another contributing factor is inflation. A key part of our outlook for China is a rise in structural inflation over the next 12-18 months from early 2007, as low-end wage pressures build, heavy industrial margins recover, and food prices continue to rise. And if CPI inflation were to increase, the authorities would come under pressure to hike deposit rates in order to keep savers' real returns positive; this has been a crucial consideration in most of the big rate adjustment decisions of the past 15 years. However, with growth rates already slowing and the economy stabilizing, it's unlikely that the PBoC would be as interested in a one-to-one offset in lending rates. In other words, rising inflation could also be a factor leading to falling bank margins.

Weakening of Implicit Guarantees

A final issue concerns a weakening of the long-standing implicit official guarantee of support for the state-owned banking system. We argued above that privatization is the only way forward for commercial banks, and the government is already well-advanced in its plans to reduce the state to a minority shareholder in the big four financial institutions. This implies that large banks will no longer be seen as carrying the full weight of the state and its resources behind it, a point made even more forcefully now that the government has decided to introduce a formal deposit insurance scheme. Of course this is nothing more than a move toward a "normal" banking system and as such is a good thing from the point of view of economic efficiency, as it puts smaller, non-state institutions on an equal footing in terms of competitiveness and removes incentives for moral hazard behavior. On the other hand, it also makes the financial institution more liable to speculative attack if China does wake up in five or ten years time with another bout of severe macroeconomic instability and sharply worsening bank balance sheets.

This is all the more so since the government will not be able to intervene so easily and effortlessly the next time around. In the earlier discussion on central bank seignorage mathematics, we showed how a combination of record-high saving rates and a banking system monopoly on financial intermediation means that the PBoC could ward off even the largest domestic financial shocks simply by printing money, without undue macroeconomic impact. However, we also saw that money demand growth will necessarily slow as the authorities liberalize the financial system, which in turn means that the PBoC's ability to create seignorage revenues will fall. If banks do get into trouble again over the next decade, the Ministry of Finance will have to finance a larger share of the burden.

7

After Hu, Who?: The Rising Stars of China's Fifth Generation

Cheng Li
William Kenan Professor of Government, Hamilton College
Visiting Fellow, The Brookings Institution

Introduction

As Hu Jintao heads into his second term as the Secretary General of the Chinese Communist Party, analysts of Chinese politics have begun to turn the spotlight onto possible candidates for the next Politburo.[1] It is expected that the Politburo of the 17th Central Committee of the Chinese Communist Party (CCP), which will be formed in the fall of 2007, will consist of many newcomers, especially new younger members who are in their 50s. This will come as no surprise, because by 2007 the average ages of the members of the Standing Committee, Politburo, and Secretariat of the 16th Central Committee of the CCP will be 67, 66, and 65, respectively. With no exceptions, all members of these three leadership bodies will be in their 60s or 70s in 2007. The recruitment of new blood into these most important decision-making institutions in the People's Republic of China (PRC) has become a major concern for Hu Jintao and the CCP leadership.

The Significance of the Upcoming Politburo Reshuffling

The reshuffling of the Politburo membership in the upcoming Party Congress is particularly important for at least three reasons.

The Consolidation of Hu's Power

It is widely recognized that in the current Politburo, Hu Jintao is surrounded by Jiang Zemin's protégés and other leaders who do not belong to Hu's own faction. Among the 24 members of the Politburo as of the end of 2006, only four, including Hu himself, have had leadership experience in the Chinese Communist Youth League (CCYL), which is Hu's power base. But even the three other members cannot be regarded as Hu's protégés because none was directly promoted by Hu. Ever since taking the post of general secretary of the Party, Hu has formed a political coalition with Premier Wen Jiabao, Vice Premier Wu Yi, and other members who lack a clear factional affiliation, in an effort to counterbalance the enormous power of his political rivals in the Politburo.

Many of Hu's protégés will likely become members of the next Politburo. Those leaders who worked in the national leadership of the CCYL under Hu Jintao in the early 1980s, the so-called *tuanpai* (Youth League clique), are considered the most likely to obtain membership. One or two of them may even obtain seats on the Standing Committee. The expected promotion of the prominent *tuanpai* officials such as Liaoning Party Secretary Li Keqiang, Jiangsu Party Secretary Li Yuanchao, and Director of the

CCP United Front Work Department Liu Yandong will significantly consolidate Hu's power base. Understanding the factional dynamics of this supreme decision-making body in the country, especially the growing presence of Hu's protégés, is important in our assessment of the next phase of Chinese elite politics. By gaining a stronger representation of his own team in the next Politburo, Hu could more aggressively reshape China's economic and socio-political development in line with his own vision and perceived mandate.

The Coming of Age of the Fifth Generation

The new faces in the 2007 Politburo may include leaders who were born in the late 1940s. For example, Liu Yandong (born in 1945), Minister of the National Development and Reform Commission Ma Kai (b. 1946), and Beijing Mayor Wang Qishan (b. 1948) are among the leading candidates for Politburo membership. These leaders are only a few years younger than Hu Jintao, and they are regarded as the younger members of the "Fourth Generation" of PRC leaders. It is also possible that a few leaders in their early 60s, such as State Councilor Chen Zhili (b. 1942), Chairman of the state-owned Assets Supervision and Administration Commission Li Rongrong (b. 1944), and Tianjin Mayor Dai Xianglong (b. 1944), will enter the Politburo for the first time. As a matter of fact, the 2002 Politburo also had a few first-timers in their early 60s, including Vice Premier Zeng Peiyan (b. 1938) and Tianjin Party Secretary Zhang Lichang (b. 1939).

Although the 17th Party Congress is not expected to see a stark generational transition of power in terms of age discrepancies, the ascension of this next batch of leaders will most likely signify the rapid rise of the so-called "Fifth Generation" of the Chinese leadership.[2] The Fifth Generation will be composed of the age cohorts who were born in the 1950s and the early 1960s. The Chinese official media call them the "Generation of the Republic" (*gongheguo yidai*) since they were all born after the founding of the PRC. They were China's "baby boomers." Many were "sent-down youths" during the Cultural Revolution when they spent years doing manual labor in the countryside. A majority of them went to college after Deng Xiaoping reinstated the national college entrance examination in 1977-78.

The Fifth Generation of leaders differs profoundly from preceding generations in terms of their formative experiences, educational credentials, political socialization, administrative background, and worldviews. The history of the PRC also indicates that each generation of leaders has brought forth its own mandate and its own policy priorities. New leaders often expend great energy trying to fix the problems created or exacerbated by their predecessors, as evident in the transition from Jiang's Third Generation to Hu's Fourth Generation of leadership. To a great extent, generational characteristics of future leaders are important—and sometimes quite reliable—predictors of China's future political trajectory.

The Selection of Hu's Successor

Hu Jintao served on the Politburo Standing Committee for ten years before becoming general secretary of the CCP. Hu's previous ten-year-long membership on the Standing Committee not only allowed him to gain leadership experience in the country's highest political institution, but also placed him as the "first among equals" in the Fourth Generation in line to succeed Jiang. Based on such a precedent, it seems necessary for the Chinese political establishment to identify Hu's designated successor in the 17th Party Congress in 2007. With an adequate "reserve" period near the center of power, that "heir apparent" will be able to take over the top leadership when Hu completes his second term at the 18th Party Congress in 2012.

Largely because of the current Chinese obsession with age in elite recruitment, "the heir apparent" is unlikely to be chosen from the current members of the Politburo. The youngest current Standing Committee member, Li Changchun, is only two years younger than Hu, and the youngest current Politburo member, Liu Yunshan, is only five years younger than Hu. The CCP's norm of promoting leaders in batches, within somewhat narrow age brackets, suggests that Hu's designated successor will most likely be a new face in the 2007 Politburo. It is unclear, however, whether the 17th Party Congress will select one single younger leader to be the successor to Hu, or will choose two to four leaders from the Fifth Generation to wait in line to succeed to the top posts. This largely depends on how much consensus or compromise competing factions can reach, and the degree of confidence the old guards have regarding the ability of the newcomers.

Group Characteristics of the Upcoming Leadership

Prior to the 17th Party Congress in 2007, Hu Jintao and other current top leaders will likely search for their successors from a sizeable pool of candidates. An analysis of group characteristics of a number of rising stars can help highlight both the intra-generational division and inter-generational differences of the Chinese leadership.

The need to identify more contenders is highlighted by the fact that in 2007, eleven (47.8%) out of 23 full members of the 16th Politburo will be over 66 years old. Table 7.1 shows the backgrounds of the original members of the 16th Politburo, including their ages in 2007. Luo Gan (72), Wu Guanzheng (69), Jia Qinglin (67), Wu Yi (68), Zeng Peiyan (68), and Cao Gangchuan (72) will most likely retire. Zeng Qinghong (68), a heavyweight in Chinese politics today, may also retire if he can place one or two of his strong allies in the next Politburo Standing Committee to counterbalance Hu Jintao's growing power. In addition, Standing Committee Member and State Council Vice Premier Huang Ju died in June 2007; former Tianjin Party Secretary Zhang Lichang retired in 2007; and former Shanghai Party Secretary Chen Liangyu was removed because of corruption charges in 2006.

Table 7.1 also shows that except for members of the Standing Committee, all other members of the 16th Politburo were first-timers to full membership in 2002. This indicates that even a few Politburo members who are under 65 (in 2007) may also step down to open their seats to newcomers. It is reasonable to expect that a half of the members of the next Politburo will be newcomers.

The seven-member Secretariat will probably undergo an even more substantial reshuffling than the Politburo. With the exception of 60 year old Liu Yunshan, other members of the Secretariat — Zeng Qinghong (68), Zhou Yongkang (65), He Guoqiang (64), Wang Gang (65), Xu Caihou (64), and He Yong (67)—will likely no longer serve in this body after the 17th Party Congress. Xu, a representative of the military, will likely be promoted to the next Politburo, replacing the 72 year old Minister of Defense Cao Gangchuan. Guo Boxiong (65), the other Politburo member from the military, will likely retain his seat. The new Secretariat formed in 2007 will largely consist of newcomers. Meanwhile, due to their age, three out of four vice premiers and four of five state councilors in the State Council will likely retire in the next National People's Congress, which will be held in the spring of 2008.

Who will fill in all these important leadership positions? Table 7.2 lists 29 contenders for the 2007 Politburo and Secretariat. They are the most likely candidates, from the civilian sector, to be chosen for these two powerful decision-making bodies. The number of the military representatives is expected to remain very small, and the question of the candidate pool of military leaders is beyond the scope of this study. The civilian leaders listed here were chosen based on a combination of factors such as their current leadership positions, administrative experiences, membership in the 16th Central Committee, age, patron-client ties, regional or bureaucratic representation, and other distinguishing factors.

A majority of them, 22 (75.9%), will be in their 50s in 2007 when the 17th Party Congress convenes. Five will be in their 60s and two will be in their 40s. The average age is 55, about eleven years younger than that of the 16th Politburo members. With the exception of Cai Wu (Director of the Information Office of the CCP Central Committee) and Miao Wei (former CEO of the Dongfeng Auto Corp. and Party Secretary of Wuhan), all others in the list currently serve in the Central Committee of the CCP as full members (13) or alternates (14). The leaders on this list are not all at the same starting point in the race for power. Some may have a chance to become members of the Politburo Standing Committee, while the others' best chance is to serve in the Secretariat.

Table 7.1. Backgrounds of All Members of the 16th Politburo (2007)

Name	Age (2007)	Sex	Likelihood to be on 17th Politburo	Current Position	Institution of Highest Level Of Education Attended	Field	Level	Year Entered CC	Year Entered PB
Hu Jintao	64	M	Retain	Sec-Gen, PRC President	Qinghua University	Engineering	Col.	1982 (AM)	1992
Wu Bangguo	66	M	Retain or Out	Chair, NPC, PB SC Member	Qinghua University	Engineering	Col.	1982 (AM)	1992
Wen Jiabao	65	M	Retain	Premier, PB SC Member	Beijing Institute of Geology	Engineering	Master	1987	1992 (AM)
Jia Qinglin	67	M	Out	Chair, CPPCC, PB SC Mem.	Hebei Engineering College	Engineering	Col.	1987	1997
Zeng Qinghong	68	M	Retain or Out	PRC VP, PB SC Mem.	Beijing Institute of Tech.	Engineering	Col.	1997	1997 (AM)
Huang Ju	69	M	Deceased June 2007	Exe. V-Premier, PB SC Mem.	Qinghua University	Engineering	Col.	1987 (AM)	1994

Table 7.1. Backgrounds of All Members of the 16th Politburo (2007) (cont'd)

Name	Age (2007)	Sex	Likelihood to be on 17th Politburo	Current Position	Institution of Highest Level Of Education Attended	Field	Level	Year Entered CC	Year Entered PB
Wu Guanzheng	69	M	Out	Sec'y of CCDI, PB SC Mem.	Qinghua University	Engineering	Master	1982 (AM)	1997
Li Changchun	63	M	Retain	PB SC Member	Harbin Institute of Tech.	Engineering	Col.	1982 (AM)	1997
Luo Gan	72	M	Out	PB SC Member	Freiburg Ins. of Metallurgy	Engineering	Col.	1982 (AM)	1997
Wang Lequan	63	M	Out	Party Secretary of Xinjiang	Central Party School	Politics	Master	1992 (AM)	2002
Wang Zhaoguo	66	M	Out	Vice Chair, NPC	Harbin Institute of Tech.	Engineering	Col.	1982	2002
Hui Liangyu	63	M	Promote to SC	Vice Premier	Jilin Provincial Party School	Economics	Col.	1992 (AM)	2002

Table 7.1. Backgrounds of All Members of the 16th Politburo (2007) (cont'd)

Name	Age (2007)	Sex	Likelihood to be on 17th Politburo	Current Position	Institution of Highest Level Of Education Attended	Field	Level	Year Entered CC	Year Entered PB
Liu Qi	65	M	Out	Party Secretary of Beijing	Beijing Institute of Iron/Steel	Engineering	Master	1992 (AM)	2002
Liu Yunshan	60	M	Retain	Dir., CCP Propaganda Dep't	Central Party School	Mgmt.	Col.	1982 (AM)	2002
Wu Yi	68	F	Out	Vice Premier	Beijing Petroleum Institute	Engineering	Col.	1987 (AM)	1997 (AM)
Zhang Lichang	68	M	Retired	Party Secretary of Tianjin	Beijing Economics Cor. Univ.	Economics	J.Col.	1982 (AM)	2002
Zhang Dejiang	61	M	Retain	Party Secretary of Guangdong	Kim Il Sung University	Economics	Col.	1992 (AM)	2002
Chen Liangyu	61	M	Removed 2006	Former Party Secretary of Shanghai	PLA Institute of Engineering	Engineering	Col.	1992 (AM)	2002

Table 7.1. Backgrounds of All Members of the 16th Politburo (2007) (cont'd)

Name	Age (2007)	Sex	Likelihood to be on 17th Politburo	Current Position	Institution of Highest Level Of Education Attended	Field	Level	Year Entered CC	Year Entered PB
Zhou Yongkang	65	M	Out	Minister of Public Security	Beijing Petroleum Institute	Engineering	Col.	1992 (AM)	2002
Yu Zhengsheng	62	M	Promote to SC	Party Secretary of Hubei	Harbin Mil. Engineering Ins.	Engineering	Col.	1992 (AM)	2002
He Guoqiang	64	M	Out	Dir., CCP Organization Dep't	Beijing Ins. Chem. Eng.	Engineering	Col.	1982 (AM)	2002
Guo Boxiong	65	M	Retain	Vice Chair, CMC	PLA Military Academy	Mil. Affairs	Col.	1997	2002
Cao Gangchuan	72	M	Out	Vice Chair, CMC	Military Eng. School, USSR	Engineering	Col.	1997	2002
Zeng Peiyan	68	M	Out	Vice Premier	Qinghua University	Engineering	Col.	1992 (AM)	2002

Table 7.1. Backgrounds of All Members of the 16th Politburo (2007) (cont'd)

Name	Age (2007)	Sex	Likelihood to be on 17th Politburo	Current Position	Institution of Highest Level Of Education Attended	Field	Level	Year Entered CC	Year Entered PB
Wang Gang (AM)	65	M	Promote to full	Director, CCP General Office	Jilin University	Philosophy	Col.	1997 (AM)	2002 (AM)

Notes: All Ages as of November 2007. Standing Committee members' names are in boldface.

Abbreviations: AM=Alternate Member, CC=Central Committee, CCDI=Central Commission of Discipline Inspection, CCP=Chinese Communist Party, Chem.=Chemical, CMC=Central Military Commission, Col.=College, Com.=Commission, Cor.=Correspondence, CPPCC=Chinese People's Political Consultative Conference, Dep't=Department, Dir.=Director, Eng.=Engineering, Exe.=Executive, F=Female, Ins.=Institute, J.=Junior, M=Male, Mem.=Member, Mgmt.=Management, Mil.=Military, NPC=National People's Congress, PB=Politburo, PRC=People's Republic of China, SC=Standing Committee, Sec'y=Secretary, Tech.=Technology, Univ.=University, USSR=Union of Soviet Socialist Republics.

Table 7.2. Contenders for the Membership of the 2007 Politburo and Secretariat

Name	Age (2007)	Sex	Likelihood to be on the 17th Central Com.	Current Position (By mid-2007)	Institution of Highest Level of Education Attended	Field	Level	Year Entered CC
Li Keqiang	52	M	SC or PB	Party Secretary of Liaoning	Beijing Univ.	Economics	Ph.D.	1997
Li Yuanchao	56	M	SC or PB	Party Secretary of Jiangsu	Central Party School	Politics	Ph.D.	2002 (AM)
Liu Yandong	61	F	SC or PB	Dir. CCP United Front Work Dept.	Jilin Univ.	Politics	Ph.D.	2002, 1997 (AM)
Wang Qishan	59	M	PB & V. Premier	Mayor of Beijing	Northwestern Univ.	History	College	2002, 1997 (AM)
Ma Kai	61	M	PB & V. Premier	Minister of Dev. & Reform Com.	People's Univ.	Pol. Eco.	Master	2002
Wang Yang	52	M	PB & V. Premier	Party Secretary of Chongqing	Univ of Sci. & Tech. of China	Mgmt	Master	2002
Du Qinglin	60	M	PB & V. Premier	Party Secretary of Sichuan	Jilin Univ.	Law	Master	2002, 1992 (AM)
Han Zheng	53	M	PB & V. Premier	Mayor of Shanghai	East China Normal Univ.	Politics	Master	2002
Xi Jinping	54	M	PB & V. Premier	Party Secretary of Shanghai	Qinghua University	Law/ Politics	Ph.D.	2002, 1997 (AM)

Table 7.2. Contenders for the Membership of the 2007 Politburo and Secretariat (cont'd)

Name	Age (2007)	Sex	Likelihood to be on the 17th Central Com.	Current Position (By mid-2007)	Institution of Highest Level of Education Attended	Field	Level	Year Entered CC
Bo Xilai	58	M	PB or Secretariat	Minister of Commerce	CASS	Journalism	Master	2002
Wu Aiying	55	F	PB or Secretariat	Minister of Justice	Central Party School	Politics	Master	1992 (AM)
Zhou Xiaochuan	59	M	PB & Councilor	Governor, People's Bank	Qinghua Univ.	Engineering	Ph.D.	2002
Liu Mingkang	61	M	PB & Councilor	Chair, Banking Regulatory Com.	London University	MBA	MBA	2002 (AM)
Li Yizhong	62	M	PB & Councilor	Chair, State Adm. of Work Safety	Beijing Oil Col.	Engineering	College	2002, 1992 (AM)
Shen Yueyue	50	F	Secretariat	Vice Director, CCP Org. Dept.	Central Party School	Pol. Eco.	Master	1997 (AM)
Ling Jihua	51	M	Secretariat	Vice Director, CCP Central Office	Hunan Univ.	MBA	Master	2002 (AM)
Wang Huning	52	M	Secretariat	Dir., CCP Ins. on Policy Research	Fudan Univ.	Politics	Master	2002

Table 7.2. Contenders for the Membership of the 2007 Politburo and Secretariat (cont'd)

Name	Age (2007)	Sex	Likelihood to be on the 17th Central Com.	Current Position (By mid-2007)	Institution of Highest Level of Education Attended	Field	Level	Year Entered CC
Cai Wu	58	M	Secretariat	Dir., Info. Office of CCP Cen. Com.	Beijing Univ.	Law	Ph.D.	
Zhang Baoshun	57	M	Secretariat	Party Secretary of Shanxi	Jilin Univ.	Mgmt.	Master	2002 (AM)
Zhao Leji	50	M	Secretariat	Party Secretary of Shaanxi	Beijing Univ.	Philosophy	College	2002
Song Xiuyan	52	F	Secretariat	Governor of Qinghai	Central Party School	Politics	Master	1997 (AM)
Yuan Chunqing	55	M	Secretariat	Governor of Shaanxi	Hunan Univ.	Mgmt.	Ph.D.	2002 (AM)
Liu Qibao	54	M	Secretariat	Party Secretary of Guangxi	Jilin Univ.	Mgmt.	Master	2002 (AM)
Li Hongzhong	51	M	Alternate PB	Party Secretary of Shenzhen City	Jilin Univ.	History	College	2002 (AM)
Zhang Qingwei	45	M	Alternate PB	Minister COSTIND	Northwestern Univ.	Engineering	Master	2002

Table 7.2. Contenders for the Membership of the 2007 Politburo and Secretariat (cont'd)

Name	Age (2007)	Sex	Likelihood to be on the 17th Central Com.	Current Position (By mid-2007)	Institution of Highest Level of Education Attended	Field	Level	Year Entered CC
Yang Jiechi	57	M	Alternate PB	Minister of Foreign Affairs	London Sch. of Eco. & Pol.	Politics	College	2002 (AM)
Miao Wei	52	M	Alternate PB	Party Secretary of Wuhan City	Central Party School	Politics	Master	
Jiang Jianqing	54	M	Alternate PB	Governor, Ind. & Commercial Bank	Jiaotong Univ.	Mgmt.	Ph.D.	2002 (AM)
Zhu Yanfeng	46	M	Alternate PB	CEO, First Auto Work Group Corp.	Zhejiang Univ.	Engineering	College	2002 (AM)

Notes: All Ages as of November 2007. Those names in boldface are front runners.

Abbreviations: AM=Alternate Member, CASS=Chinese Academy of Social Sciences, CC=Central Committee, CCP=Chinese Communist Party, Cen.=Central, Com.=Commission, Dept.=Department, Dev.=Development, Eco.=Economics, F=Female, Ind.=Industrial, Info.=Information, Ins.=Institute, M=Male, MBA=Master of Business Administration, Mgmt.=Management, Org.=Organization, PB=Politburo, Pol.=Politics, PS=Party Secretary, SC=Standing Committee, Sch.=School, Tech.=Technology, Univ.=University, COSTIND=Comm. of Sci., Tech. and Ind. for National Defense.

Institutional Representation

These candidates come from four general bureaucratic sectors: 1) the State Council, 2) the departments and institutions under the CCP Central Committee, 3) the provincial and municipal leadership, and 4) major enterprises.

Candidates from the State Council

Because a majority of vice premiers and state councilors in the State Council are expected to retire in 2008, candidates from various ministries have an advantage for winning membership in the next Politburo. The leading contenders include Minister of State Development and Reform Commission Ma Kai (b. 1946), Minister of Commerce Bo Xilai (b. 1949), Minister of Justice Wu Aiying (b. 1951), Governor of People's Bank Zhou Xiaochuan (b. 1948), Chair of the State Banking Regulatory Commission Liu Mingkang (b. 1946), and Minister of Foreign Affairs Yang Jiechi (b. 1950). Some of them are currently running some of the most important ministries in the country.

Although Wu Aiying has only recently taken her current position, she has served on the CCP Central Committee as an alternate member since 1992 (one of the three with the longest membership in the list). In light of the rapid legal development in the country, her ministry seems to have gained more weight in the eyes of the political establishment. Wu not only had work experience under Hu Jintao two decades ago when both served in the leadership of the CCYL, but she also served as Deputy Party Secretary in Shandong between 1998 and 2002 when Wu Guanzheng was the Party boss there. Wu Guanzheng, a member of the Politburo Standing Committee, is currently in charge of the Central Commission of Discipline Inspection of the CCP. It was believed that Wu Guanzheng nominated Wu Aiying for the position of Minister of Justice. As is the norm in Chinese elite politics, Wu Guanzheng will likely use his own retirement in the Politburo Standing Committee in 2007 to promote his friends, including Wu Aiying, to higher positions.

Minister of Foreign Affairs Yang Jiechi seems to need more leadership credentials in order to obtain a seat in the next Politburo. In recent years, the full Minister of Foreign Ministry, Tang Jiaxuan or Li Zhaoxing, was not able to obtain a Politburo seat. But all senior career diplomats in China, e.g., State Councilor Tang Jiaxuan (b. 1938), Minister of Foreign Affairs Li Zhaoxing (b. 1940), Director of the Foreign Affairs Office under the State Council Liu Huaqiu (b. 1939), and Executive Vice Minister of Foreign Affairs Dai Bingguo (b. 1941), will be in their late 60s in 2007. Yang Jiechi is more appealing than others among his age cohort in the Ministry of Foreign Affairs because he is an alternate member of the 16th Central Committee and has served as Ambassador to the United States.

Candidates from the Departments under the CCP Central Committee

Five leaders are chosen from the institutions under the CCP Central Committee. Ling Jihua (b. 1956) and Cai Wu (b. 1949) are two confidants of Hu Jintao. Vice Director of CCP General Office Ling Jinhua began to serve as Hu's personal secretary in 1983 when Hu was Secretary of the CCYL Central Committee. Soon after Hu became a member of the Politburo Standing Committee of the CCP in 1992, Ling began to serve as chief-of-staff for his old boss. As Hu's power increases, Ling may soon succeed Wang Gang as director of the General Office of the CCP Central Committee.

Similarly, Cai Wu also began to work under Hu's leadership in 1983 when Cai served as director of the Department of International Liaison of the CCYL Central Committee. He worked there for 12 years. In 1995, Cai moved to the Department of

International Liaison of the CCP Central Committee where he served as head of the research department, deputy chief of staff, and vice director. Cai was expected to become the director of the department, but the position went to Wang Jiarui, Jiang's protégé and former mayor of Qingdao. Because of both his professional expertise and current position, Cai has become a key player on Hu's foreign policy team.

Director of the CCP Institute of Policy Research Wang Huning (b. 1955) used to be Jiang's advisor and strategist. In recent years, Wang has often traveled with Hu, especially during Hu's trips to foreign countries. This seems to indicate that Hu also thinks highly of Wang and may continue to benefit from Wang's wisdom. If this observation is correct, Wang should not have too much difficulty in obtaining a seat in the Secretariat, especially considering the fact that Wang is already a full member of the 16th Central Committee.

Vice Director of the CCP Organization Department Shen Yueyue (b. 1957) is Hu Jintao's "appointed person" in the crucial area of personnel matters. Like many other protégés of Hu Jintao, Shen advanced her career from the CCYL, attended the Central Party School, and had broad experience in municipal and provincial leadership. In recent years, Shen has been extremely effective in "recommending" many *tuanpai* leaders to important leadership positions. Having served in the Central Committee as an alternate member for two terms, Shen is in line for further promotion.

Candidates from the Provincial Leadership

Province leadership has become, over the past decade, the most important stepping-stone to high national posts. A recent study shows that the percentage of Politburo members who served as provincial leaders (deputy party secretaries and vice governors, or above) rose sharply over the decade: 55% in 1992, 68% in 1997, and 83% by 2002. The percentage of Politburo members who were provincial chiefs (party secretaries and governors) increased from 50% in 1992 to 59% in 1997, and again to 67% by 2002.[4]

Meanwhile, China's province-level administrations have enjoyed more autonomy than ever before to advance local economic interests. They often do so with support from representatives among top national leaders. Shanghai's rapid development during the 1990s, for example, has been closely linked to the enormous power of Jiang Zemin and the "Shanghai Gang." The more recent policy shifts to more balanced regional development and the reallocation of resources to China's inland provinces are related to the fact that President Hu has spent much time in his career in the western part of China and that he built his power base there.

The trend of overrepresentation of Politburo members with provincial administrative backgrounds will likely continue in the 2007 Politburo. The CCP recent norm for such a selection has four main considerations: 1) Party secretaries in Beijing, Shanghai, Tianjin, Chongqing, and some rich provinces on the coast such as Guangdong, Jiangsu, and Shandong will have seats; 2) inland provinces will have one to three representatives; 3) some of the provincial chiefs who obtain Politburo seats may soon be transferred to the national leadership, serving as vice premier in the State Council or heads of the departments of the CCP Central Committee; and 4) most of the provincial leaders who obtain Politburo seats are selected because of factional consideration, especially their patron-client ties with top leaders, but occasionally leaders without clear factional affiliation are also selected because of their public popularity and administrative achievements.

Thirteen provincial and municipal leaders are on this list of Politburo hopefuls. Former Zhejiang Party Secretary and present Party Secretary of Shanghai Xi Jinping (b. 1953), Shanghai Mayor Han Zheng (b. 1954), and Shenzhen Party Secretary Li Hongzhong (b. 1956) have been close to Jiang Zemin and Zeng Qinghong. They are likely to be nominated by the Jiang-Zeng faction, especially at a time that Hu's *tuanpai* leaders are overrepresented in the provincial leadership. Shanxi Party Secretary Zhang Baoshun (b. 1950), Chongqing Party Secretary Wang Yang (b. 1955), Sichuan Party Secretary Du Qinglin (b. 1946), Shaanxi Governor Yuan Chunqing (b. 1952), Guangxi Party Secretary Liu Qibao (b. 1953), and the only female provincial chief in the country, Qinghai Governor Song Xiuyan (b. 1955), are all *tuanpai* leaders who worked under Hu Jintao in the CCYL leadership two decades ago. Shaanxi Party Secretary Zhao Leji (b. 1957) does not belong to any faction, but has the advantage of being the youngest provincial Party secretary in the country. Prior to this, he was also the youngest provincial governor.

Candidates from Major Enterprises

Although the CEOs of China's flagship companies usually hold the official government rank of vice minister or vice provincial governor or above, they usually are not contenders for Politburo seats. But at the 16th Party Congress, for the first time in history, the Central Enterprise Work Commission and the Central Financial Work Commission had their own delegations at the Party Congress.[5] Seventeen representatives of the entrepreneurial class became members of the presidium of the Party Congress.[6] A total of 24 entrepreneurs from large state-owned enterprises, collective firms, joint ventures, and commercial banks were selected to serve on the 356-member 16th Central Committee as full or alternate members. They include Zhang Qingwei (43-year-old former CEO of China Aerospace Science & Technology Corp. and present Minister of the Commission of Science, Technology and Industry for National Defense (COSTIND)), Su Shulin (42-year-old vice president of China National Petroleum Corp.), and Liu Shiquan (41-year-old deputy general manager of the Sanjiang Space

Group). Zhang is the youngest full member of the 16th Central Committee, and Su and Liu are the two youngest alternates.

Because of the growing importance of enterprises and the young age of CEOs of China's flagship companies, prominent business leaders may be considered as "dark horses" for the future Politburo or the Secretariat. The list includes Zhang Qingwei (b. 1961), a leader for China's space program; Zhu Yanfeng (b. 1961), the CEO of the largest auto company in China; Miao Wei (b. 1955), former CEO of Dongfeng Auto Company and presently Party Secretary of Wuhan; Jiang Jianqing (b. 1953), the governor of China's largest commercial bank, and Li Yizhong (b. 1945), the chair of the State Commission of Work Safety of the State Council.

Li Yizhong is, of course, not a young rising star, but as one of the most trusted friends of Premier Wen Jiabao, he is expected to continue to take on important tasks. Prior to his current position, he headed the State-Owned Assets Administration Commission, another crucial institution for the issues of social justice and social stability. Li has more than 30 years of management experience in the petroleum and petrochemical industry. Between 1998 and 2003, Li served as CEO of Sinopec Corp., the world's ninth largest oil company. He has also been on the CCP Central Committee since 1992.

The institutional division of political elites in China is not stagnant because leaders often switch from one to another organization. Yet, the career paths and institutional affiliations of political rising stars are important in our assessment of the policy orientation of the new leadership. It should also be noted that the list of potential candidates is always subject to change due to unexpected circumstances. For example, Yang Chuantang, Party secretary of Tibet (b. 1954), was often regarded as a rising star in the Fifth Generation. Unfortunately, he suffered a cerebral hemorrhage in 2005 and is therefore considered out of the race for power, at least for now. Zhang Zuoji (b. 1945), Governor of

Heilongjiang, had broad leadership experiences in both central and local governments. He was a major player in the so-called "northeastern rejuvenation." But the pollution scandal revolving around the Songhua River severely damaged his public image because Zhang was believed not only to be ineffective in dealing with such a crisis, but also to be responsible for the government's cover-up. His chance for a Politburo seat has become slim. Similarly, the slave labor scandal in Shanxi province will harm the chances of promotion for the province's Party Secretary, Zhang Baoshun.

New Trends in Educational and Occupational Backgrounds

Three trends can be found in the data about the schooling and professions of the upcoming leadership.

Higher Degrees

Among these 29 leaders on the list, 23 received post-graduate education. Eight leaders hold Ph.D. degrees. They are Li Keqiang (granted in 1994), Li Yuanchao (g. 1995), Liu Yandong (g. 1998), Zhou Xiaochuan (g. 1985), Cai Wu (g. 1999), Xi Jinping (g. 2002), Yuan Chunqing (g. 1997), and Jiang Jianqing (g. 1999). In contrast, none of the current members in the Politburo holds a doctoral degree and only four have a post-graduate education. However, all of these doctoral degree holders in the Fifth Generation pursued their graduate studies through on-the-job programs, usually after they became provincial- or ministerial-level leaders.

Most of those who hold master's degrees also pursued their post-graduate education on a part-time basis. While almost all of these leaders attended month-long training programs at the Communist Party School (CPS), some also obtained their degrees there. Three female rising stars, Wu Aiying, Shen Yueyue, and

Song Xiuyan, all received their masters' degrees from the CPS. The Chinese leadership apparently uses the CPS to enhance the educational credentials of some young leaders on the fast track for promotion.

Politics and Law: Popular Academic Fields

Perhaps the most important difference between the Fourth and Fifth Generations of leaders lies in their educational and occupational backgrounds. Among the 24 full members of the 16th Politburo including the recently purged former Shanghai Party Secretary Chen Liangyu, 18 (75%) majored in engineering. All nine members of Politburo Standing Committee are engineers by training. In a sharp contrast, among the 29 leaders on the list, thirteen (44.8%) majored in politics and law, eight (27.6%) specialized in economics and management, four (13.8%) studied humanities (including history, philosophy, and journalism), and only four (13.8%) majored in engineering.

Hu Jintao and other top politicians now speak often of the need to strengthen the country's legal system. Jiang's work report for the 2002 Party Congress specified that the nation should establish a new Chinese-style legal system by 2010. More recently, Hu has made widely publicized speeches in which he stresses the rule of law. This suggests that lawyers may become an important elite group in the near future. In fact, receiving a law degree has become a valuable credential for party leadership. Some leaders on the list did undergraduate work in engineering or science, but studied law at the graduate level. Xi Jinping, for example, majored in engineering at Qinghua University in 1979, but more recently received a Ph.D. in law and politics from the university. Liu Yandong received her undergraduate education in engineering at Qinghua University, and then received her master's degree in sociology at People's University and a Ph.D. in politics at Jilin University.

The Fourth Generation of leadership is known for the predominance of Qinghua University graduates. Four of nine members of the 16th Politburo Standing Committee, Hu Jintao, Wu Bangguo, Huang Ju, and Wu Guanzheng, graduated from Qinghua. Although Xi Jinping, Liu Yandong, and Zhou Xiaochuan attended Qinghua, a larger number of rising stars in the upcoming generation are graduates of Beijing University (*Beida*) and Jilin University. Li Keqiang, Cai Wu, Zhao Leji, Bo Xilai, Li Yuanchao, and Yuan Chunqing all studied at *Beida*. In fact, with the exception of Zhao, all other *Beida* graduates attended the university in the same year (1978). Most of them grew up during the Cultural Revolution and did not receive formal elementary or middle school education. Many were sent-down youths who worked as farmers for many years before entering college after the Cultural Revolution. Table 7.2 also shows that five leaders, Liu Yandong, Du Qinglin, Zhang Baoshun, Liu Qibao, and Li Hongzhong, studied at Jilin University. All except Li Hongzhong who attended the university as a full-time undergraduate between 1978 and 1982, pursued on-the-job studies.

The Emergence of Western-Educated Returnees

Another important trend in the educational backgrounds of the upcoming leadership is the emergence of the returnees from study in Western countries. Table 7.1 shows that in the current Politburo two leaders of the Third Generation, Luo Gan and Cao Gangchuan, studied in the former Soviet Union.[7] Table 7.2 also shows that with the exception of Zhang Dejiang who studied in North Korea, Fourth Generation leaders generally have attended China's own universities. This is unsurprising since throughout the 1960s and 1970s China hardly sent any students abroad. Only after 1978, when Deng Xiaoping began the educational open door policy, did a large number Chinese students and scholars travel abroad to pursue academic studies.

The Chinese authorities claim that they have made an effort to recruit Western-educated Chinese nationals into the political establishment. In 2000, Zeng Qinghong, then the head of the CCP Organization Department, stated that students and scholars returning from study abroad should be seen as an important source for political recruitment. Zeng also specified that some outstanding returnees be immediately appointed to leading bureau-level posts (*juzhang*). According to Zeng, these leaders with foreign educational backgrounds may be promoted to even higher posts after serving as bureau heads for a few years.[8]

Some Western-educated returnees have indeed been integrated into the Chinese leadership, although the number in the high positions is still quite small. They usually serve in functional areas such as education, science and technology, finance, foreign trade, and foreign affairs. Among the 29 leaders in this study, only the Chair of the China Banking Regulatory Commission, Liu Mingkang, can be considered a "returnee." Liu studied at London University between 1985 and 1987, and received an MBA degree there.

However, six other leaders had some sort of experience in foreign studies in the West. Yang Jiechi studied English at Bath University and international affairs at the London School of Economics and Politics between 1973 and 1975.[9] Zhou Xiaochuan, Jiang Jianqing, Wang Huning, Li Yuanchao, and Li Hongzhong all studied in the United States as visiting scholars (Zhou at the University of California at Santa Cruz in 1987-88, Jiang at Columbia University in 1995, Wang at the University of Michigan and Iowa State University in 1988-89, and both Li Yuanchao and Li Hongzhong at Harvard University's Kennedy School of Government, in 2002 and 1996-97, respectively).

These leaders' respective sojourns in foreign countries were usually brief and very few have solid academic credentials or broad professional experiences which they have obtained abroad.

Nevertheless, the likely emergence of top leaders in the next Politburo with doctoral degrees, law education, and/or Western training is an important development that deserves attention. This trend indicates that the career paths of Chinese political elites are increasingly divergent. Although the diversity of the educational, occupational, and administrative backgrounds of leaders is perhaps a positive development that can potentially contribute to political pluralism in China, the history of contemporary China has shown that differences in the educational backgrounds and career experiences of political leaders are often the source of tensions and conflicts.

Factional Divisions and Policy Issues

Patron-client ties and factionalism have played important roles in the career advancements of the newcomers. Their rise to the national leadership and their dynamic interactions will likely reshape the factions or coalitions to which they belong. To a great extent, their factional divisions also reflect the different socio-economic groups and geographical regions they represent. Although they all want to ensure the survival of the CCP rule at home and retain China's status as a major international player abroad, they differ on some important political and socio-economic policies.

The Populist Coalition led by Tuanpai vs. the Elitist Coalition led by Princelings

Two political coalitions are presently balancing each other within the CCP leadership. One coalition can be identified as the "populist coalition" led by Hu Jintao. The core faction of the populist coalition is the *tuanpai* who advanced their political careers primarily from the CCYL. The other coalition might be called the "elitist coalition," previously led by former Party chief Jiang Zemin and now largely led by Vice President Zeng Qinghong. The core of this elitist coalition has been the Shanghai Gang. Because of the relatively declining power and influence of the Shanghai Gang at present, it is most likely that princelings will rise to become the core group of this elitist coalition. An assessment of the strengths and weaknesses of these two coalitions will help to elucidate the major issues and policy initiatives that will be undertaken by the upcoming 17th Party Congress and beyond.

The Coming Era of the Tuanpai *Dominance*

Officials of the CCYL have long been a major source of recruitment for the Party and government leadership in the PRC. The mission of the CCYL states explicitly that this political organization is the "reserve army" (*houbeijun*) for the CCP. The CCYL is one of the largest political institutions in the PRC. In 2006, the CCYL had a total of over 72 million members, including 191,000 full-time CCYL cadres.[10] For most of PRC history, the number of leaders with CCYL backgrounds in the Chinese top leadership has been quite small. Although Liu Shaoqi intended to promote some CCYL leaders, Mao chose to persecute them during the Cultural Revolution. Deng promoted Hu Yaobang, Hu Qili, and Wang Zhaoguo, but all of them lost favor in the late 1980s. Jiang did not value Party functionalists with CCYL backgrounds as much as technocrats with economic expertise. Very few of Jiang's close associates previously worked in the CCYL.

This trend will likely change in the next Politburo, in which Hu will be firmly in charge. Even now when *tuanpai* officials do not hold many seats in the Politburo, they have the largest representation on the 16th Central Committee of the CCP. Altogether 47 *tuanpai* officials currently serve on the committee as full or alternate members. Since Hu became General Secretary of the Party in the fall of 2002, a large number of officials with CCYL backgrounds have been appointed to positions in the ministerial and provincial levels of leadership. According to a recent study, about 150 *tuanpai* officials currently serve in the ministerial and provincial levels of leadership.[11]

Among the 29 contenders for the next Politburo seats examined in this study, 13 (45%) are *tuanpai* leaders (see Table 7.3). Mayor of Shanghai Han Zheng is not considered as a *tuanpai* leader despite the fact he served as Deputy Secretary and Secretary of the CCYL Shanghai Committee between 1990 and 1992. He is closer to Jiang and Zeng than to Hu and is widely seen as a member of the Shanghai Gang. Similarly, Li Yuanchao and Liu Yandong are considered core members of *tuanpai* despite their princeling family backgrounds and/or the Shanghai connection. The overlap cases of Han, Li, and Liu, however, are exceptions.

All 13 *tuanpai* leaders worked in the national or provincial leadership in the CCYL in the early 1980s when Hu was in charge of that organization. Li Keqiang, Li Yuanchao, Liu Yandong, Cai Wu, Zhang Baoshun, and Yuan Chunqing directly worked under Hu's leadership at the CCYL Secretariat or Central Committee. Ling Jihua was Hu's personal secretary (*mishu*). Hu promoted Liu Qibao and Wang Yang to the CCYL provincial leadership posts in Anhui province in early 1980s. Hu also provided some good opportunities to other *tuanpai* officials to broaden their leadership experiences. For example, Liu Qibao served as deputy editor-in-chief of the *People's Daily* in 1993 and then deputy chief-of-staff in the State Council between 1994 and 2000; Zhang Baoshun served as deputy director of the Xinhua News Agency; Wang Yang served as executive deputy chief-of-staff of the State Council; and Yuan Chunqing served as chief-of-staff of the Central Commission of Discipline Inspection (CCDI) of the CCP.

Table 7.3. The Populist Coalition: Contenders with *Tuanpai* (CCYL) and Inland Backgrounds

Name	Current Position (By mid-2007)	Factional Identity	Factional Ties and Defining Experience With Dates (or years)
Li Keqiang	Party Secretary of Liaoning	*Tuanpai*	CCYL Secretariat, 82-98
Li Yuanchao	Party Secretary of Jiangsu	*Tuanpai*	CCYL Secretariat, 82-90
Liu Yandong	Director, CCP United Front Dept.	*Tuanpai*	CCYL Secretariat, 82-91
Du Qinglin	Party Secretary of Sichuan	*Tuanpai*	CCYL Jilin Dep. Sec., & Sec., 79-84
Wu Aiying	Minister of Justice	*Tuanpai*	CCYL Shandong Dep. Sec., 82-89
Shen Yueyue	Vice Director, CCP Org. Dept.	*Tuanpai*	CCYL Ningbo Dep. Sec. and Zhejiang Sec., 83-93
Ling Jihua	Vice Director, CCP Central Office	*Tuanpai*	CCYL Central Com., 79-95 (Hu Jintao's *mishu*, 82-85)
Cai Wu	Director, Info. Office of CCP Cen. Com.	*Tuanpai*	CCYL Central Com., 83-95
Zhang Baoshun	Party Secretary of Shanxi	*Tuanpai*	CCYL Central Com., 78-93 (Secretariat, 82-93)
Wang Yang	Party Secretary of Chongqing	*Tuanpai*	CCYL Anhui Com., 82-84 (Dep. Sec., 83-84)
Song Xiuyan	Governor of Qinghai	*Tuanpai*	CCYL Qinghai Dep. Sec. & Sec., 83-88

Table 7.3. The Populist Coalition: Contenders with *Tuanpai* (CCYL) and Inland Backgrounds (cont'd)

Name	Current Position (By mid-2007)	Factional Identity	Factional Ties and Defining Experience With Dates (or years)
Yuan Chunqing	Governor of Shaanxi	*Tuanpai*	CCYL Central Com., 80-97 (Secretariat, 92-97)
Liu Qibao	Party Secretary of Guangxi	*Tuanpai*	CCYL Anhui Dep. Sec. & Sec. 82-83, CCYL Secretariat, 85-93
Zhao Leji	Party Secretary of Shaanxi	*Inland G.*	Provincial leadership in Qinghai, 86-05

Abbreviations: CCP=Chinese Communist Party, CCYL=Chinese Communist Youth League, Cen.=Central, Com.=Committee, Dep.=Deputy, Dept.=Department, Dir.=Director, G.=Group, Info.=Information, Org.=Organization, Sec.=Secretary.

Like Hu, most of these *tuanpai* officials have had provincial leadership experience, especially in the inland regions. Li Keqiang, Du Qinglin, Shen Yueyue, Zhang Baoshun, Wang Yang, Song Xiuyan, Yuan Chunqing, and Liu Qibao all have had administrative experience in inland provinces. Meanwhile, the *tuanpai* faction has formed their coalition primarily with provincial leaders in poor inland regions. This alignment was largely due to the fact that in the Jiang era, inland provinces were often marginalized, in terms of both economic resource allocation and political power, by Jiang's development strategy that favored the coastal regions, especially Shanghai. Inland leaders on the list, for example, Party Secretary of Shaanxi Zhao Leji, are often seen as supporters of Hu's policy shift to promote a more balanced regional development strategy.

Protecting the Interests of the Elitist Coalition

The growing power and influence of *tuanpai* leaders and the populist coalition under Hu has been at the expense of the influence of the Shanghai Gang and the elitist coalition. However, the Shanghai Gang and the elitist coalition still remain very powerful, especially in the Politburo and its Standing Committee. At a time when Hu Jintao and his team are laying the groundwork for the 17th Party Congress, Zeng Qinghong and others in the elitist coalition also will make sure that their interests will be protected. Specifically, they seek to secure as many seats as possible for the next Politburo.

Among the 29 leaders in this study, 12 (41%) candidates are from the elitist coalition, which consists of princelings, members of the Shanghai Gang, provincial and municipal leaders from the coast regions, and CEOs of flagship enterprises (see Table 7.4). Their political alliance is based on a combination of factors such as more privileged personal backgrounds, similar political values, and loosely defined common interests.

Three leaders in this study, Li Yizhong, Zhang Qingwei, and Liu Mingkang, do not have any factional affiliation.

The persistence of, and the resistance to, nepotism and favoritism in elite recruitment are seemingly contradictory developments in China during the present Reform Era. Political rising stars often have strong patron-client ties, but at the same time both the general public and the political establishment are quite critical of this trend. For example, many candidates on the ballot for the Central Committee did not get elected despite (or perhaps as a result of) their high-ranking family backgrounds. The Fifteenth Congress, like the two previous congresses, formed its

Table 7.4. The Elitist Coalition: Contenders with Princeling or Shanghai Faction Backgrounds

Name	Current Position (By mid-2007)	Factional Identity	Factional Ties and Defining Experience
Wang Qishan	Mayor of Beijing	Princeling	Son-in-law of Yao Yilin (former vice premier)
Ma Kai	Minister of Dev. & Reform Com.	Princeling	Son of a revolutionary veteran leader
Bo Xilai	Minister of Commerce	Princeling	Jiang's protégé, son of Bo Yibo (former vice premier)
Zhou Xiaochuan	Governor, People's Bank	Princeling	Jiang's protégé, son of Zhou Jiannan (former min.)
Xi Jinping	Party Secretary of Shanghai	Princeling	Son of Xi Zhongxun (former vice premier)
Han Zheng	Mayor of Shanghai	Shanghai Gang	Jiang's protégé
Wang Huning	Dir., CCP Institute on Pol. Research	Shanghai Gang	Jiang's protégé, Chair & Dean at Fudan U., 89-95
Jiang Jianqing	Governor, Ind. & Commercial Bank	Shanghai Gang	Shanghai Branch of Ind. & Commercial Bank, 86-99
Yang Jiechi	Minister of Foreign Affairs	Shanghai Gang	Jiang's protégé, a native of Shanghai
Li Hongzhong	Party Secretary of Shenzhen City	Coast Group	Jiang's protégé
Miao Wei	Party Secretary of Wuhan City	Enterprise Group	CEO of Dongfeng Auto Work Group Corp., 99-05
Zhu Yanfeng	CEO, First Auto Work Group Corp.	Enterprise Group	Zeng Qinghong's protégé

Abbreviations: CC=Central Committee, CCP=Chinese Communist Party, Com.=Commission, Dev.=Development, Ind.=Industrial, Min.=minister, and Pol.=Policy.

Central Committee by an "election with more candidates than posts." Many princelings were among the small percentage of candidates who were defeated. They included Chen Yuan, Wang Jun, and Bo Xilai, all sons of veteran Communist leaders. Among the ten elected alternate members receiving the lowest votes, five were princelings, including Wang Qishan, Liu Yandong, and Xi Jinping (who received the lowest number of votes).

Princelings are, of course, not necessarily unqualified for their leadership posts. Some princelings have changed bad public images by exhibiting good administrative performance. The drastic change in the public image of Beijing Mayor Wang Qishan is a good example. Members of emerging middle class, especially those associated with the new economic sector, will soon seek its own representatives in the top leadership, especially from those in the elitist coalition.

Interdependence of the Two Coalitions and New Policy Priorities

An analysis of the leadership experiences of the rising stars of the two coalitions also illustrates that they generally have divergent career paths. Table 7.5 compares leaders of these two coalitions in terms of their leadership experiences in eight functional areas: 1) foreign trade, 2) banking and finance, 3) industrial firms, 4) rural administration, 5) CCP organization work, 6) propaganda, 7) legal and disciplinary affairs, and 8) united front work. All the information is based on the biographies published by official Chinese sources.[12]

One of the most astonishing findings of this comparison is that none of the *tuanpai* candidates for the next Politburo have had work experience in foreign trade, finance, or banking. Of course, some of these leaders previously served as mayors, and some currently serve as governors whose primary responsibility is to promote economic growth in their cities or provinces. Those who serve as Party secretaries are also required to make important economic decisions. In a way, these *tuanpai* leaders are not necessarily ignorant of, or incapable of, handling economic issues. Nevertheless, none of the main work experiences of the most prominent *tuanpai* leaders has been in economic and financial administration, especially in the international area. *Tuanpai* leaders usually have had leadership experiences in non-economic fields such as CCP organization, propaganda, legal and disciplinary, and united front work. These experiences make them especially strong in rural administration. Some served as Party secretaries of the People's Communes and/or county early in their careers. These credentials may not be valuable in a country that prioritizes industrialization, foreign trade, and economic globalization, but are essential since the Hu administration emphasizes the need to pay more attention to social problems and political tensions among various interest groups.

In contrast, Table 7.5 also shows that the leaders of the elitist coalition are strong in industrial administration, foreign trade, finance and banking, but weak in the non-economic CCP functionary areas. With the exception of Bo Xilai who served as director of the Propaganda Department of the CCP Municipal Committee of Dalian between 1988 and 1989, these leaders do not have any leadership experience in these areas.

The divergent work experiences and administrative skills between these two coalitions suggest that neither the *tuanpai* nor the elitists is willing or able to defeat the other. This is partly due to the mutual recognition that they are in the same boat, and partly because these coalitions complement each other with respect to leadership skills and professional expertise. *Tuanpai* officials' lack of credentials in economics, especially in foreign trade and finance, is an inherent disadvantage for this group. Consequently, Hu's *tuanpai* officials must cooperate—and share power—with other groups. This fact reveals that although Hu is in charge, other political forces may be able to restrain his power. But this tension is a healthy political situation that may help prevent Hu and his protégés from wielding excessive power or achieving social fairness at the expense of economic development. Nevertheless, if the expected large increase in the number of like-minded *tuanpai* leaders manifests in the next Politburo, Hu will be more determined to carry out his own policy initiatives in the years to come.

Table 7.5. A Comparison of Leadership Experiences between the Populist Coalition and the Elitist Coalition

	Foreign Trade	Banking/ Finance	Ind. Exp.	Rural Exp.	CCP Org. Work	Propaganda	Legal & Dis. Affairs	United Front Work
Populist Coalition								
Li Keqiang				X				
Li Yuanchao						X		X
Liu Yandong					X		X	X
Du Qinglin			X	X	X		X	
Wu Aiying				X			X	X
Shen Yueyue					X			
Ling Jihua				X		X		
Cai Wu						X		
Zhang Baoshun						X		X
Wang Yang				X		X		
Song Xiuyan				X	X			X
Yuan Chunqing							X	
Liu Qibao						X		
Zhao Leji			X		X			

Table 7.5. A Comparison of Leadership Experiences between the Populist Coalition and the Elitist Coalition (cont'd)

	Foreign Trade	Banking/ Finance	Ind. Exp.	Rural Exp.	CCP Org. Work	Propaganda	Legal & Dis. Affairs	United Front Work
Elitist Coalition								
Wang Qishan		X		X				
Ma Kai	X							
Bo Xilai	X	X	X	X		X		
Zhou Xiaochuan		X						
Xi Jinping				X				
Han Zheng		X	X					
Wang Huning								
Jiang Jianqing		X						
Yang Jiechi								
Li Hongzhong	X		X					
Miao Wei			X					
Zhu Yanfeng			X					

Abbreviations: Dis.=Disciplinary, Exp.= Experience, Ind.=Industrial, and Org.=Organization.

Front Runners for the Next Politburo

Among all the candidates for membership to the 2007 Politburo, four leaders—Li Keqiang, Li Yuanchao, Wang Qishan, and Liu Yandong—are apparently the front-runners in the race for power. Their advantages over others are largely due to their current administrative positions, broad leadership experience, strong patron-client ties, educational credentials, and/or political achievements. None of them is new to the Chinese public, and, in fact, all four of them have served on the vice-provincial and ministerial level of leadership for about two decades.

Three of these upcoming leaders (Li Yuanchao, Wang Qishan, and Liu Yandong) are princelings (people who come from high-ranking official families), and three of them (Li Keqiang, Li Yuanchao, and Liu Yandong) are *tuanpai* who advanced their careers primarily from the CCYL. As they move into the highest level of authority, patron-client ties or family background that previously enabled them to succeed may become a liability. Their political credentials should now increasingly focus on their ability, skills, performance, and achievements—factors beyond their political networks.

Li Keqiang: A "Carbon Copy of Hu Jintao"

There are several important similarities between Li Keqiang and Hu Jintao. Both come from humble family backgrounds; both are natives of Anhui; both were student leaders in their college years; both advanced their political careers primarily from the CCYL; both served as provincial party secretaries at a relatively young age; both were long considered as candidates for top national leadership posts; both have the reputation of turning potential rivals into political allies; both have photographic memories when giving public speeches; and both have low-profile personalities and are known for generally not losing their tempers under difficult circumstances. Not surprisingly, some foreign observers refer to Li Keqiang as "a 13-year-younger carbon copy of Hu."[13]

Li Keqiang's political career thus far, however, has not been as smooth as that of Hu. Whereas Hu often received strong endorsement (and a large number of votes) from the political establishment, Li lost a few elections early in his career. In 1982, in the election of Beijing delegates to the 11th National Conference of the CCYL, Li failed to become a delegate despite the fact that he held the post of Secretary of the CCYL Committee of Beijing University. In the election to the Central Committee of the 14th Party Congress, Li was on the ballot as an alternate member, but was among the small number of candidates who failed to be elected. It was widely speculated that Li was nominated for a membership seat on the 16th Politburo, but was not successful because of his lack of accomplishments in Henan province.

Neither Hu nor Li can claim much success during their tenures as provincial heads. But in the case of Li, his provincial leadership accomplishments have, until now, been overshadowed by one disaster after another. In March 2000, two years after he became Henan Governor, a fire in a video theater of Jiaozuo city killed 74 people. Nine months later, another fire in a dance club in Luoyang city killed 309 people, which was the second largest deadly fire in PRC history. In addition, during his tenure as Henan Governor and Party Secretary, the province has been notorious for its "AIDS villages," coal mine explosions, and the prevalence of various sorts of fake goods produced in the province.[14] Li's bad luck seemed not to end after he moved to Liaoning in December 2004. Within a month after he was appointed Liaoning Party Secretary, a gas explosion ripped through the Sunjiawan coal mine in the province, killing 114 miners.

All these terrible incidents have apparently caused some delay in Li's further career promotion. But Li's capacity and "good luck" when it comes to his personal political survival have been remarkable. For example, Li was in charge of college affairs for the CCYL Central Committee during the 1989 Tiananmen student protest movement. This major event jeopardized the careers of many people on both sides of the conflict, including some of Li's friends and colleagues. Li not only survived the crisis, but also further advanced his political career.

Compared with other rising stars in his generation, Li currently demonstrates several advantages:

- Li not only has the longest tenure as a full member of the CCP Central Committee, but also has experience in running the country's two largest provinces, one predominantly agricultural and the other industrial.

- His main competitors, Li Yuanchao, Wang Qishan, and Liu Yandong, are all princelings who come from high-ranking official families. In contrast, Li Keqiang does not come from a high-ranking family, which is regarded unfavorably in the eyes of the Chinese public.

- Industrial accidents, coal mine explosions, health crises, and other disasters are not unique to Henan and Liaoning. Many other provinces in the country have also experienced similar incidents. It is interesting that most of Li's critics have attributed Li's poor performance in Henan to his "bad luck" rather than his lack of leadership ability. Those who have known him, including those who were Li's schoolmates at Beijing University and later became political dissidents in exile, often describe Li as "sharp, intelligent, thoughtful, and open-minded."[15]

- Li served in the CCYL central leadership for 16 years. Now that the CCYL has become Hu Jintao's most important powerbase, Li is expected to play a greater role in the future.

- Li apparently has been an enthusiastic supporter of Hu's agenda and policy initiatives. Under Li's leadership, the CCYL launched the young volunteer program to help relieve poverty in rural China in the late 1990s. Henan and Liaoning are the two provinces that have greatly benefited from Hu's two new development strategies—"the rise of central China" (*zhongyuan jueqi*) and "the northeastern rejuvenation" (*dongbei zhenxing*).

Li Yuanchao: A Princeling Turned **Tuanpai** Leader

Li Yuanchao's background is unusual. He began his political career in Shanghai, but he has not been associated with the Shanghai Gang since he left Shanghai in 1983, two years before Jiang Zemin and Zeng Qinghong arrived in the city as top municipal officials. He is a princeling (his father once served as Vice Mayor of Shanghai), but Li advanced his career primarily from the CCYL. During the reform era, princelings usually have taken positions in business firms or local governments in coastal cities, which provide more opportunities for financial profits and/or political careers. CCYL officials, in contrast, usually come from humble family backgrounds, and many from poor inland provinces.

Hu has long been known for his liberal views and his protection of CCYL officials who were targeted for their sympathetic position toward the 1989 Tiananmen student demonstration.[16] In 1990, Li himself was also demoted from a vice-minister level position in the CCYL to be a bureau director of the International Publicity of the CCP Central Committee. For the following decade, Li Yuanchao was not regarded as a rising star because he spent that time working in the areas of China's international publicity and cultural exchanges, which are generally not considered areas that breed future central political leaders. In the 1990s, he appeared to spend much of his time pursuing on-the-job postgraduate studies in economics and law.

A major turning point in Li's political career occurred in 2000 when he (at age 50) was appointed to be Deputy Party Secretary of Jiangsu Province. One year later, Li also assumed the post of Party Secretary of Nanjing, Jiangsu's capital city. This arrangement indicated that he would be the first in line to become full Party Secretary of the province, but also allowed him to show his ability and achievements in running the capital city of the province. Chinese journalists later called this arrangement "the Li Yuanchao model." Yuan Chunqing (consecutively Deputy Party Secretary of Shaanxi and Party Secretary of Xi'an) and Jiang Daming (consecutively Deputy Party Secretary of Shandong and Party Secretary of Jinan) followed suit. Both Yuan and Jiang are also *tuanpai* leaders.

To a great extent, Li Yuanchao's performance in Nanjing and Jiangsu can be perceived as a showcase for the coming-of-age of Hu Jintao's *tuanpai* leaders. During the past few years, especially after Li Yuanchao assumed the post of Party Secretary of Jiangsu at the end of 2002, Jiangsu Province has been the frontier of the country's political and administrative reforms. Li Yuanchao has arguably been tougher and more outspoken on issues regarding official corruption, government accountability, and the election of local leaders than any other provincial chief.

- In 2004, several high-profile leaders in Jiangsu were arrested on corruption charges. The most noticeable figures included the head of the Organization Department of the Jiangsu CCP Committee, the head of Jiangsu's Anti-Corruption Bureau, and the Chairman of the Jiangsu State Assets Commission.

- Li Yuanchao has initiated the concept of "service-oriented government" (*fuwuxing zhengfu*). He has also adopted the measure of public evaluation of leading officials in governmental institutions. Usually more than 10,000 citizens were asked to publicly evaluate local leaders each time. In 2002, for example, five heads of departments in the Nanjing Municipal Government who received poor evaluations were either demoted or fired. They included heads of the Environmental and City Planning Bureau and the Real Property Bureau.

- In both Nanjing and Jiangsu, Li has routinely implemented intra-Party elections of top local leaders. All 34 members of the Nanjing Municipal Committee of the CCP, for example, voted to select four district heads out of eight candidates. Similarly, all members of the Jiangsu Provincial Committee of the CCP voted on deputy-bureau-level leaders of the province. The purpose of this practice is to reduce the power of the Party chief (*diyibashou*) in decision-making bodies.

These measures described above, though not really democratic, are in line with Hu's populist approach. At a time of rapid socio-economic change in the country, Li seems to understand that these measures are far from sufficient to foster adaptation and growth. He recently criticized the mentality of some leaders who are "obsessed with stability" (*taiping guan*) and who refuse to try new political experiments.[17] Li believes that this mentality, though seemingly safe, is, in fact, dangerous because they may result in losing the good opportunity to effectively prevent more serious crises. According to him, Chinese leaders do not lack wisdom or ideas, but need more courage and "guts" to pursue bolder reforms. Only time will tell what Li hopes to accomplish through his "bolder reforms," and whether he will have the opportunity to play a larger role in the national leadership in the next decade.

Wang Qishan: "The Chief of the Fire Brigade"

Wang Qishan, widely known as "the chief of the fire brigade" (*jiuhuo duizhang*), is regarded as a leader who is capable and trustworthy in times of emergency or crisis. At the peak of the severe acute respiratory syndrome (SARS) epidemic in the spring of 2003, Wang Qishan was appointed to be Acting Mayor of Beijing, perhaps the hardest hit city. The day he arrived in the city, the number of people who were affected with SARS increased from 37 to 339.[18] Patients were dying, medical facilities were far from adequate, residents were in panic, alarming rumors were widespread, the government lost credibility, and some foreign observers called this crisis "China's Chernobyl." Some of the responses that Wang initiated were incredibly successful. For example, with the help of the military, an infectious disease field hospital with 1,000 beds was established in the suburb of Beijing within eight days. Not surprisingly, in the Beijing municipal congress meeting in the following year, Wang was confirmed mayor of Beijing with 742 "yes" votes and only one "no" vote from the delegates.

Wang's two previous appointments were also made in times of emergency. His appointment as Executive Vice Governor of Guangdong in 1998 was due to the need for Wang, an expert of finance and banking, to handle the bankruptcy of Guangdong Enterprises, a case he was viewed to have successfully managed. Wang's appointment as Party Secretary of Hainan in 2002 was related to attempts to solve a decade-long real estate bubble in Hainan. Wang's mission for Hainan was apparently unfinished due to his transfer to Beijing. Although he worked in Hainan for only five months, his emphasis on environmental concern and rural development was well received.

Wang Qishan is often perceived as a leading candidate to succeed Wen Jiabao as Premier in the future. Although Wang and Wen have different personalities and leadership styles, they are similar in many aspects. Both were born into intellectual families; both had the experience of working in poor rural areas; both are self-taught economists; both are favored by their common mentor (Zhu Rongji); neither is heavily associated with any political faction, although Wang is a princeling and has close personal ties with Jiang; both are popular administrators who communicate well with the ordinary people; and both pay great attention to detail. Wang's favorite quote is: "The devil is in the details."[19] Neither is hesitant to apologize for their mistakes. Wang often says: "No one can avoid making a mistake, but one should not repeat the same mistake."[20] Just as Wen Jiabao is an exceptional leader in the Fourth Generation, so is Wang Qishan in the Fifth Generation. Very few leaders in the Fifth Generation have the same combination of broad experience, professional expertise, and administrative skills of that of Wang. All these factors make Wang a formidable contender for a top post in the Chinese leadership in the future.

Liu Yandong: "A Lady Harmonizer"

Liu Yandong currently serves as director of the CCP United Front Work Department. This department has two primary missions: 1) to build ties between the Chinese Communist Party and various elements of Chinese society; and 2) to exert China's influence in Hong Kong and to win the hearts and minds of people in Taiwan with regard to peaceful unification with the Mainland. Both missions are crucial components of Hu Jintao's political agenda to build a harmonious society at home and strive to foster China's peaceful rise in the world. As she has gradually moved to the spotlight of Chinese politics, Liu often presents herself as "a lady harmonizer" who is sensitive to different opinions and able to reconcile contrasting interests in light of Chinese nationalism. On a visit to Hong Kong, Liu said to the media, "Keeping on good terms with others who hold different opinions is the essence of the Chinese nation."[21]

Liu's role as a harmonizer of tensions also extends to factional politics in the Chinese leadership. Liu has known Hu Jintao for over three decades, first at Qinghai University where both served as political councilors, and then in both the CCYL Secretariat and All-China Youth Federation where Liu served as Hu's deputy. Liu is also very close to Jiang Zemin and Zeng Qinghong. It was reported by the Chinese official media that Liu's father, Liu Ruilong, introduced Jiang's foster father Jiang Shangqing to the Communist movement in 1927.[22] The family ties between Liu and Zeng also can be traced to the early 1950s when both families were in Shanghai. Liu Ruilong served as Chief-of-Staff of the CCP Shanghai Municipal Committee while Zeng's father, Zeng Shan, served as Vice Mayor of Shanghai. During their years in Shanghai, Zeng Qinghong's mother, Deng Liujin, one of the few women who participated in the Long March, established a kindergarten exclusively for children of high-ranking officials. Liu attended the kindergarten. It was reported that Liu and other students visited Deng Liujin during holidays until Deng's death in 2003 at age 92.[23]

Liu has been considered a rising star for over two decades. In 1981, at age of 36, Liu was appointed as Deputy Party Secretary of the Chaoyang District in Beijing. A few other princelings who served as district-level leaders in Beijing at that time, for example, Chen Yuan and Tian Chengping, were soon promoted to more important positions. It was believed that the delay of Liu's promotion was largely due to the fact that during the 1989 Tiananmen movement, Liu argued that the authorities should have continued the dialogue with students instead of enforcing a military crackdown.[24]

Like many of her colleagues in the CCYL Secretariat, Liu is liberal-minded. Under her leadership, the Academy of Socialism, which is often regarded as the "No. 2 Central Party School," has launched many research projects for political reforms since the late 1990s.

All the factors discussed above—the growing importance of the united front work, Liu's strong ties with Hu Jintao and Zeng Qinghong, and her liberal-minded public image—seem to indicate that she will most likely obtain a seat in the Politburo, perhaps even becoming the first ever woman Standing Committee member in the CCP's history.

Potential Areas of Policy Change

As a result of the upcoming reshuffling in leadership, policy changes will most likely take place in the following three interrelated broad areas:

In economic development strategy, Hu's new team will place emphasis on three key aspects. First, while the new team understands that China cannot afford to lose foreign trade and foreign investment, they have also come to believe that the Chinese economy is too dependent on the outside world. The new leaders will gradually shift economic priority to the stimulation of demand in the domestic market, especially in the inland provinces. Second, partly because of their strong background and expertise in rural areas, Hu's new team will more aggressively seek to improve China's agricultural sector and enhance the standard of living of peasants through measures such as state bonds, favorable policies, tax breaks, and an increase of the price of agricultural goods. Third, inland developments (including western, central, and northeastern regions) will accelerate, but a large portion of resources will be allocated to Tianjin's New Binhai District with a plan to develop it as "North China's Pudong," in the hope of stimulating the economic development in the northern and northeastern regions of the country.

In terms of social policy, most leaders in the Fifth Generation, especially *tuanpai* officials, have been enthusiastic supporters of Hu's new initiatives for social policy. At a time when China faces serious challenges such as environmental degradation, energy scarcity, employment pressure, and economic disparity, Hu's team has come to realize that the Chinese leadership should pay more attention to the issue of social fairness. Two particular social policies may have far-reaching implications. First, China presently has 114 million migrant workers. It is expected that 200 million more will migrate to urban areas in the next 15 to 20 years. For over 50 years, the urban residence permit system (*hukou*) has prevented rural residents from settling down in urban areas by treating these migrants as second-class or third-class citizens. In the interests of social justice, Hu's new populist team will likely abolish the *hukou* system in the next few years. Second, China now has 130 million elderly people (who are 60-years old or above), accounting for 10.2% of the population, and the number and percentage will increase to 200 million (14%) in 2015. As China rapidly becomes an aging society, new leaders will have to make efforts to establish a social welfare system, especially a health care system in the country. Top leaders admitted recently that China's healthcare reform has failed. Hu's new team will make new experiments in this area.

The real dramatic change in Hu's second term will most likely be in the political arena. Many rising stars, e.g., Li Yuanchao, Li Keqiang, and Liu Yandong, are known for their open-mindedness and liberal views. These new leaders may be able to look beyond the burdens of events such as the Cultural Revolution and the 1989 Tiananmen Incident and are probably less scared of social protests and religious movements than were their predecessors. Consequently, these rising leaders may be bold enough to pursue more aggressive political reforms and elections. In addition, a large number of candidates in both coalitions for the next Politburo have received their education in the field of law and politics.

Tuanpai leaders are particularly strong in the area of non-economic functional areas. Their leadership legacy should be in the area in which they have an advantage. Also due to their functional work areas, *Tuanpai* leaders are arguably less corrupt than others. They may be more inclined to adopt anti-corruption measures and regulations.

The Chinese public discourse on democracy, the rule of law, human rights, political reforms, governmental accountability, NGOs, and civil society has arguably been more dynamic during the past two years than at any previous time in PRC history.[25] An encouraging sign is that two prominent scholars in this discourse, Yu Keping and Xia Yong, have served as advisors to Hu Jintao, and have been recently appointed to the posts of Deputy Director of the Central Bureau of Translation of the CCP and Director of the State Bureau of Secrecy, respectively. Both have written numerous books on these subjects.[26] The increasingly commercialized mass media will have independent voices, especially with China's further opening to the outside world with events such as the 2008 Beijing Olympics and 2010 Shanghai World Expo.

The recent peaceful and institutionalized transition of power from Jiang to Hu, the drastic changes in socio-economic policy as a result of the political secession, the dynamic balance of power that has arisen between the populist coalition and elitist coalition (especially with respect to the geographic regions and socio-economic interest groups represented by these two coalitions), and group characteristics of the Fifth Generation of leaders are all fascinating institutional developments that will likely engender further political changes. Recent political changes in both Taiwan and Hong Kong may provide more incentives and further confidence for Beijing to make political reforms. Any shrewd Chinese leader realizes that the peaceful reunification between the Chinese Mainland and Taiwan has the rise of China's own political democracy as a precondition.

No one should expect that China will develop a multi-party system in the near future. The Chinese democracy will, and should, have its own unique features. However, institutional checks and balances, political choices, constitutionalism, the independence of media, and civil liberty are the essential components for any democracy. Despite some understandable hesitance, China seems to be moving in this direction. The next decade or so will further test the wisdom and capabilities of Hu Jintao and his colleagues in the Fifth Generation.

Notes and References

1. The author is indebted to Yinsheng Li and Xiaobo Ma for their research assistance. The author also thanks Sally Carman, Michael Enright, and David Sands for suggesting ways in which to improve the chapter.

2. At the 16th Party Congress, the Third Generation of leaders was replaced by the Fourth Generation. With the exception of Hu Jintao, all other members of the previous Politburo Standing Committee retired. At the 17th Party Congress, the Fourth Generation of leaders—Hu Jintao, Wu Bangguo, Wen Jiaobao, and Li Changchun—will likely retain their seats on the Standing Committee.

3. Cheng Ying, *"Jujiao Zhonggong shiliujie wuzhong quanhui: Zhongguo de zhuanzhe"(Focusing on the Fifth Plenum of the Sixteenth Central Committee of the Chinese Communist Party: China's transition), Liaowang Dongfang Zhoukan (Oriental Outlook Weekly)*, October 9, 2005. Also see http://www.xinhuanet.com. October 9, 2005.

4. Cheng Li and Lynn White, "The Sixteenth Central Committee of the Chinese Communist Party: Hu Gets What?," *Asian Survey*, Vol. 43, No. 4 (July/August 2003), pp. 553-597.

5. The 16th Party Congress included 38 delegations. In addition
    to the two new delegations from enterprises and financial
    firms, there were 31 provincial and municipal delegations,
    one from the People's Liberation Army (PLA), one from the
    Central Party, one from the central government, one from
    Hong Kong and Macao, and one representing Taiwan.
6. *Shijie ribao (World Journal)*, November 12, 2002, sec. A, p. 3.
7. On the 1997 Politburo, seven (29%) studied in the Soviet
    Union or other East European countries; and other members
    of the Third Generation also had Soviet experience.
8. See http://www.chinesenewsnet.com. September 25, 2000.
9. During the early and mid-1970s, China sent a small number
    of students abroad to study foreign languages. This was largely
    to fill the growing need for interpreters following President
    Nixon's visit to China in 1972 and the PRC's newly-established
    or resumed diplomatic relations with Japan, Great Britain, and
    France.
10. See http://vweb.cycnet.com/cms/2004/ccylorg/index/
    introduction/t20060405_310720.htm. In 2002, the total
    number of CCYL members was about 68 million, including
    some 181,000 fulltime cadres. *Shijie ribao*, May 3, 2002, p.
    7, and http://cyc7.cycnet.com/zuzhi/worksnew/80year/
    introduce/index.htm.
11. *Zhongguo shibao* (China Times), July 13, 2005, p. 1.
12. The information is available from the Xinhua News Agency.
    See http://www.xinhuanet.com.
13. Peter Harmsen, "Mining Disaster Bad Luck for Rising Political
    Star," *The Standard*, February 21, 2005.
14. Li Keqiang was, of course, not responsible for the spread of
    the AIDS virus in the province caused by the poor standards
    for blood transmission because this problem occurred before
    his arrival in Henan. However, human rights groups often
    criticized Li for his cover-up of the extent of the AIDS problems
    in the province.

15. Wang Juntao, "*Beida fengyun jiuyou dianping*" *(Comment on a few distinguished alumni of Beijing University)*. See http://www.blogchina.com. December 25, 2005.

16. Soon after the 1989 Tiananmen movement, a group of CCYL officials, including Li's long-time colleague from Shanghai, Chen Haiyan, were purged or forced to leave the CCYL Central Committee. It was believed that Li tried to protect them. Ding Wang, *Hu Jintao yu gongqingtuan jieban qun (Hu Jintao and the successors of the Chinese Communist Youth Leagues)*, Hong Kong: Hong Kong Celebrities Press, 2005, p. 278.

17. See http://www.xinhuanet.com. August 11, 2005.

18. *Beijing ribao (Beijing Daily)*, April 23, 2003.

19. See http://www.chinanews.com.cn. January 26, 2005.

20. *Xinjing bao (New Capital Newspaper)*, January 26, 2005, p. 1.

21. *Taipei Times*, May 27, 2004, p. 5.

22. See http://www.xinhuanet.com. October 16, 2005.

23. Zi Ping (ed.), *Zhonggong zhengyao furen (Wives of Chinese Communist Leaders)*. Hong Kong: Globe Co., 1999, pp. 192-201.

24. Ding Wang, *Hu Jintao yu gongqingtuan jieban qun (Hu Jintao and the successors of the Chinese CommunistYouth Leagues)*. Hong Kong: Hong Kong Celebrities Press, 2005, p. 272.

25. For example, *Liaowang zhoukan* and *Liaowang dongfang zhoukan*, two official news magazines run by the Xinhua News Agency, frequently published articles on these topics.

26. For example, Yu Keping, *Shequn zhuyi (Communitarianism)*. Beijing: Beijing University Press, 2005; Yu Keping, *Zhongguo gongminshehui de xingqi yu zhili de bianqian (The emergence of civil society and its significance for governance reform in China)*. Beijing: Shehui kexuewenxian chubanshe, 2002; Xia Yong, *Yifa zhiguo – guojia yu shehui (Rule of law in governance: State and society)*, Beijing: Shehui kexue wenxian chubanshe, 2003; and XiaYong, *Zhongguo minquan zhexue (The philosophy of civil rights in the context of China)*. Beijing: Sanlian shudian, 2004.

8

Different Futures for China

Robert C. Broadfoot
Managing Director of Political &
Economic Risk Consultancy, Ltd.
and
Michael J. Enright
Director Asia-Pacific Competitiveness Programs, Hong Kong
Institute of Economics and Business Strategy
Sun Hung Kai Professor, University of Hong Kong
Director, Enright, Scott & Associates

Introduction

The purpose of this chapter is to provide the reader with a framework to assess the issues, variables, and uncertainties that will influence China's development over the next five to ten years. The chapter is not intended to forecast where China will be 10 years from now. Rather, it is structured around key uncertainties that China faces and five different, mutually exclusive scenarios for the future. The idea is to provide logical and alternative ways of thinking that the reader can use to test his or her own assumptions, think through logical consequences of certain developments, and create more robust long-term strategies.

The key uncertainties and descriptions discussed in this chapter are not scientifically or empirically determined, but to a large extent are the product of experience and imagination. The key uncertainties used in the analysis are the ability of China to maintain rapid economic growth, the cohesiveness of society on the Chinese Mainland (particularly the relationship between the Chinese government and its citizens), the state of relations across the Straits of Taiwan, and China's relations with the world's other great powers (proxied by China's relations with Japan).

Each uncertainty is associated with signposts that are worth close monitoring. With respect to economic developments, a rapid slowing of GDP or China's export growth could be a harbinger of economic difficulties. The number and extent of protests, noticeable frustration over corruption, and use of force to suppress demonstrations could be forerunners of deteriorating relations between the Chinese government and the Chinese people. Signposts concerning relations across the Taiwan Straits include the statements of the leaders on either side of the Straits, the next election in Taiwan, and the extent to which the Mainland leadership appears compelled to use nationalism and the "Taiwan issue" to shore up support at home. Signposts of China's relations with other powers will include the number and types of senior level government meetings; the degree of rhetoric over "historical issues," textbooks, and visits to the Yasukuni Shrine in Japanese relations; China's relations with "rogue states"; and trade tensions with the West.

In order to simplify the analysis, two potential outcomes were posited for each of the major uncertainties. Four uncertainties with two possible outcomes for each yield 16 potential scenarios. For the sake of space and simplicity, five specific scenarios were selected for further description and analysis. These were chosen to illustrate the analytical techniques, and to provide insights that go beyond the conventional wisdom, rather than as the most or least likely scenarios. Each of the five represents a unique combination of outcomes of the uncertainties with its own set of implications for corporate strategy for China operations, as well as for China's potential impact on the global economy and on global geopolitical conditions. Each will be associated with its own signposts, which could provide an early view as to which scenario might actually be evolving.

Building the Scenarios

Scenario analysis attempts to construct a set of different, but internally consistent pictures of the future as an aid to planning and decision making. Scenarios are not forecasts, in that they do not attempt to predict the future. Instead, by portraying a number of potential futures, they encourage individuals and organizations to think out of the box, to be prepared for eventualities outside the conventional wisdom, and to develop signposts that they can use to monitor future developments.

There are four basic criteria for valid sets of scenarios. The scenarios should be *plausible*, within the limits of what might conceivably happen, and without built-in inconsistencies that would undermine their credibility. They should be *different*, that is, not be simply variations of a base case but structurally different. They should be *useful for decision making*, each contributing insights into the future that will shed light on the opportunities and threats that an organization will face. Finally, scenarios should *challenge* the organization's conventional wisdom about the future.

We start by identifying what we assume are "constants" for any scenario for China's future. These "givens" need to be specified upfront because other analysts may choose to treat some of them as uncertainties rather than givens. Next we will identify the key uncertainties and potential outcomes that will underpin the scenarios. Some sense of the potential interactions of the uncertainties will also be explored. We will then build up a picture of the potential scenarios that can logically emerge from the outcomes of the critical uncertainties. A limited number of these scenarios will be fleshed out in order to provide greater insights into different paths for China's future. Finally, perspectives and implications will be drawn from the overall scenario analysis.

Key Assumptions and Critical Uncertainties

There are a number of key assumptions and critical uncertainties that underpin the scenario analysis of China's future. The assumptions are the givens that are expected to hold true, no matter which scenario eventuates. The uncertainties are those that are used to generate the scenarios.

Key Assumptions

In thinking about different futures for China over the next several years, it is useful first to identify major assumptions and "givens."

First, we assume that the Chinese Communist Party (Party) will place a high priority on retaining undisputed political power. Moreover, power at the top of the Party will not be so heavily concentrated in one person that factional interests become unimportant. A key role of the State President and Party General-Secretary will be to mediate the interplay of different factions and shape a consensus on key policy issues that preserves the semblance of political unity and cohesiveness.

Second, we assume that the Chinese government will remain unified on several important policies, such as Taiwan reunification and the need to maintain social stability. The government will tightly control and sometimes proscribe religious and other groups that are seen as potential threats to the Party's authority. The government will also appear very unified in its foreign policy toward such matters as Japan, U.S., and E.U. relations; in the management of China's special relationship with Hong Kong; and in China's position with respect to ASEAN, Russia, India, and the countries of Central Asia. Within the highest levels of government there might be differences of opinion on how best to implement these policies, but there will be a consensus on the ultimate policy goals and the desire to shield any differences of opinion from public view.

Third, we assume that although China is moving toward a more market-oriented system, China's leaders will continue to prefer administrative guidance over market tools like flexible interest rates and a freely floating exchange rate. In other words, when the Chinese government wants to cool down a sector it considers to be overheated or performing in a way other than desired, the authorities will feel more comfortable giving instructions to address the problem directly rather than relying solely on monetary or fiscal policies to bring about the desired result.

Fourth, China will not completely solve its institutional shortcomings in the next several years. This means that the big state-owned banks will continue to have problems with weak management and non-performing loans. The legal system will continue to lack independence from both the government and the Party. Corruption will remain a serious problem, as will physical problems with the local environment like air and water pollution. The local media will remain tightly controlled by the Party and the government, and will reflect official views and successes more than opposition or alternative views and failures.

Fifth, the struggle for power and resources between the central and local governments will remain a constant feature of the system.

Sixth, energy and raw materials security will remain a high priority for the government, as will the government's desire to move up the technology ladder and to create national state-owned companies (SOEs) that can compete with major multinational companies (MNCs) both at home and abroad.

Seventh, the relationship between the U.S. and Japan will remain extremely strong during the coming years. The two governments might have policy differences over exchange rate and trade issues, but these will be managed smoothly and will not detract from aligned views over North Korea, Taiwan, and most foreign policy matters. The U.S. will also remain very committed to Japan's defense and Japan will remain the closest ally of the U.S. in Asia.

Critical Uncertainties

China faces many uncertainties. For the present chapter, we will focus on four uncertainties that we believe are critical for China's future. These include China's ability to maintain rapid economic growth, the cohesion of China's society, the state of cross-Taiwan Straits relations, and the state of relations between China and the world's other great powers.

China's Economic Development

Although it experienced considerable volatility in the early years of the reform period, China's economy has grown at an average rate of approximately 10.5% per year for two decades. This growth has allowed China to bring more people out of poverty than in any other place at any other time in history. It also has cushioned the pain of one of the most far-reaching reform processes ever attempted. Many analysts believe that sustained economic growth has been perhaps the most important feature that has served to maintain the legitimacy of the Chinese Communist Party rule for the bulk of the populace. In addition, given the ongoing reform process and new entrants to the workforce, it has been estimated that rapid economic growth (on the order of 7% per year or more) is necessary to keep the process going and any backlash in abeyance.

Most analysts that follow China, forecast that the country can continue its rapid economic growth for at least another decade. They focus on how far China still has to go, the increasing sophistication of its economy, the expansion of domestic demand, the improvements in infrastructure, and the process of market-oriented reform that is likely to lead to the more efficient utilization of resources. Others point to problems in the financial sector, potential resource shortages, regional disparities, trade tensions, and problems associated with the growing rich-poor divide—and predict that China will be unable to sustain rapid economic growth. On balance, China's economic position seems strong and it would take a very significant event or events to push China off its development trajectory. However, the resolution to this uncertainty will determine if China will have the resources and will to continue its reform process, and whether China's leadership can continue to use economic growth as a legitimizing feature.

Cohesion in Chinese Society

The cohesion of Chinese society in general and the relationship between the Chinese government and people in particular represents another critical uncertainty for China. The arrangement that the Government has with the general population in China is not particularly well balanced. The Chinese government is not elected democratically and corruption is a persistent and damaging force. Since it is extremely difficult for average people to go through institutional channels to fight abuses, and the government's approach to fighting the problem is selective rather than comprehensive, people do not see the government (at least at local levels) so much as an ally in the fight against graft but as a central part of the problem. The lack of a comprehensive national welfare program is becoming a particularly glaring weakness, as the old method of fulfilling the basic housing, health, and education needs of the population through work units is being dismantled. Furthermore, regionalism and competition between municipalities and provinces has resulted in internal protectionism that fragments the economy and detracts from the government's ability to forge a strong national consensus. There are barriers to internal trade flows, infrastructure development, and dealing with environmental problems. Laws and regulations are implemented differently depending on the region. And local politics frequently interfere with national programs such as banking reform, the consolidation of certain over-crowded industries, and the adoption of national standards that could lead to greater economies of scale.

This combination means that the social contract between government and people in China is much weaker than in more advanced countries, and the Party stays in power largely because of its ability to prevent any opposition that can mount a serious challenge from emerging. The central government sets the rules and local governments implement them. People are expected to follow the rules, not to question or fight them. Many of the rules are deeply resented, but people feel pressured into obeying them. While there is far greater consensus in China today than during the Cultural Revolution, or during the days of the Tiananmen Square incident, there is no national consensus on issues like freedom of speech, freedom of press, religious rights, and birth control. In the absence of a national ideology that binds the country together, the Party uses its track record on economic development over the last two decades and nationalism over issues like Taiwan or Japanese textbooks and Prime Ministerial visits to the Yasukuni Shrine to enhance its position as leader and defender of the nation. The question is whether China will develop a more or less cohesive society than it has today and whether relations between the Party and the people will improve or deteriorate. The outcome of this uncertainty will go a long way toward determining how China develops and how open it ultimately becomes economically and politically.

Relations Across the Taiwan Straits

Uncertainties concerning the evolution of relations across the Taiwan Straits also will be critical for China. The PRC government has clearly made reunification, or at least not "losing" Taiwan, a national priority—probably only second after maintaining Communist Party rule. The differences between Taipei and Beijing go deeper than government-to-government relations. Taiwanese have no desire to go to war and would like to be able to take advantage of business opportunities on the Chinese Mainland, but there is a consensus within the island's population that prefers the island's democratic political system to the Mainland's authoritarian system. A growing sense of Taiwanese identity has been translated into support for the DPP of Chen Shui-bian, and a mounting sense of separation across the Straits.

Chinese leaders, for their part, describe Taiwanese independence as "a cancer" that could spread and, therefore, is something that cannot be permitted. This helps explain the sensitivity of PRC leaders to any hint or reference that might be construed as indicating that Taiwan has national status or independence, even to the extent of preventing Taiwan from obtaining observer status at the World Health Organization. The use of Taiwan as a rallying point for support of the Chinese Communist Party on the Chinese Mainland also implies that Taiwanese independence could shake the perceived legitimacy of the Party as the defender of the nation.

Relations with the World's Other Great Powers

The state of China's relations with other great powers, the U.S., the E.U., and Japan in particular, represent yet another critical uncertainty for China. While the China-U.S. relationship is probably the most influential in global terms, China's bilateral relationship with Japan is perhaps more interesting to analyze. This is because Japan and China are the major powers in East Asia, they face deep divisions over Japan's treatment of China in the 1930s and 1940s, and they are already coming into direct competition over energy resources. However, at the same time, there is much greater scope for China-Japan cooperation than China-U.S. cooperation, given the proximity of the Asian neighbors, their presence in a variety of Asian forums, and the fact that the economies of China and Japan are largely complementary. In addition, since Japan is increasingly acting as Washington's ally-proxy within Asia politically, militarily, and economically, the China-Japan uncertainty provides a proxy for China-U.S. relations as well. After all, Japan is almost certain to follow the U.S. line toward China on many issues, such as exchange rate matters, the treatment of Taiwan, and pressure on China to improve its protection of intellectual property.

China's relations with Japan could go in one of two directions in the years ahead: they could become more confrontational or they could become more cooperative. In 2004 and 2005, bilateral relations were marked by increased confrontation—as shown by the anti-Japanese demonstrations that took place in China in April and May 2005 over textbook changes in Japan; Chinese Vice-Premier Wu Yi's decision to cut short her trip to Japan and not meet with Prime Minister Junichiro Koizumi; Japan's announcement of a deadline for stopping aid to China; and Japan's decision to counter China's oil exploration activities in disputed waters with plans to mount its own exploration and development. While there were some signs of a thaw after new Prime Minister Shinzo Abe took office in 2006, elements of both confrontation and cooperation remain, with a changing balance between the two. China still wants to expand its exports to Japan and have access to Japanese technology. Japanese companies want access to the China market, and Japan already has a formidable investment presence in the Chinese Mainland that it wants to protect. One possible outcome is that China and Japan learn to accommodate each other, without becoming particularly close allies or irreconcilable enemies.

Outcomes of the Uncertainties and Scenarios

Each of the uncertainties can have a nearly infinite number of potential outcomes. While a number of the uncertainties could have "middle of the road" outcomes, for purposes of generating scenarios, it is useful to think in terms of extremes, since this reveals how the status quo could change in quite different directions. For this reason, and for ease of exposition, we will therefore assume that each major uncertainty has dichotomous outcomes.

The potential resolutions of the uncertainties then are as follows: In terms of China's economic performance, "Good Performance" will be taken as China's economy continuing to grow at a rapid rate, allowing for increasing individual and national prosperity and the redeployment of the vast majority of people displaced by the reform process. "Poor Performance" will be taken as a situation in which China's economic growth slows to much lower levels than in the past 20 years, causing incomes to stagnate and making the reform process more difficult to take forward.

In terms of China's internal cohesion, "Good Cohesion" is defined as Chinese society becoming more unified, with grievances of the people being addressed, and few challenges to Party rule. "Poor Cohesion" would be Chinese society becoming more fragmented, with the government and the Party being ineffective in dealing with grievances, and protests spilling over into direct challenges to Party rule.

In terms of relations across the Taiwan Straits, "Good Relations" would imply that overtures made by China's leadership to opposition forces and to business interests become decisive in Taiwan politics, leading to a Taiwan regime more amenable to linkages and discussions with the Mainland. Meanwhile, China would become more willing to keep the status quo and forego the military option. "Poor Relations" would involve clear movements towards independence within Taiwan, China's military build-up creating additional threats to Taiwan, cross-Straits rhetoric ratcheting up, and the potential for war escalating.

In terms of relations with foreign "Great Powers," "Good Relations" will be taken as China being increasingly viewed as a "responsible power" helping to resolve difficult international issues, human rights in China improving in the eyes of foreign powers, and China becoming less concerned that foreign powers are trying to contain its emergence. "Poor Relations" would involve China being viewed as an "irresponsible power," unwilling to help resolve international issues, human rights in China considered to be deteriorating, and China perceiving that foreign powers are trying to contain China internationally and are interfering in China's domestic affairs.

The uncertainties provide a rich set of possibilities. Four uncertainties, each with two potential outcomes results in 16 potential scenarios. These are depicted in Figure 8.1. Note that the uncertainties could in theory be listed in any order. We have chosen to portray them in the order listed above since China's economic performance will influence its ability to foster internal cohesion, which in turn will influence its posture toward Taiwan and foreign "Great Powers," though of course other causal patterns are possible.

There are a number of potential interactions among the uncertainties that yield interesting possibilities regarding China's future. For example, continued economic growth may allow China's leadership to work toward a more cohesive society by recognizing

Figure 8.1. The Scenario Tree

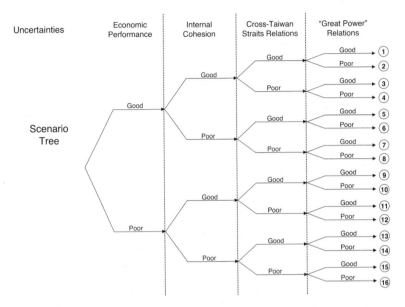

Source: Political and Economic Risk Consultancy, Limited and Enright, Scott & Associates, Limited

and dealing with the frustrations of many within the nation in a positive manner (Scenarios #1 through #4). On the other hand, if China's economy continues to grow rapidly, but only a small portion of China's population benefits from increased prosperity, the gap between the "haves" and "have nots" could create social pressure and unrest, resulting in poor internal cohesion (Scenarios #5 through #8).

Should China's economic performance suffer, China's leadership will have a more difficult time in fostering a cohesive—or in the words of President Hu Jintao—"harmonious" society (Scenarios #13 through #16). On the other hand, if the economy is in disarray, nationalism over Taiwan or historical issues with Japan might be used to create cohesiveness on the Mainland (Scenarios #9 through #12). Such nationalism might prove inconsistent with good relations across the Straits of Taiwan or with foreign great powers, making Scenarios #9, #10, and #11 possible, but perhaps not likely.

Perhaps the most likely cause for a massive deterioration of China's relations with foreign powers would be tensions across the Straits of Taiwan. This would be consistent with Scenarios #4, #8, #12, and #16. However, it is also possible for China's relations with foreign powers to deteriorate even if relations across the Straits of Taiwan become more cordial. In such cases, deterioration could be due to trade tensions, competition for resources, developments in North Korea, China's relationships with rogue states, or a failure to bridge the gap over historical issues with Japan. This would be consistent with Scenarios #2, #6, #10, and #14. There is even a case that could be made that it is logically possible for a worsening of tensions across the Straits of Taiwan not to create intractable problems in China's relations with foreign powers, if the Taiwan-related tensions were perceived as having been due to unilateral moves on the part of Taiwan. This would be consistent with Scenarios #3, #7, #11, and #15.

Scenarios for the Future

Instead of working through all the potential scenarios in Figure 8.1, it is useful to choose a limited number for further elaboration and illustration. We will focus on five scenarios corresponding to Scenarios #2, #1, #13, #16, and #8 in Figure 8.1. The reader can readily work through the remainder. The analysis used for these alternative scenario discussions will consider what must happen in order for each scenario end-state to arise. We are not trying to forecast any particular scenario. Instead, we think that the lack of predictability in each of the uncertainties employed in our scenarios is so great that none of the scenarios can be completely discounted. On the contrary, each has a sufficiently high probability of occurring that it has to be factored somehow in an organization's strategic thinking.

Scenario #2: Every Country for Itself

Sample Signposts for Scenario #2

- Elections are expanded and held at the township level.

- The Chinese government makes headway in dealing with such demographic problems as care of the elderly and medical obligations.

- Japan, the U.S., and the E.U. governments try to put new obstacles in the way of global acquisitions by China's top 200 firms, but these firms keep growing and at the expense of foreign competition.

- China reverts to a more hard-line approach toward Taiwan, forcing the issue in ways that Taiwanese and the island's current allies might not like but feel powerless to oppose. Taiwan conceptually capitulates, giving up hopes of independence, thereby reducing Taiwan as an international flashpoint, but continues to maintain its own system.

- Heavy costs of past unilateralism induce a U.S. withdrawal from certain military commitments in Asia, such as in Okinawa, Korea, and the Philippines, leaving Japan more responsible for security in the region.

- Beijing and Tokyo have conflicting and mutually exclusive leadership initiatives in East and Southeast Asia. China's economy is growing so strongly that Japan becomes more isolated in the region.

- The Japanese government raises its assessment of China's military threat, and vice versa.

The major features of this scenario (see Figure 8.2) are increasing confrontation between foreign powers and China, a growing national consensus in China that sees the general population throwing its support behind the government, and an easing of tensions across the Straits of Taiwan. For this to happen, China's economy will probably have to keep growing briskly. Its trade surplus and foreign exchange reserves will keep rising, prompting the U.S., Japan, and the E.U. to complain that the country continues to enjoy an unfair trading advantage. The government enjoys relatively high approval ratings and there is no groundswell in demand for change at the top. The Party continues to experiment with democracy at the very local level of government, but not at the provincial or national level. However, even limited democracy at the local level improves the transparency and accountability of the echelon of government that is most relevant to average Chinese.

Figure 8.2. Every Country for Itself

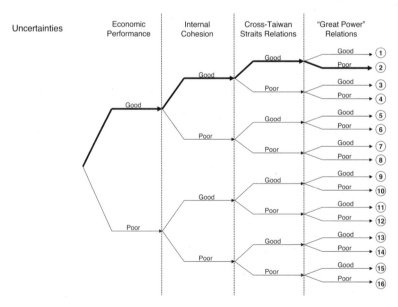

Source: Political and Economic Risk Consultancy, Limited and Enright, Scott & Associates, Limited

This scenario sees a narrowing of the disjuncture between the professed ideology of the Party and the way people experience everyday lives. The Party develops the governing capacity to deal with the multiple challenges it will be facing. Economic growth remains robust, agricultural producer prices remain reasonable, and some progress is made in income re-distribution to poor provinces/counties. The judicial system remains deficient, but the government earns respect as a referee that intervenes in ways that preserve what the people perceive to be "fairness," limiting extremes of corruption and other abuses that could upset social stability. The number of channels through which people can express their grievances increases and their quality improves. This does not mean these types of problems are solved, but it does mean they are not allowed to build to the point where they cause a destabilizing crisis. The government's attempts to make SOEs better managed and more competitive at home and abroad are largely successful.

However, the SOE-centered model that is a source of national pride in China becomes the target of foreign complaints. China's rapid growth increases its reliance on imported sources of oil and other commodities, so it will try to secure these materials by undertaking direct foreign investments and entering into bilateral agreements with supplying countries, irrespective of their international image. China thus moves closer to countries like Iran, Venezuela, and Sudan. China will also try to invest in developed markets like the U.S., but will encounter stiff opposition from governments and special interest groups in the developed countries. Although the developed countries voice a range of complaints against China, including human rights violations, lack of democracy, and lack of access for their companies to Chinese markets, the main argument against Chinese investment centers on the state ownership and control of the companies doing the investing. Japan and the West are increasingly afraid that China might have an economic model that can beat their own systems and create economic, social, and political problems for them.

Instead of bowing to foreign pressure and genuinely privatizing the SOEs that are turning into successful national champions, in this scenario China does exactly the opposite. The Chinese government intervenes in ways that consolidates state-owned industries, creating even more effective national champions. For example, the government orders PetroChina, Sinopec, and CNOOC to merge their foreign operations into a single entity so they are not competing against each other in the same markets. This would make it easier for China to negotiate long-term supply contracts and also to bid for certain foreign projects.

Because China's economy is growing rapidly in this scenario and its demand for energy and raw materials is rising, upward pressure on global commodity prices remains strong. This creates problems for other countries, including Japan, that are also competing for the same raw materials. The more that these countries use their political powers to interfere with China's investment and sourcing plans, the more that Beijing attaches national security considerations to its business initiatives. This means that Beijing will be willing to pay higher prices for its investments and raw material purchases than private companies from the U.S., Japan, and Europe that have to base their decisions strictly on commercial considerations.

Japan, for its part, will try to ensure that Russia builds an oil pipeline across Siberia to Nakhodka on Russia's east coast, where the fuel can be shipped to Japan, and it will try to block any attempt by China to build a spur to this pipeline that can channel supplies directly to China. Beijing and Tokyo will also step up oil exploration and development efforts in disputed waters in the East China Sea. Japan will argue that the need to defend these oil exploration exercises against Chinese threats is one reason why the country needs to enhance its military capabilities. The competition for energy resources will result in intensified confrontation between China and Japan—to the point where the military on both sides is called in to support commercial initiatives. In Japan, the government of Shinzo Abe favors a more assertive foreign policy and is supported by the United States government.

The U.S. will have enough problems on its hands fighting its global war on terrorism, trying to install stable, democratic governments in Iraq and Afghanistan, countering Iran's nuclear ambitions, and dealing with a domestic population that is increasingly tired of expanding foreign entanglements. Washington will not turn its back on Asia, but it will rely more on Japan to push the American agenda in the region. North Korea will remain a problem that the U.S. has to deal with directly, but in this scenario China will not use its leverage over Pyongyang to push for a settlement of the problem. In this scenario, Beijing does not want a war to erupt in the Korean Peninsula, but neither does it see much to be gained from helping to arrange a permanent solution.

Taiwan is a different matter. In this scenario, the Kuomintang (KMT) wins back the presidency and control over both the Executive and Legislative branches of the government. Beijing feels more comfortable with the KMT leadership than with the present DPP leadership, and enters into negotiations with the KMT that result in at least modest breakthroughs on direct trade and travel. Taiwan abandons its arms purchases from the U.S., on the grounds that they do more to aggravate Beijing than to offer any real protection to Taiwan. Thus, although China and Japan (as well as the U.S.) will see increasing friction over trade, investment, and many other issues, Taiwan will become less of a flashpoint, and there will be less cause for either Japan or the U.S. to confront Beijing on this issue.

The first tangible example of China's expanding international influence and the defusing of cross-Straits tensions will be the 2008 Beijing Olympics, when Chinese athletes perform exceptionally well and the facelift the government gives Beijing not only makes China look good in international eyes but also from a domestic perspective. Every time a Chinese athlete defeats Japanese or U.S.

athletes, local feelings of nationalism will be particularly noticeable, just as will Chinese support for the athletes of countries like Korea, India, African countries, and Latin America, but the really strong crowd support will be for athletes from Taiwan. The Games will be a unifying event for China and will generate support for the government, helping to give its leaders the confidence they need to act as if they have a genuine mandate. Confronting countries like Japan and the U.S. will serve as a unifying factor that gives Beijing even greater leeway at home.

If Taiwan can be removed as a variable in the equation, it will be much easier for China to adopt confrontational tactics against Japan and the U.S. without risking military retaliation. When Japanese leaders visit the Yasukuni Shrine to stress their nationalist credentials and use Japan's naval capabilities to confront China directly in the East China Sea, there will be a popular backlash in China with widespread demonstrations. Young, educated middle-class Chinese—without any encouragement from the government—will mount a consumer boycott of Japanese products, and Chinese workers at Japanese factories in China will go out on strike. Foreign investors' supply lines in China will be disrupted, and several will experience threats to property and personnel. In response, some Japanese companies will close their China operations and there will be a shift in investment focus by Japanese companies away from China to other countries like the Philippines, Vietnam, and India.

Protectionist sentiments against imports from China will grow not only in Japan, but also in the U.S. and the E.U. Companies from these countries that have substantial investments in China and are trying to develop both export business and the local market will find it much more difficult to lobby their home governments, as being seen as supportive of China risks a labor and investor backlash at home.

In this environment, the World Trade Organization (WTO) becomes much less effective at promoting free trade, since the former promoters of free trade, the U.S. and the E.U., are unilaterally adopting more protectionist policies in the face of growing competition—from China in manufacturing and India in services. Globalization suffers a serious setback. China, for its part, will focus more on entering bilateral trade agreements that build alliances and help sustain economic growth. Relations between China and ASEAN grow much closer, as do relations between China and the republics of Central Asia, a number of African countries, and several major Latin American countries like Venezuela and Brazil, which have their own reasons for decreasing their dependency on the U.S. and view China as an attractive alternative market.

One of the main developments in this scenario is that China succeeds in turning its domestic market into a powerful growth engine. China does not divest itself of its big holdings of U.S. Treasury Bills initially, but it stops investing in U.S. assets, placing pressure on U.S. interest rates and property prices, hurting consumer spending, and potentially sending the U.S. economy into recession. In response, China focuses much more on improving investment returns in China and the quality of life there. It focuses on such projects as housing, public transportation, electrification, and cleaning up the environment. These projects stimulate growth, but they also draw in more imports. Because developed countries have taken the lead in discriminating against Chinese exports and the WTO is ineffective as an organization, China is able to retaliate by being very selective in the types of imports it admits and by using its purchasing clout to build strategic alliances.

In this scenario, the imbalance between U.S. domestic and international commitments and U.S. budget capabilities seriously strains Washington's capacity to carry out multiple missions. The U.S. is forced to rely on Japan to shoulder the cost and burden of Asian leadership. But the unwillingness or inability of the U.S. to project its own influence directly in Asia makes China much less reluctant to adopt a much more confrontational approach versus

Japan. China is particularly active in forging closer economic relationships with its immediate neighbors, from Thailand to Korea and even with India, but the scope of its influence will be far greater than its immediate region. Chinese markets and investments will be engines for growth in much of the developing world, although not with the same strings attached as the U.S.

Scenario #1: One for All and All for One

Sample Signposts for Scenario #1

- Same as the first two points in Scenario #2, i.e., hard evidence that the government is building a more inclusive system and addressing the problems of the most disadvantaged segments of society.

- Clear moves toward accommodation with the increasingly complex and pluralistic society would begin with the revival of the 1987 political reform program and see China evolve in the direction of its East Asian neighbors.

- There is hard evidence of state resources being redirected away from the inefficient parts of the state sector towards the more productive private sector.

- Increasingly frequent visits by top leaders of both China and Japan illustrate both the desire for comprehensive agreements and the scope of the problems to be resolved.

- Foreign investment in service industries is liberalized very rapidly, generating a boom in service sector jobs.

- There are a growing number of investments not only by Japanese companies in Chinese companies, but also by Chinese companies in Japanese companies.

- China's gamble on a policy aimed at gradual absorption of Taiwan rather than one focused on militancy starts to pay off, as can be seen by progress in cross-Straits negotiations.

- The U.S. and the E.U. remove their embargo on the sale of arms to China.

- China is invited to join the larger G8 community.

- Tokyo and Beijing begin negotiations for a bilateral free trade agreement.

This scenario (see Figure 8.3) is similar in some ways to Scenario #2. Many of the same developments that result in a much stronger national consensus occur in this scenario too. These include the continuation of rapid economic growth, some progress in income re-distribution to poor provinces/counties, and successful experiments with elections at the local level. Key institutions like the banks and the local stock market are strengthened. China bows to international pressure and adopts a flexible exchange rate. China's exports keep growing, but the growth of imports is even more rapid, creating opportunities for Japanese, U.S., and European exporters that keep protectionist pressures in these countries in check.

Exactly as in Scenario #2, the 2008 Olympic Games are a strong unifying event for China. They become a building block for better relations with Taiwan, where political developments have evolved in a way that sees independence advocates marginalized, and a general consensus emerges for closer relations with Beijing.

Figure 8.3. One for All and All for One

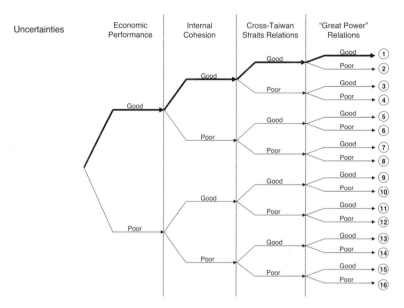

Source: Political and Economic Risk Consultancy, Limited and Enright, Scott & Associates, Limited

China reciprocates by toning down its military rhetoric, moving missiles away from its borders facing Taiwan, and enters into serious negotiations that will permit the resumption of direct cross-Straits trade and travel. Japan, the U.S., and other foreign governments welcome this improvement in cross-Straits relations and try to encourage it.

In Japan, nationalist forces are kept in check by more pacifist segments of society. Leaders start to shun Yasukuni Shrine visits, reduce the whitewashing of Japanese atrocities during World War II, and enter into negotiations with China to resolve issues that affect the national interests of both countries. These negotiations result in a cooperative rather than a competitive approach on energy and environmental problems. Eager to expand their presence in the China market, Japanese car companies agree to transfer some of their energy-saving technology to China to help reduce emissions and save on gas consumption. Instead of competing for the same supplies of oil and gas, China and Japan agree to cooperate on ways that open up new supplies. The two countries reach a formula for jointly developing and sharing oil and gas resources in the East China Sea and sharing access to Siberian oil. China signs oil exploration and development deals with the Central Asian republics, gaining new supplies that do not have to be transported on international shipping routes and helping to promote the development of western China. Japanese and Western oil companies participate in this new pipeline construction in China, which is a joint venture rather than 100% state-owned.

One key to this scenario is growing involvement of Japanese and other foreign companies in China, and the involvement of Chinese SOEs in the Japanese, U.S., and European economies. China's national champions such as Lenovo and Haier become genuinely competitive multinationals, with accepted international brands, investments in the developed world that are major employers in these countries, and listed entities with significant foreign equity and dividend payments to foreign shareholders. Forces in Japan and the West that are trying to block the foreign investments of Chinese SOEs are overruled by other interests that see these investments as positive. In addition to the commercial incentives for allowing such investments, the argument that holds sway is that the greater China's involvement in the Japanese and U.S. economies, the bigger its stake in their success and the more powerful is China's incentive to avoid bilateral frictions—political as well as economic. In an extreme version of this scenario, China and Japan would sign a free trade agreement, prompting other Asian countries to seek similar favorable treatment, and pushing Asia in the direction of a genuine common market.

In short, this is a scenario in which Japan and China learn to accommodate each other and China is accepted by the major countries in the world as a team player, not an enemy. Stability is fortified by the mutual dependency between the economies, and forces of nationalism—although always a concern—are not allowed to dictate the agendas of either China or Japan (or the U.S., for that matter).

The U.S. remains closely allied with Japan in this scenario, but it is not so overstretched by its other international and domestic commitments that it becomes less involved in Asia. Moreover, China cooperates with the U.S. on endeavors such as in discouraging North Korea from developing nuclear weapons while helping it develop a more successful economy of its own. Beijing also supports the U.S. initiative to stop Iran from developing nuclear capabilities. In other words, while there are points of disagreement and friction, they are managed, and there is also a strong emphasis on cooperating on issues that are of mutual interest.

Scenario #13: The Gorbachev Scenario

Sample Signposts for Scenario #13

- Environmental problems, disease, and natural disasters overwhelm the Chinese government's capabilities to deal with them, forcing Beijing to look to Japan, the U.S., and other countries for help.

- Economic growth slows, causing increased tension among different domestic groups over how the economic pie should be split. Beijing adopts market-solutions, such as higher interest rates, a reduction of subsidies, and other measures that cause pain to certain groups, but receives the backing of foreign governments that have long advocated such reforms.

- Initial attempts at democracy at the village level release pent up frustrations and the voicing of complaints, but there is no quick or easy way to address these complaints.

- Labor unrest is sparked by high-profile bankruptcies of major state-owned companies, resulting in major layoffs.

- In the longer term, the lack of channels to express legitimate grievances results in a mushrooming of demonstrations, which are mainly directed at the local level, but the government does not crack down. Instead, debates surface within the top level of the CCP over the need for reform and how to provide better representation for disadvantaged groups so as to stabilize the system. Actual reform is too slow to stop demonstrations. Instead, the loudest protestors get priority attention in resolving their grievances.

- Social problems are further compounded by a rise in crime, corruption, money laundering, and other ills that anger the local population, much as organized crime grew rapidly in Russia once the Communist Party there started losing its grip. Beijing and foreign governments cooperate to fight this crime.

Scenario #13 (see Figure 8.4) is an environment in which there is little domestic harmony, but the international community is largely supportive of China. This implies two possible outcomes. First, that Beijing seriously addresses many of the systemic deficiencies and other problems which Japan, the U.S., the E.U., and other major trading partners have pointed out. Second, that dislocations to domestic life caused by reforms are so grievous that they generate serious resistance, and turn large parts of the population against the government.

Figure 8.4. The Gorbachev Scenario

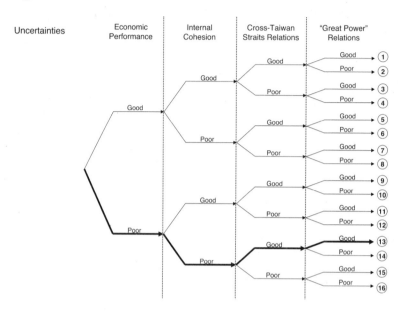

Source: Political and Economic Risk Consultancy, Limited and Enright, Scott & Associates, Limited

In this scenario, accommodation is reached with Taiwan, but in a way that splits society on the Mainland, as some criticize the PRC leadership for perceived weakness. Beijing would also probably be cooperating with Japan, the U.S., and South Korea in pushing North Korea to refrain from developing nuclear weapons. China would be an active member of the World Trade Organization and would make substantive progress in bringing its own practices like intellectual property rights protection, foreign investment regulations, and corporate governance standards more into line with international standards.

In this scenario, China liberalizes controls on its television and radio stations, permitting foreign broadcasters to operate channels and relaxing what censors refer to as "political standards." The Internet and the new generation of cellular telephone technology facilitate the spread of uncensored information, particularly among more educated, middle-class Chinese. The government also experiments more with democracy at the local level. Village elections in the countryside and neighborhood committees become more common, raising popular assertiveness on policy issues and sparking debate in Beijing as to if and how electoral experiments should be expanded to higher levels. However, just because there are more outlets for people to express their grievances does not mean that there is fast progress in fixing these problems. The government lacks the resources to do so and must therefore prioritize. It addresses those problems first where there is the biggest public outcry to do so, which creates an incentive for people to adopt disruptive pressuring tactics.

Further into this scenario, the government decides that it wants an efficient stock market rather than a politically-dominated one. It lets ailing local financial companies die and invites experienced foreign firms to build the markets. More Chinese companies are allowed access to capital markets. People avoid firms with non-tradable shares and, instead, money flows to genuine private firms and foreign-owned investments that gain the right to list on Chinese exchanges. China's leadership decides that the duds among Chinese listed companies should be de-listed and allowed to wither. The remaining state-owned enterprises are sold as quickly as possible and investors left to set their value. This set of reforms seriously disrupts the market—something reformers in Beijing, backed up by foreign advisers and governments, argue is the only way to put the local capital market on a solid long-term footing.

Unfortunately from the perspective of many local Chinese, this shock therapy is all shock and no therapy, as the harsh reality of the competitive marketplace is a rude awakening for many Chinese banks and companies. Today, many of China's leading state-owned companies are confident that they are about to join the ranks of the world's largest and most successful companies. But several years into this scenario makes it clear that these firms are not really up to the competitive challenges abroad. Market conditions turn sharply against them. Indeed, market conditions are the primary catalyst of developments in this scenario. The government in Beijing has used rapid economic growth as the main way to keep the public behind it, but in this scenario growth slows sharply—not just for six months or one year, but for two or three years.

Part of the slowdown takes place internationally. The Japanese government contributes to the economic problems by raising taxes in order to address the burgeoning government debt problem, snuffing out the country's recovery. The real culprit, however, is the U.S., which sees consumer spending go into a deep slump once the U.S. housing bubble bursts. With the Chinese currency having been de-linked from the U.S. dollar, the greenback's slump in the foreign exchange market in this scenario results in a drop in U.S. demand for imports, including from China.

As China's export sector slips into low gear, profits at many Chinese firms slump. Moreover, in the early stages of this downturn, foreign companies perceive the Chinese market to be one of the few bright spots in the world. They therefore intensify their push into the country both through direct investments and exports. This further cuts profit margins for both foreign and Chinese companies, resulting in hard times for many local manufacturers. Residential property prices in Guangdong, Shanghai, and Beijing fall sharply in this environment and people who had been counting on a steady increase in their incomes to finance a housing purchase suddenly find themselves strapped for cash. Families that purchased their homes at the height of the market suddenly find their asset values have fallen sharply. Consequently, consumer spending in China weakens markedly and deflationary conditions set in.

The weak local and international environments cause commodity prices to fall sharply, making foreign assets purchased by Chinese interests when prices were at their peak look like bad deals. Investors turn against the companies involved and their share prices fall sharply. Agricultural producer prices also weaken, making life very difficult for Chinese farmers and increasing the flow of migrant labor in search of work, which is harder to come by, into the cities. The government does not have the resources to spend its way out of these problems. The Chinese economic pie, which had been expanding so rapidly for nearly two decades, suddenly stops growing, making it impossible to redistribute income to poorer provinces when they are most in need.

In this scenario, fault-lines develop between provinces that the central government is unable to mediate effectively. Wealthier provinces and municipalities are unwilling to transfer their wealth to poorer areas of the country. All provinces are competing for the same investment and export markets and oppose attempts by the government to dismantle internal barriers to business. The fault-lines extend to the cultural level—with people from Shanghai, Beijing, Guangdong, and other areas—reluctant to cooperate with people who are not from their particular area.

Some of the government's biggest problems in this scenario occur with average middle-class households in major urban areas. For the first time in China's post-1949 history, these households have significant assets of their own other than deposits with state-owned banks that the government always supports. These households have residential properties and own shares of companies listed on China's stock market. They also have many more personal financial obligations, including health and education expenses, than was the case when the work unit took care of such needs. In this scenario, average Chinese resent the sharp fall in their asset wealth that takes place because of what they see as the government's mismanagement. Demonstrations increase and the government finds itself very much on the defensive. In other words, China might still have good international relations, but could find itself in domestic disarray. This is our Gorbachev scenario.

Scenario #16: Tiananmen II

Sample Signposts for Scenario #16

- An increase in domestic repression in the name of maintaining social stability and a more xenophobic international posture results in the CCP becoming widely viewed within China as the instrument of rule for the new Chinese economic and power elites, rather than a force acting for China's people as a whole. The share of the economy in the hands of the 10% of the population expands to 60% from the current 45%.

- Pandemic outbreaks, compounding other growing health crises cause a much greater loss of life in poorer rural areas than in wealthier urban areas. One response by local governments is to enforce the isolation of the poor from the rich.

- Corruption intensifies but the government clamps down on information flows, preventing an open discussion of increasingly overt problems. Disaffected groups decide they have nothing to lose and take to the streets. Protests start to focus more on the mistakes and shortcomings of the central government, not just on those of the local governments.

- National champion companies that have listed on international markets lose out to international competition and suffer an adverse swing in market conditions, leaving foreign shareholders and joint venture partners with an unfair share of the losses.

- Nationalism is manifested too forcefully, causing major Japanese and other foreign companies to pull out of China.

- Taiwan holds a national referendum despite threats from Beijing to use military force. Tokyo and the U.S. come to the protection of Taiwan and Beijing is unable to carry out its threats.

The above scenario posits a difficult environment for China's Communist Party and the Chinese government (see Figure 8.5). Beijing is increasingly locked in conflict with major foreign governments like Japan, the U.S., and key members of the E.U., while it also is facing mounting challenges to its leadership at home in the form of greater regionalism, corruption, crime,

Figure 8.5. Tiananmen II

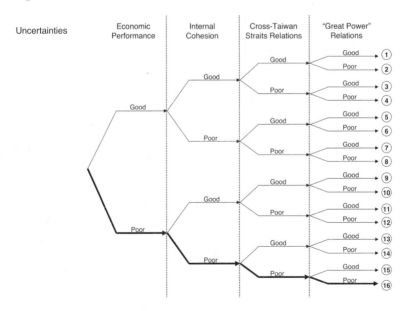

Source: Political and Economic Risk Consultancy, Limited and Enright, Scott & Associates, Limited

and demonstrations by people who feel they have been unfairly victimized and are frustrated by the lack of official channels to seek redress. China's so-called "sustainable model for development" that calls for a balance between economic growth, environmental conditions, social stability, and national security interests starts faltering badly.

Early in this scenario, it will become clear that the world has become more protectionist against Chinese exports and China's merger and acquisition efforts. The E.U. erects more barriers to Chinese exports, while the U.S. Department of Commerce and International Trade Commission find in favor of U.S. companies seeking import duties to offset what they claim are unfair subsidizes from Beijing. The U.S. and Japan take punitive trade action against China on the grounds that China is not in compliance with its trade commitments in areas such as intellectual property rights and agriculture. The U.S. government also passes a bill that would give the federal government the right to veto any proposed merger or acquisition of a U.S. company involving a government-controlled foreign company.

The decision to revalue the *yuan* and to attach it to a basket of currencies instead of just to the U.S. dollar does not reduce foreign complaints against China. Instead, the move merely convinces foreign governments like Japan and the U.S. that the only way to get Beijing to act on an issue is to force it to do so. Beijing might argue that outside pressure will not force its hand, but its actions speak otherwise, prompting foreign governments to step up their confrontational tactics.

The U.S. and Japan also increasingly view China as a national security threat in this scenario. The Pentagon's 2005 report on China asserting that Beijing's military buildup could pose a threat to U.S. allies in Asia and upset the regional balance of power prompts Washington to encourage Japan to raise its own military profile, which it does by reforming its Constitution.

The government changes in South Korea, with the Uri Party losing the next presidential election to the opposition GNP, which also increases its majority in the National Assembly. The new Korean president tries to improve the South's ties with Washington by dropping President Roh Moo-hyun's conciliatory policy toward North Korea and, instead, supporting the more hard-line, non-compromising approach of the U.S.

In Taiwan, the infighting within the opposition parties prevents the KMT from unifying behind a single presidential candidate, opening the door for the DPP not only to retain the presidency but also to gain a majority in the legislature. Taipei does not formally pursue independence, but it does invest heavily in new weapons systems and institutionalizes the process of holding national referendums on important issues—a policy that Beijing strongly opposes. Cross-Straits relations deteriorate badly in this scenario. China threatens to use military force if Taiwan does not behave, but both Japan and the U.S. intervene with comments that they will continue to support Taiwan's autonomy, provided the island does not formally declare independence.

Japan also confronts China in the East China Sea. Japan's oil exploration efforts anger China and lead to a flexing of military muscles by both sides, but the exploration does not turn up significant amounts of oil or gas, which also means there are no oil and gas deposits on the Chinese side of the border. This intensifies China's desire to secure foreign sources of petroleum supplies, but it is frustrated in these efforts by Japan's success in securing a deal with Russia and by U.S. and European interests locking up oil resources in the Central Asian republics. China is also unable to buy major foreign oil companies because of the unwillingness of the U.S. or European governments to allow the acquisitions to go through. China therefore deals more with rogue states like Iran and sides with those states in their disputes with the U.S.

As bad as this external picture is for China, the country's leaders are more concerned with domestic problems. The deceleration in China's exports to the U.S., Japan, and Europe hurts China's domestic growth rates. The government is embarrassed by the failure of its national champion companies to perform well internationally. Foreign investors lose their appetite for the shares of these companies, and China's domestic stock market fails to develop, because of the poor performance of the listed companies and the overhang of state-owned shares. Fraud in the securities industry costs Chinese their private savings and sparks a backlash against the government for permitting this to happen. The government fails to develop public trust in the equity and bond markets, keeping the country's financial foundations shaky.

In this scenario, environmental problems like air and water pollution intensify, creating real hardships for many regions. The situation is so bad in Hong Kong that it becomes a political issue that strains the territory's relations with neighboring Guangdong province, where most of the pollution originates. China's government also fails to develop adequate infrastructure, so power blackouts worsen. A serious flu epidemic originating in Southern China hurts the government's reputation with the local population as well as with the outside world.

The less confident the political leadership is at home, the more aggressively nationalist it is likely to be abroad. Beijing actually encourages anti-Japanese sentiment over the use of school textbooks that downplay the nation's wartime atrocities in Asia and Japan's assertive posture in disputed territories in the East China Sea. Average Chinese use their cellular phones and the Internet to mobilize demonstrations against the Japanese. Some Japanese property in China is damaged and workers at Japanese-owned companies go out on strike. This prompts Japanese and other foreign companies to reconsider investment plans in China.

But the protests do not stop with the Japanese. Although feelings against the Japanese are strong, many of the Chinese who join the anti-Japanese demonstrations have more serious grievances that they also start expressing in their demonstrations, and many of these complaints are directed against China's Communist Party and government. People blame the country's leaders for allowing growth to slow, for permitting corruption to flourish, for environmental problems, for the falling local housing prices, and for failing to provide basic social welfare needs. What starts out as protests with an anti-foreign focus therefore turn into demonstrations about domestic grievances.

The 2008 Olympics turn into a nightmare for the Chinese leadership. They had hoped to use the Games as a "coming out party" for China, to show the world and average Chinese that China has finally become one of the world's great powers. Instead, the Games take place in an extremely divisive atmosphere. Foreigners like Japanese and Americans feel uncomfortable with the way they are treated, and instead of putting on a unified face for the world, the Chinese public shows it is very unhappy with its situation. The government responds with force, clamping down on any forms of unrest, but this merely creates more discontent. People are also extremely unhappy about the cost of the Olympics. They are told—not asked—to dig into their own pockets to cover the cost of the Games. This creates huge resentment directed against the government.

If we take this scenario to its extreme point, China's current leadership under President Hu Jintao faces an internal rebellion. To be sure, there is no alternative domestic group in a position to take over the government. However, it is possible that rival factions within the CCP could allow their differences to surface in this kind of stressful environment. President Hu and his supporters could be accused of allowing social instability to intensify to the point where the Party is threatened. This would open the door for one of the rivals to Mr. Hu to make a bid for power, or for the Party's old guard (who have retired from active office but still wield considerable influence) to order a major shake-up in China's Party and government, similar to what happened in the wake of the 1989 Tiananmen demonstrations. This is why we have named this scenario Tiananmen II.

Scenario #8: The China First Scenario

Sample Signposts for Scenario #8

- The economy continues to grow rapidly, but increasing tensions between China and major Western countries force China to focus less on trade with these countries and more on trade and investment with the developing world.

- Major headway is made in developing internationally competitive domestic industries, but foreign companies are increasingly excluded from this development. Instead, it is led by Chinese companies.

- Regional and urban-rural disparities, as well as wealth disparities within major metropolitan areas are exacerbated, leading to tension and instances of localized unrest.

- Corruption intensifies, but the government clamps down on information flows, preventing an open discussion of increasingly obvious problems. Protests start to focus more on the mistakes and shortcomings of the national government, not just the local governments. The government responds with force, suppressing discontent, but failing to address its root causes.

- The central government tries to reign in rapidly growing provinces, but is only partially successful.

- China increases the pressure on Taiwan by steadily increasing its military capability and by wooing Taiwan's leading business people. Taiwan reacts by electing independence-minded politicians.

- China's "go it alone" approach to obtaining natural resources and supporting "rogue" states sours relations with foreign powers. China competes with the U.S. and other developed countries for influence in Southeast Asia, Africa, and Latin America.

- Trade tensions mount as China's trade surplus and foreign reserve position balloons.

- Economic nationalism in China further hinders the development of positive investment and trade relationships.

In this scenario (see Figure 8.6), China's economic growth continues nearly unabated. However, one of the major features of this scenario is that the engine for this growth progressively shifts to domestic-led sources rather than external ones, and foreign companies are increasingly excluded from participating in these

Figure 8.6. The China First Scenario

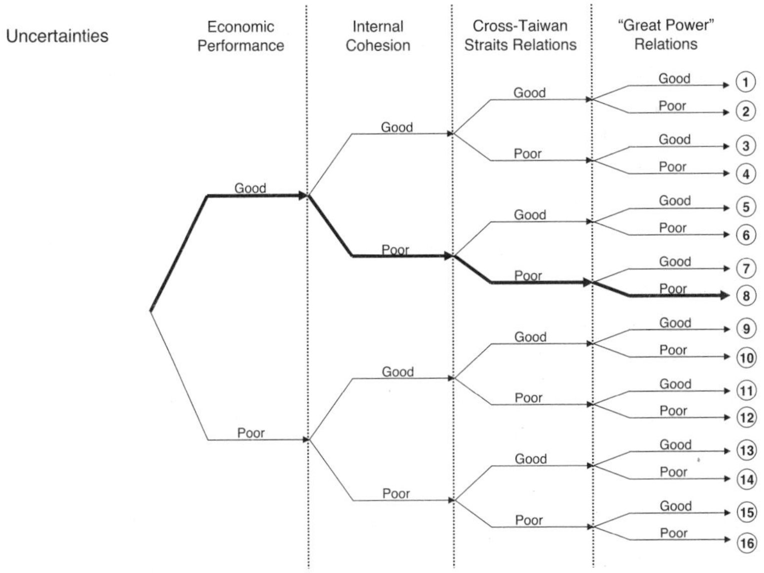

Source: Political and Economic Risk Consultancy, Limited and Enright, Scott & Associates, Limited

domestic industries. Instead, Chinese companies pioneer solutions to Chinese problems like housing, energy, and transportation, and in the process they develop new technologies and business models that are internationally competitive. The developed West finds China to be even more of a competitive threat, while the developing world finds China an attractive alternative business partner to the West. China's influence on the international stage therefore increases, but in ways that put it more at odds with the U.S., the E.U., and Japan.

In this scenario, China's export machine still drives record trade surpluses which foreign governments try, but fail, to contain. China's own domestic market becomes a true growth engine as the country's second and third tier cities, now linked with highways and rail lines, start developing rapidly. Attempts to avoid overheating are partially successful, but not successful enough to reduce economic growth to the targeted rates. Greater reliance on domestic growth makes China less beholden to international interests and international organizations. As a result, China starts to make it more difficult for foreign firms operating in China, which are increasingly seen as having profiteered at the expense of the Chinese people.

In this scenario, the main reason internal coherence is poor is widening disparities in wealth. There is a growing sense of injustice as the have-nots begin to covet the wealth of the haves, but the government uses force to prevent these frustrations from erupting on a scale that could disrupt the economy or threaten the dominant position of the Communist Party. Corruption and connections are seen as the path to wealth. Efforts to redistribute wealth and development are more symbolic than substantive and fail to take hold. Growing unrest is dealt with harshly, but mostly at a local level, with national officials occasionally seen as saving local populations from unscrupulous local officials. As a result, an uneasy calm at the national level masks problems at the local level. The authoritarian nature of the system still makes the relationship of the government to the population more forced than naturally self-sustaining. The authorities can claim they have a national consensus that gives them a mandate to govern, but the absence of democracy makes it difficult, if not impossible, to prove this claim.

A more ideologically-oriented leadership focuses greater attention on limiting Taiwan's freedom of action, heightening pressure on regimes that still recognize Taiwan, and increasing the military presence on the Mainland side of the Taiwan Straits. Ironically, policies designed to prevent the loss of Taiwan push moderate Taiwanese further away from the PRC position on Taiwan and to independence-minded politicians. The resulting tension also contributes to a deterioration in China's relationships with Japan, the E.U., and the U.S.

Failure to reign in North Korea's nuclear ambitions creates additional impetus for a reform of the Japanese constitution and a build up in Japanese military capability. In order to obtain support for these measures, Japanese politicians are forced to at least pay lip service to more conservative influences within Japan, further complicating relations with China. Competition for resources between China and Japan becomes open. The competition starts as economic and diplomatic, but it could also develop a military dimension. China responds to what it perceives as a growing threat from Japan by stepping up its own military spending and developing new and much more effective offensive and defensive weapons systems. It also develops a blue-water navy and tries to reduce its vulnerability to blockades along China's eastern coast by obtaining port access through Southeast Asia (via rails and ports it helps develop in Cambodia and Burma) and through Central Asia (via rails, highways, and pipelines it helps finance and build in this region).

The U.S. and E.U. become more and more impatient with perceived foot dragging by China on its WTO accession agreement commitments. U.S. and E.U. interests become more vocal in their complaints about lack of access to China's markets, subsidization of Chinese companies through the financial system, currency manipulation, and other unfair trading practices. Stung by the imposition of competition, labor, and unionization laws perceived as targeting foreign companies, leading multinationals that have been supporters of China in debates over trade issues at home fall silent. Trade disputes spill over into and then out of the World Trade Organization, which proves ineffective in managing China-U.S. and China-E.U. trade relations.

China accelerates its efforts to build relationships with Third World nations that are resource-rich, or strategically located, but have strained relations with the West. International sanctions against such nations become impossible to impose or ineffective in practice. Chinese investment and loans, given without conditions on governance reforms, replace those from Western countries or multilateral agencies that have strings attached. As a result, it is Chinese companies that grasp the lion's share of economic opportunities associated with the development of these nations. Chinese companies use protected positions at home and in the Third World to launch attacks against leading firms worldwide. China begins to exercise leadership among Third World nations in international forums, further isolating Western and Japanese interests. Meanwhile, China continues to expand its military and continues to stray into areas, such as space armament, that cause concern in various quarters around the world.

In this scenario, the rest of the world confronts a China that is far more economically and politically powerful in world affairs, yet at the same time is more ideological and inward focused than it had been under the previous leadership. Crackdowns on the press, economic nationalism, aggressive international diplomacy, more redistributionist thinking, and less willingness to compromise on some issues may be signs of a very different China going forward than some had hoped for.

In many ways, this "China First" scenario is a natural extension of trends that have emerged in the Hu Jintao-Wen Jiabao era. It appears that the Hu-Wen team fears that this scenario will lead to domestic unrest and isolation from the "Great Powers" and therefore China needs to be self-sufficient and maximize its position. While the moves undertaken may quell domestic unrest, ironically, they make it more likely that relations with Taiwan and the "Great Powers" will be strained. The danger is not only that this may hurt China's ultimate development, but that attempts to rein in the economy could succeed too well and take away some of the growth that has allowed China to deal with its challenges for the last 25 years. This could shift the ground from a challenging, but manageable Scenario #8 to an intractable Scenario #16.

China Scenarios in Perspective

We have not tried to forecast the future. We have not even provided a probability for any one of our scenarios occurring. Hopefully, the logic of each scenario is sufficiently well grounded that each is seen as having a high enough probability so as to be worthy of consideration. What we have tried to do is provide a framework for understanding the parameters of uncertainty that China, and therefore the world, faces. Any one of the futures we have outlined here could unfold during the coming five to 10 years. Indeed, it is possible that China could move through more than two different scenarios during this period. The future is not pre-ordained, nor is the path of change likely to be linear. However, the future is likely to lie somewhere within the overall set of scenarios.

The value of the uncertainties and signposts we have identified is that they can be used to track China's development over time. We have focused on a limited number of uncertainties in order to develop clear pictures to provoke thought, but many other things could happen that could change the pace and direction of change for the country. The international price of oil, the performance of the U.S. economy, the outcomes of elections in Taiwan and Korea, the future of the Kim Jong-il regime in North Korea, the international war on terrorism, and how attempts to dissuade Iran's nuclear ambitions play out are some examples of forces that are largely beyond the ability of the Chinese government to control, but will still have important implications for the nation. We also have not focused on the potential for a return of SARS, a bird flu pandemic, or natural disasters as well, as they could arise to reshape any scenario.

Closer to home, the Chinese government might like to give the impression that it is in complete control of the country, but there are plenty of examples where this is not the case. Corruption scandals in major Chinese state-owned banks and SOEs are clearly against the wishes of the central government, yet they still happen with depressing regularity. The country's leaders publicly admit that corruption, if it is not contained, has the potential to create social instability and undermine the government. The SARS epidemic caught the government by surprise and was a reminder of the types of serious health and environmental risks that exist and that could have a disruptive impact on the economy, social conditions, and China's ability to interface with the rest of the world. Moreover, new technology like the Internet and cellular phones is facilitating domestic and international communications to such an extent that it is interfering with the government's ability to control the flow of information to the population.

The specific signposts we identify might never materialize, but being aware of these and similar signposts should make it easier to spot parallels with actual developments as they occur. Greater awareness of an event's significance in terms of pushing China in a particular direction should improve the speed and quality of an organization's reaction to that event. After all, that is what will really distinguish the winners from the losers in China. It is less important to accurately predict the future (such a feat is almost impossible) than it is to understand and react to change faster and better than competitors.

For any organization dealing with China, it is important to review current assumptions about China and strategies that are in place. How do those assumptions stand up to the different scenarios? Would existing strategies work well in every scenario or are there weaknesses that could be improved or modified? Trends may be headed in one direction, but that direction could change. What early signposts would indicate that a direction change is taking place? It is critical that strategic plans have enough flexibility so that an organization can make adjustments if the signposts indicate some critical assumptions might be wrong. Strategies that lack such flexibility are extremely dangerous and have a greater potential to lead to disaster than they have to result in a huge success.

In a business sense, the important point to note is that there is a way for companies to profit in every scenario we have discussed. By the same token, there is no scenario discussed in which a company could not lose money if it is badly positioned. Every scenario has its special challenges and opportunities. This implies that there is an appropriate strategic response for any company in any scenario. The response differs not only based on the particular scenario, but also on the industry and, in many cases, the particular company. However, it is the companies that assess the potential scenarios, the "different futures for China" and prepare for the unknowns and uncertainties that are most likely to survive and thrive regardless of what the future holds.

Index